The Making of Superstars

Artists and Executives of the Rock Music Business

By Robert Stephen Spitz

ANCHOR PRESS/DOUBLEDAY
GARDEN CITY, NEW YORK
1978

FERNALD LIBRARY
COLBY-SAWYER COLLEGE
NEW LONDON, N. H. 03257

The Anchor Press edition is the first publication of
The Making of Superstars.
Anchor Press edition: 1978
Copyright © 1978 by Robert Stephen Spitz
All Rights Reserved
Printed in the United States of America
First Edition

Library of Congress Cataloging in Publication Data

Spitz, Robert Stephen.
  The making of superstars.

  Includes index.
  1. Rock musicians—Biography. 2. Music trade—
United States. I. Title.
ML385.S64   784'.092'2

ISBN: 0-385-12413-9
Library of Congress Catalog Card Number 76–56338

The author would like to acknowledge the use of the following songs which have been excerpted in the text. Their inclusion in the book has immeasurably enhanced its readability.

"Your Song," words and music by Elton John and Bernie Taupin, copyright 1969 by Dick James Music Inc.

"Music," words and music by John Miles, copyright 1975, British Rocket Music, Inc.

"Beautiful Music," words by Marty Panzer and music by Barry Manilow, copyright 1975, Kamikazee Music Corp.

"Talkin' New York," words and music by Bob Dylan, copyright 1962, Duchess Music Corp.

"Be Free," words and music by Jim Messina, copyright 1974, Jasperilla Music Co.

"Stars," words and music by Janis Ian, copyright 1972, Mine Music Ltd./April Music Inc.

"Your Favorite Entertainer," words and music by Neil Sedaka and Phil Cody, copyright 1974 and 1975, Don Kirshner Music Inc. and Kirshner Songs Inc.

"Sunshine Lady," words and music by Dion DiMucci, copyright 1974, Skinny Zach Music, Inc.

"Success Story," words and music by John Entwhistle, copyright 1975, Track Music Inc.

"Crossroads," words and music by Neil Sedaka and Phil Cody, copyright 1974 and 1975, Don Kirshner Music Inc. and Kirshner Songs Inc.

"Love Is a Beautiful Thing," words and music by Felix Cavaliere and Eddie Brigati, Jr., copyright 1966, Slascar Publishing Co., Ltd.

"Everybody Needs Somebody to Love" © Controlled by Caesar and Dino Music (B.M.I.)

"I've Got So Much to Give," words and music by Barry White, copyright 1973, Sa-Vette Music Co. and January Music Corp.

"I want to Go to the Sun," words and music by Peter Frampton, Copyright 1974, Almo Music Corp. and Fram-Dee Music Ltd.

"Mau Mau (Amerikon)," words by Paul Kantner, Grace Slick, and Joey Covington, music by Paul Kantner, copyright 1970, God Tunes.

The author wishes to express his gratitude for permission to quote excerpts from "The Drifters," by James Michener, copyright © 1971 by Random House, Inc., reprinted by permission of the publisher.

For Vicki

"I hope you don't mind that I put
down in words,
How wonderful life is while you're
in the world."

Playlist

Acknowledgments

Approximately a century ago, a noted philosopher said, "After the verb *To Love, To Help* is the most beautiful verb in the world." I cannot imagine anyone appreciating the simplicity of that statement more than an author about to embark on a first, factual book. Because there were so many people who cared about my writings, I am indebted to those who gave of their valuable time *To Help* me collect the information and organize the interviews contained in this book.

The people at the record companies opened every conceivable door for me and put up with my seemingly endless phone calls concerning their artists' schedules and requests for interviews. I am particularly grateful to Soozin Kazick, who, at the time, was at Columbia Records and has moved on to bigger and better horizons; Alan Rosenberg, Marion Perkins, and Beth Naranjo at Warner Bros. Records; Janice Circone and Martin Kirkup at A&M Records; and the elusive Ruth Gonzales, who, one day, will make one helluva record executive. You are all overworked and underpaid. Peter Jay Philbin of Columbia Records (who is neither overworked nor underpaid—sorry Philby!) is an exceptional friend who spent many hours discussing rock music and my book with me before deserting New York for (questionably) greener pastures on the West Coast. His advice during the first few months of preparation was much appreciated. I hope that he'll soon tire of Hollywood and come back East.

Fran Curtis of Rogers and Cowan rushed back from a vacation in the Hamptons to return my affairs to a state of transient "confusion unconfused" and, on several occasions, delivered to me interviews in a matter of minutes which I had been trying to secure for months. This occurred far too many times to write it off to coincidence; may I never learn how she obtained them. Carol Strauss Klenfner offered me priceless encouragement and assistance and was directly responsible for my completing two chapters of this book.

No words can describe how extraordinary a university is the New School. Every professional having the desire to teach should be as fortunate as I am in my association with them. Teaching at the New School—the first prominent school to offer rock as a course—has brought me hours of pleasure and gratification. Besides being a stimulating facility in which to learn, they are one of the few institutions on this earth to recognize the relevance of rock culture and to encourage its growth through education. Mike Engl, the assistant dean, offered me the rare opportunity to teach there, and his guidance (and patience) has been an inspiration. If he ever decides to leave his post there, he has a brilliant future awaiting him as a salary negotiator.

Everyone should have friends as understanding as mine. Allen LeWinter *knew* everything would come together for me in the end. He's a promotion man at heart and could have probably convinced me of anything. Marc Greenberg is an incomparable person who knows me almost as well as my wife does—almost. There were times when I wanted to sit down and quit but he wouldn't let me. He stood by me when I had tough decisions to make; his presence in my life carefully defines the meaning of "friendship." Sam McKeith, one of the wisest and craftiest individuals I know, taught me the value of confidence and relying on first instincts. His confidence in me never faltered. And my thanks to Bryan Lurie for an afternoon of intense proofreading. I sincerely hope that the book lives up to his evaluations.

My editor, Marie Brown, is as creative as she is constructive. Her contributions over the months have given my perspective new depth and challenge. There have been times when I've been intimidated by her extensive knowledge of rock and the music business, but she's from Philly and grew up listening to Hy Lit, Jimmy

Acknowledgments ix

Bishop, Georgie Woods and the Geator With The Heater, and she still has the audacity to claim she's been to more Uptown shows than I. She hasn't.

If there are any souls looking forward to publication of this book more than I, it is my parents. Their patience and love have been like a shadow; I don't have to turn around to know that it's always there.

How can I ever express the gratitude and love I feel for my beautiful wife, Vicki? What can I tell her that she doesn't already know? She, in essence, wrote this book with me, experienced my pain, my frustration, my elation; we are extensions of one another, and this book reflects much of that. She often wore the hat of the editor, typist, mimeographer and correspondent. Vicki exhibited an extraordinary amount of patience and faith in me—especially when it came to some of my more volatile qualities—and wrote off to "artistic temperament" far more than I had even hoped I'd get away with. How can I help but respect and admire her. And love her.

Thank you all.

Postscript: As this book was being prepared to go to print, I was shocked, as was every other rock devotee, by the early and tragic death of Elvis Presley. It would be unfair to you, the reader, and to myself not to pay tribute to the man who started all this called rock and roll. He was a hero to me throughout my entire life, an innovator, and a gentleman. Elvis earned the title The King and was, indeed, our first superstar. His presence will be greatly missed by all who admired him. In Memoriam: Elvis Aaron Presley (1935–1977).

R.S.S.

"Music was my first love, and it
will be my last,
Music of the future—the music of
the past
To live without my music, would
be impossible to do.
'Cause in this world of troubles
my music pulls me through."

JOHN MILES, *Music*

I listened to the records, watched the reactions of the young people, and entered a world more powerful than the world of marijuana, more persuasive than that of LSD.

When I finally heard the music, I was struck by how varied it was: what I had once lumped together as noise, now separated into a wider variety of sound than what I had known in my youth, and I began slowly to pick out selections in each category that seemed to me to have musical merit; with each discovery I moved closer to the world which the young people around me were inhabiting. Music thus became a passport to terra incognita, and now as I look back upon those idle days in Torremolinos, they seem among the most productive of my life.

JAMES A. MICHENER, *The Drifters*

Introduction

Incongruity has always been the mainstay of the American ideal, the flexible cement of transition. Who would have imagined twenty years ago that anyone would devote serious study to the evolution of rock and roll music? For that matter, who would have predicted it would even *last* for twenty years, let alone assume its many musical forms and sociological roles? The small cult following which rockabilly—one of its early predecessors— had accumulated at the outset of the 1950s among people in mostly Southern, rural areas was the antithesis of the majority of that day's audience. And as the new music spread into urban centers, it borrowed heavily from gospel music and rhythm and blues, and it found its way to the street corners where groups of four and five teenagers harmonized *a cappella* to what we now refer to as "doo-wop." Electronics came much later.

However, the postwar music establishment—the patrons of such stolid musical citizenry as Billy Eckstine, Eddie Fisher, Patti Page, and the Mills Brothers (among others)—viewed rock as an apocryphal bastardization of pop, a compendium of muddled, dispassionate arrangements sketched loosely in a four-chord disguise. One early critic, obviously ignorant of the innovative sound, borrowed from Shakespeare when he described rock music as "a tale told by an idiot, full of sound and fury, signifying nothing." Rock and roll lyrics were generally assumed unintelligible and obscure, a gobbledegook of nonsense viewed by a jaundiced eye. And the precognition that rock would one day become universal in scope, would become the lifeline of youth culture, was considered preposterous.

Who would have dared to presume that the bohemian architects of this new musical medium would unfold into the creative and administrative artisans, the culture scholars, the teachers? They were looked upon as offbeat dreamers, children on a lark whose self-indulgence would soon be rudely taught the simple economic principles of survival. To regard people like the Ertegun brothers or Chuck Berry or Albert Grossman or Carole King as harbingers of a rejuvenated way of life was considered absurd by the prosaic pop music crowd. John Hammond, Sr.'s introduction of Bob Dylan as the poetical/musical composer of tomorrow was openly referred to as Hammond's Folly, the long shot of long shots.

And yet, as incongruous as the events of life are, no one predicted the extent or magnitude that rock music would have in the twentieth century. We should have. The clues were there: the daily lines of teenagers down Market Street in Philadelphia, waiting to be admitted to dance on "Bandstand," the small groups of kids who jammed in the tiny studio while Allen Freed played the newest diet of 45's, words like *bop* and *stroll* and *hand jive*, sock hops, short shorts, ducktails—and the necessary ingredients of rebellion and pandemonium. Rock and roll had it all. But few envisioned what has today become such a vast financial empire upward of four billion dollars a year. Or the musical genius (and credibility) of a Lennon and McCartney, Aretha Franklin, Elvis Presley, or a Stevie Wonder. Or that hundreds of thousands of young people would make an attempt to formulate careers as composers or vocalists or executives from a music which had been referred to as artless and irresponsible—which had become the ground swell of a common teenage identity. An intelligent music with a definite form and permeable boundaries for creative experimentation. A respected music boasting its distinguished contributors. An exciting music which has introduced countless innovative instruments with which to create its multidimensions. A competitive music demanding integrity, patient listening, and superior quality.

What, then, is restraining this far-reaching medium from becoming a studied art? Why do we persist to treat rock as a secondary music, to tread gently and subserviently in the shadows of the traditional, jazz, and classical compositions when we contend that its creators and promoters express the same amounts of integrity and skill as, say, Johann Sebastian Bach or Benny Goodman? Quite basically, the requirement for accepting rock, for understanding rock music and its culture, is for those people who hold it in intangible esteem to divest themselves of the sophomoric discriminations which have been attached (not always unduly) to the music since its inception. For what rock was born out of, and what rock has developed into today, are related only out of consequence of a rhythm that has sustained the lifetime of the music.

Paralleling its demographics quite closely, the rock industry itself has sprouted from small, family-operated businesses into finely tuned corporate assembly lines on which thousands of employees concern themselves with such diversities as the quality of plastic (and, coincidentally, the price and politics of the oil industry—necessary components for its manufacture), mass media technology, million-dollar accounting practices, the temperament of the country, public and artist relations, marketing and long-term experimentation and development. Excess earnings, made from extraordinary rock profits, are very cautiously counseled into shrewd investments by rather staid Wall Street banking houses who, only years earlier, spurned its bankability. Today, rock music is considered one of the most stable and durable industries, and those same banking houses have even gone as far as to place their own capital behind managers' and artists' existing contracts in an attempt to gain a quick return on their investment. Today, successful touring acts can gross up to $150,000 a night playing at arenas and sporting complexes across the country. Coupled with healthy royalty percentages of hit albums and songwriters' royalties, it is plausible for a superstar-ranked artist to earn upward of a million dollars a year. Managers and agents, at fifteen per cent of the take, respectively, don't fare badly either. And even within the bureaucratic levels of the major recording companies, executives in various departments earn in excess of $40,000 a year; highly respected promotion men can demand incomes exceeding $50,000 and $60,000. Economically, rock is reaching maturity; artistically, it is still the new kid on the block, still considered obscure and untenable by older generations, still watered down and administered in small doses until palatable to those who have not grown up with it (for example, "television rock": Tony Orlando and Dawn, Sonny and Cher, The Captain and Tenille—as opposed to the more eclectic talents such as Jackson Browne, the Jefferson Starship, Queen, etc.).

It is important for us to accept the new American imagery created by the perceptive young talents who have expanded their rock music beginnings. Their artistic writings are certainly as valid as those who have made an impression before them. Like Carl Sandburg, Stephen Crane, Archibald MacLeish and Robert Frost, whose reflections of life have sustained decades, so too will the words of Bob Dylan, Paul Simon, Laura Nyro, Bruce Springsteen, and Joni Mitchell be remembered by those whose lives their words represent. Stevie Wonder's art is as poignant and new as the precepts of the vital black identity movement, and they will continue to pioneer social relevancy and advancement through his lyrical urgings. He has educated us all.

But still we continue to place the older, more established American poets and musicians on a pedestal, out of reach of their younger, elucidated counterparts as if there can never be that bridge between the philosophies of the generations. Yet rock culture is clearly just an extension of our musical history and of our culture. Isaac Stern and Eric Clapton—both musicians of awesome talent—Henry Wadsworth Longfellow and Paul Simon—peers separated by a century of technology. That their audiences are separate and apart from each other is only a matter of time; thank God for their distinction of styles.

However, for rock music, time has ironically added another evaluative aspect: maturity—in both the artist and the audience. Superstar longevity seems to have become more prominent and what was once a music for teenagers *by* teenagers has evolved into a culture whose heroes represent a thirty-year age span. Some of those artists began their careers in their early teens and have grown up with the business; others merely play to a larger, heterogeneous audience. And, at the same time, those rock audiences of the late 1950s and early 1960s who characterized the frenzied musical energy have grown up, retaining their rock and roll roots. In fact, it presents an interesting irony: How are parents able to advise their child about some of the more theatrical improprieties used by groups like Kiss and Alice Cooper when it was they who ripped the theater seats during previews of *Love Me Tender* and who were dragged by police out of Shea Stadium in New York for attempting to jump onto the stage where the Beatles were performing?

Rock music has, indeed, outlasted and usurped its former age and reckless identities. It is no longer specifically a teenage music or, necessarily, restricted to younger audiences. It is no longer characterized by physical gyrations and unintelligible lyrics. It is no longer a phenomenon.

Rock and roll is a way of life.

It has given us new heroes, new thoughts and philosophies through well-constructed lyrics and—oh yes—new musical inspiration. And in the end, all good music lives forever.

During my years in this business, I have had several opportunities which afforded me a unique vantage point from which to observe the superstar process. That process, I found overwhelming—hourless days, months, even years spent grooming the artist, creating a public image, selecting the right manager and producer to suit the artist's talent and personality, establishing the artist's own or aligning him with a music publishing company that will exploit the full potential of his catalogue, choosing an agent to book tours and convince promoters to spend a thousand dollars on an unknown act—an agent who will "get behind" the act (all too often, an agent will add another artist to his roster to protect himself from someone else signing the act, should that act become big), negotiating a record deal, hyping the press. The obligations to the artist are endless.

As the general manager of Dick James Music, Inc. (a variegated British company which had represented aspects of the careers of the Beatles, Gerry and the Pacemakers, the Hollies, Spencer Davis, and other constituents of the early British invasion), I found myself in the midst of one of the most colossal music business phenomena with one of James's clients—Elton John.

Elton had exploded, although not in the usual rock "overnight monster" way—he had spent several years and albums traveling the world, playing obscure clubs and paying the proverbial dues— and it looked as though nothing was going to stand in his way. Nothing did. But it was not as though he had suddenly created something extraordinarily unique to take him to the heights of superstardom. Rather, he had succeeded in transcending the pedestrian innuendos of rock and had become recognized as a *universal* talent, not just a *rock* music talent.

Needless to say, the offices were besieged with calls about Elton John. But the curious thing about the majority of the calls (from fans and members of the press) was that they wanted to know far more than where Elton would be appearing next or his favorite color or his astrological sign. They wanted to know how he managed to see his life within the context of the music he wrote and performed. How did he work with Bernie Taupin, his lyricist? What motivated him to create? From where were his influences drawn—not just musically, but philosophically as well? How was he able to cope with his success? They wanted to know what went on inside Elton John's mind. What were his ultimate statements? Elton John the person had become as important to them as Elton John the performer. He was no longer justanotherrocksinger.

If there is a journalism characteristic of rock music in the 1970s as opposed to the earlier days of the rock press, it is that there is more depth to a rock artist than only his music. There are his ideas concerning life, politics, ideals, careers, frustrations, and anything else that crosses a mind. And, in turn, the listening public is better able to associate with the motivations found in the music. What might have passed by as an introspective lyric now takes on a meaning reflective of the artist's comments in a particular story or interview.

It has become apparent that there is a growing need to study the contributions of the rock music community, to go beneath the surface achievements and to determine why the people involved have had such a profound effect on millions of people using this music as their common denominator. Names of the industry executives are regularly cropping up in tones of familiarity in major press releases. Producers and arrangers have deservedly drawn attention to their recording techniques and are quietly moving into the heretofore restricted areas of television and motion pictures. Unrecorded songwriters are becoming personalities on nationwide talk shows because people have become aware that there are more people behind a hit record than just the recording artist. Managers' promotional tactics have become favorite stories of the fans. Specifics have replaced sensationalism in an industry built on the creation of mystique and hype.

But while we have been listening, collecting, and deciphering or just plain humming along, rock music has developed its own short, vivid history. Companies that once capped the charts week after week—companies like Gone and Sun and Carlton and Cameo/Parkway and Imperial—have either disappeared, been swallowed up by corporations, or have been replaced by newer ones such as Arista and Rocket and Asylum and Island, and, well, the list could probably stretch on for an entire chapter. The young, cocky kids who actually pursued their first love and called themselves record people have became corporate executives. Ahmet Ertegun still maintains creative control over Atlantic Records although the company no longer sells records out of the trunk of his automobile; Don Kirshner is still a young publisher, yet he wields control over a multimillion-dollar privately owned entertainment corporation; Jerry Wexler continues to produce fabulous records. And even some of those "long shots" like Elvis, Paul Anka, Dion, Carole King, and Neil Sedaka are still around twenty years later—still singing, still composing, still performing, still relevant to several generations.

This book is about some of those people, their lives and their music. It is a behind-the-scenes view of why they were drawn to music, how they got into the business, and what happened once they got there. But more important, it is a look at people who, in addition to creating musical expression, are intelligent, witty, compassionate, and philosophical human beings. Without those qualities (and without these people) the music might never have achieved the degree of success it enjoys today.

I could have written another thousand pages and included twenty-five more profiles (easily!). But at a certain point, a judgment had to be made, and I selected those included on their credits and on my personal expectations. As each person relates his or her life in the music business, so unfolds a delineable, multifaceted history of rock and roll—the artists, executives, shenanigans, scams, frustrations, and gratitudes; only they could tell the stories behind the making of superstars without losing the color and qualities, and, subsequently, I have left the profiles in the narrative form.

There are a few people I sincerely regret omitting, but because of their hectic schedules there was not enough time to capture the full scope of their personalities and contributions and any less would have been an injustice. I think it is fair to assume that the history of rock and roll is ongoing and infinite, and I hope they will all be included in future books.

The people contained here have been a part of my life since I was old enough to put the needle on the record. In the following chapters, they have shared with me their innermost feelings, made me laugh, made me angry, and made me understand more about my own cultural heritage. I hope they will remain active in the music business for many, many years. They and their associates have created our music and our heroes through a long, difficult process which I feel is best summed up as the Making of Superstars.

R.S.S.

New York
February 1977

Jim Messina

"I want to get away and live my life
near the rivers and trees,
I want to spend my days making
rhyme
And be free."

J. MESSINA, *Be Free*

Few professional musicians ever realize the fruition of their artistic reason for being. The commercial competitiveness which unsympathetically governs and restricts the select status of renown drives a hard bargain and frustration is most often the by-product of their eagerness. To others who have partially mastered the rigors of endurance, self-imposed trials minimize their contentment; as with most perfectionists, standards are set, achieved and re-established at impossibly lofty heights. Jim Messina has pulled the inconceivable hat trick in less than ten years as a professional musician achieving recognition in three of the most distinguished groups in the short history of rock and roll. Rather curiously, he appears unintimidated by his accomplishments, secure that he possesses the ability to destine his future. Some interpret his confidence as arrogant egotism; however, underscoring Messina's implicit poise is a devisiveness supported by talent and a well-developed business sense with which he communicates his energies. Few artists have a balance of these crucial qualities, and even less channel them as adeptly as Jim.

Actually, Jim Messina makes it rather easy to understand his convictions and affect his friendship. He is a casual, gracious person whose seriousness is mixed evenly with sensitivity and wittiness. Upon first meeting him, one cannot help but assume that he has been deprived of his youthful innocence by his inundation to the business of music at a very early age. When he was only nineteen, after having been the engineer on their previous album, he became a member of the legendary Buffalo Springfield (replacing Bruce Palmer). Since that time, he has been on the road and in the studio with Poco and with Kenny Loggins as a band member and a producer and writer. In between, he has negotiated several of his own affiliations with his record company, manager, agent, and attorney and has undauntedly traversed the country on promotional campaigns to his personal satisfaction. All that cannot somehow have taken its toll. However, Messina manages a perspective on his life's work which equalizes his maturity into more of a development of talents. It is his chosen world, and he moves comfortably within it.

Messina has become the musical auteur and speaks of his work in terms of subjectivity as opposed to his earlier collectivity. His recordings are a collaborative effort, but they bear distinct marks of his contribution to the extent that his earlier, personal styles have dominated his more recent work. This is demonstrated in his work with Kenny Loggins, which began as a solo effort by Loggins but needed the direction and nuances of Messina's experience. That the group became Loggins and Messina was inevitable, but the input of Messina's creativity stems not only from his wishes for creative control but also is proportionate to the extent of his contribution desired by his associates—here, namely Kenny Loggins. All of this, of course, must be equally evaluated in the innovator's absolute and creative use of a luminous ego. To this, Jim Messina is no exception. He is fully aware of his part in his own success and is equally perceptive of the successful capacities he's fulfilled with his contemporaries. He speaks easily about his work and is just as easily critical about it.

Most of Messina's compositions are marked by their simplicity of lyrics and assuming melodies. But he has made the musical interlude expressively dominant in many of his compositions—most

*notably "My Music," "Be Free" and "Pretty Princess." This arises
from creative production, but also from Messina's desire to experiment with other sounds and rhythms. In this, he has a preference
for Latin and reggae—the Latin influence being superior in
"Vahevala," the reggae never fully reaching above a pedestrian
white American interpretation. He has mastered the country
approach—more so, he has adopted it as his own and has worked
hard at refining it from Springfield to Poco to Loggins and Messina.*

*Jim Messina has grown with his music. He has become more
perceptive as a person and more expressive in terms of his artistic
talents, and many people—many people—are watching to see the
direction in which he moves next.*

IN THE BEGINNING

When I was growing up, we were listening to artists like Chuck
Berry, Fats Domino, Elvis Presley, and Ricky Nelson. And on the
other side was the country stuff, which was predominant in our
house. My stepfather was from Arkansas, and when Johnny Cash
first debuted in the late Fifties, that was played *all* the time in my
house. Johnny Cash was one of the first trips that I got into, too,
as far as country was concerned.

My father played guitar, and that's how I got introduced to the
instrument. He was not a very good guitar player, but he was interested in Merle Travis and Jo Maphis and people like that. And
he would take me to see them on weekends at a place called Cal's
Corral Worthington Dodge, which was a big thing in Los Angeles
in the Fifties. My dad encouraged me to play all music, no matter
what. It was never a matter of having to play country music and
not playing rock and roll.

But my stepfather didn't like black music—which made me all
the more want to find out what it was all about. And I think black
music has been very important and influential in my life, probably
more so than any of the other types of music, because it's the one
thing that country music and rock and roll sometimes leave out—
the soul, the feeling, the rhythm and blues. That and Cuban and
Latin music are extremely exciting to me. Those influences show

up in the things I've written in a sense that the pulse, the back-bone of what I like to do, is highly influenced by them.

It's funny, but I've never really latched onto anybody who I could pinpoint as having been a mentor to my musical development. Probably the closest I've come to being influenced at a developing stage where I wanted and needed very much to be recognized in terms of just a musician was when I was thirteen years old. In the surf music days. The only big group I'd ever seen perform was Dick Dale and the Deltones, and their type of music was very much a part of the California scene. And in order to work at a lot of the gigs—they had what were called Surfer Stomps—you had to play that type of music. So, at thirteen, I started to get a little band together, and we played Beach Boy songs, Dick Dale songs, things by Bill Black's Combo, the Champs. The very first group I had we called the Buttonaires. We had little buttonaire-type carnations in our lapels. After that, we called ourselves the Pendletons cause that was more surfy, and we wore Pendleton shirts.

GETTING INVOLVED

The turning point, when I finally broke in as a professional, was when I came to Hollywood. I realized that there was no more room for what I was doing. There was no more Chuck Berry music, no more surf music. The Righteous Brothers were happening, and the whole music scene was changing. And when I moved to Hollywood there was no more room for me. I was a little discouraged, and I decided that if I was going to give up being a musician, I had to be around it—no doubt about it! So I started an apprenticeship as a recording engineer and worked in a recording studio for three solid years. During my high-school years, I worked on the weekends for Emperor Hudson, who was a very successful disc jockey. Bob Hudson is his real name; they're Hudson and Landry now. So, I started there, under the direction of an engineer named Mike Dorro, and went on to become a recording engineer working for Harmony Recorders, Audio Arts, and after that I went to work for Tuddy Camorata, who owned Sunset Sound and was a good orchestrator who also did a lot of work for Disney productions.

By then, I was playing bass. During my recording days as an engineer I still wanted to become a musician and I had met a fellow by the name of Joe Osborne, who was a studio bass player, and Mike Dorro. And we built Joe's studio in his house, and while building that studio, I got to know him and a lot of musicians. I met James Burton there, Dorsey Burnett, and Jerry Allison, the drummer of the Crickets.[1] Joe Osborne had been involved with the earlier rock scene, and most of the good musicians who had made those earlier days happen all congregated at his place. We built another little studio called Universal for two guys by the names of Sonny and Al Jones, whose sister had been married to the late Hank Williams and the late Johnny Horton, as well. And I started working for those guys as a recording engineer, setting up all the balances. And then they'd ask me to pick for them at some of the sessions. After I set up all the balances, I would move in under a mike. I had a chance to play with some really fine players. And that got me back into music [as a musician].

ON ENGINEERING

Engineering was something I definitely wanted to pursue as a career. I had no idea what I would end up doing or being. I knew that if engineering was the least that I did, I could enjoy it. Because I loved music, and that way, I had a chance to do all kinds of music, to be around all different kinds of artists. I just knew that I had to keep my professional awareness up in terms of new equipment, new procedures and things like that—because those things were my ticket into working at a bigger studio.

I engineered Lee Michaels' first album. Bruce Botnick was the engineer for the Doors, and occasionally he would ask me to help him out on their stuff—which I didn't enjoy too much. I just didn't dig their music, and that's very important to me. It's one of the things that can really turn an engineer off because when you're mixing personality and lifestyle into a recorded piece of music, they really affect each other. I've never been into hard drugs at all. But, in those days, I was into uppers to stay awake and downers to go to sleep, but strictly medicinal in terms of what I needed to

[1] Buddy Holly's band.

get done, and they wore me out and depressed me. So, when I ran into this group [the Doors] whose music was kind of drunk and druggy—I didn't even like their music—well, that's a couple reasons why I did very little with the Doors. Really, [I worked with them] to help Bruce out and keep their sessions going. I liked doing Lee Michaels' [album] very much, and I also liked doing Joni Mitchell's first demo before she got started. [David] Crosby was producing her and had come to me and asked me if I wanted to help him out on a small project. And that's when I first met Joni Mitchell. I loved her songs, I loved her guitar—she was really magical.

One thing I've learned having been an engineer, having been a musician, having been a producer, is trying to approach all those areas with as much objectivity and detachment as I possibly can. And I've found that each one of those areas is a major part of the over-all project, and if the engineer is not good, his insecurity will create an air of confusion. If there are certain things he can't do, if his most basic tools are no good, he will start justifying why certain things can't be done. The same thing with a producer. If he doesn't understand the music enough to explain what he feels is wrong, the same insecurity will show through to the group. You can tell a guy who *does* understand music. He's sitting out there in the studio and he says, "Hey, man, that lick just ain't right," and you think it's great. So you ask him what isn't right about it and he says, "I don't know, I just don't dig it." You've got to have a lot of trust and respect for the producer to accept that in the first place. And if the guy has no musical scruples at all, eventually it's going to wear on you. My being a musician really helps in engineering and producing because an engineer has to know music because he's basically in the same situation as the artist. That does not exclude the people who don't sing or don't play and have a real good musical sense. But I think that those people usually develop something else called *tact*. And they probably spend a lot of time with the act before they go into the studio. An engineer should spend a lot of time with the artist, listening to the demos, seeing how they sing, how they feel, how their personality shows through their music—study all the aspects of the artist so that they can record the artist the way he really is.

MEETING BUFFALO SPRINGFIELD

I was working at Sunset Sound in 1967, and I was finishing up engineering an album for an artist who was on A&M Records. Neil Young had come in, and I had never heard of the Buffalo Springfield. At that time, they had just come off a record called "For What It's Worth," which was on their first album. And being in the studio a lot, I worked anywhere from twelve to fifteen hours a day. I usually got to the studio at one o'clock in the afternoon and left at six in the morning, so I really had very little time for listening to the radio. And whatever time I did have off I usually spent doing maintenance work on the equipment. So, when I met Neil Young, I really had no idea who he was or what he did.

He approached me and said, "I understand you're an engineer here. I'd like to book some time and wanted to know if you'd like to work with me." I said, "Sure!" I would have said that to anybody at that time, 'cause in those days I was trying to get clients. But Gypsy—the lady who used to run the studio—booked them in with a fellow named Bill Lazarus. He was a fellow who had just started working there and was still very unfamiliar with the equipment. So a couple days went by, and I saw Bill and asked him how things were going. He said, "I'm having a little trouble." I went in there and realized that the group was getting frustrated and Bill was getting frustrated, so I took him outside and asked him that, if he wanted, I would take over the date until he had a chance to get more familiar with the equipment. And that was the first time I worked for Springfield.

At the time I took over the sessions, they had recorded a whole lot of stuff at the Columbia Recording Studios, and it was just atrocious. Basically, in those days, they recorded with just drums, bass, and one guitar—three or four pieces—and the sound was just horrible, really fucked. They brought in "Child's Claim to Fame," and James Burton had overdubbed two Dobros [steel-bodied, rounded guitars] on it. That was good, but it still needed bass and vocals. The acoustic guitars were really dirty, so we had to put new acoustic tracks on. Basically, what it was was taking old tapes and starting over with them, redoing them. They weren't a group that rehearsed together very much. That was an unfortunate thing, because if they had spent a lot of time rehearsing, they could have walked into the studio, said, "This tape is real bad. Why don't we cut another one?" and in two hours we could have made a real nice-sounding tape. But they weren't into that. They wanted to clean up what they already had, salvage it. So, "Child's Claim to Fame" was one of the first things I heard. And "Expecting to Fly" and "Bluebird" had already been recorded and done very well. Jack Nietzche had taken them into the studio earlier and had done that, so that was finished—that was on the "Buffalo Springfield Again" album.

I had enjoyed the music, because it was exactly the type of influences I had grown up with. I didn't think these guys were really great, by any means. In fact, I think they lacked a lot of technical abilities on their instruments. They were very sloppy and took a lot of time to get things done. Remember that my criteria for judging their musical ability were compared with guys like Joe Osborne, James Burton, Jerry McGee, Glenn D. Hardin—really proficient musicians. And the Buffalo Springfield was really a folk group that played rock and roll.

The person who really stuck out in the group the most was Stephen Stills. He really had a nice feel about his guitar and vocals, and I felt he was definitely an asset. And Richie Furay. He had a real good sound to his vocals and his songs. Stephen and Richie were really the two guys in my mind who stood out. And Neil Young. I mainly looked at Neil as an adequate guitar player who had a lot of drive to come up with something new. Neil really took on the position of being the group producer when I first met them.

Their music was special. It was unique, each tune was different, it wasn't the same tune rewritten twelve times. And they seemed to really *love* what they were doing.

WE NEED A BASS PLAYER

Around the end of 1967, I decided that I was tired of working as an engineer. It was taking too much of a toll on me. I was putting in too many hours and was exhausted all the time. My real ambition was to become a record producer. I had mixed many albums and had sat next to a lot of producers; I felt as though I could do a better job of it. But I was very young—I was nineteen years old. I decided that I was going to do just that. I had had some discussions with A&M [Records]—nothing really positive —but I felt as though I could get a job there. Plus, they were building a recording studio, so I felt that, if worse came to worse, I could say that I was willing to start out as an engineer and work my way up from there, because I saw a future with them.

At that point, we had already finished the *Buffalo Springfield Again* album, put in a *lot* of work on it. Everybody liked it and we had already started on the third album. I called the guys together and said, "Look, I'm not going to be able to finish this album. I'll help you until you get somebody you want, but I'm going to try to get a job with A&M." So Neil said, "How much money do you think you would make?" I said, ". . . don't know." I was only making $180 a week then. "I don't know. I'm going to shoot for $200, $250." And he said, "Well, before you do anything, why don't you wait a week because I have some ideas." A couple weeks prior, the bass player, Bruce [Palmer]—something happened to him legally which caused him to leave the band, and Neil came back to me later and said, "We need a bass player. I hear you can play bass. Do you think you could do this gig?" And I said, "I don't know." And he said, "Well, we have another guy coming out from New York that we used to play with, and we'd like to audition him and we'd like to audition you." So I said, "What songs are you going to do?" And they turned out to be basically the ones we recorded which I was pretty familiar with anyway. And I said, "Okay—could I sit down and go over a couple of these things?" And they said, "No. Let's just do it then [onstage]." So I agreed and showed up at rehearsal, and this guy had already shown up from New York, and he was already playing onstage with them. I listened to what he was doing, and I said to myself, "I know I can play better than him." At least, my feel would be better than that. I was really scared, really afraid, 'cause I had never done anything like this before.

So I got onstage and they started playing, and the moment the music started up, I just *knew* this was great! I was having a great time. And they all knew that it was the right feel, too. That was sort of what decided it like with anything else—just sitting down and playing.

I know now what I must have put some of the guys through who auditioned for Loggins and Messina. Because now I realize the feelings of insecurity one goes through. But it was neat. So, after that, Neil and Stephen said, "I think you can do what we need, and we'll pay you five hundred dollars a week. You can engineer and produce our albums." I thought to myself, There's really no better opportunity to produce and engineer and still go out on the road and be a part of the music. So I decided to accept their offer.

A VERY STRANGE MAN

I've been fortunate enough to have worked with people who have appeared, on the surface, that they're really honest people. My first experience with a record company executive was with Ahmet Ertegun. I was nineteen years old when I first met him. I got the feeling that he was a very strange man.

The first time I met him, I was with Stephen Stills and Neil Young. It was in a hotel room. They were doing all the talking because they knew him, and I was there as a guest. And after I had been introduced to him, he asked, "What's happening? What's the state of things?" And Stephen said, "Well, we're in the process of finishing our album. Bruce has left the band and, in fact, we have a new guy with us. This is him—Jimmy Messina—our new bass player, and he's also our engineer and producer." I was very curious as to what was going on in Ahmet's head because he was looking at a nineteen-year-old kid and probably wondering, Am I gonna get a fucking album out of this group?

He was always polite to me, but *always* a real nervous guy. The next time I met him, I called him and told him the album *The Last Time Around* was not coming along too well. There was everybody's old ladies hanging around offering opinions and causing trouble. And I told Ahmet that the best thing to do would be to get everybody to New York, put us up in a hotel, and record in studios there. That way, we'd just get it done. So Ahmet flew us all to New York, and we finished most of the album.

Working with Springfield was a real opportunity to get started in the business and Ahmet certainly helped me to do it.

THE LAST TIME AROUND

As all this was going on, the group started having their problems again. The leaving of Bruce really disappointed Stephen because they were very close, he liked him very much. And they got it into their heads that the band couldn't survive unless all the original members were there. Stephen and Neil were having their difficulties creatively. They were fighting and not getting along. And it was getting to the point where it was hard for everybody to enjoy what they were doing. That was about six or seven months later, after the *Buffalo Springfield Again* album was done.

The group was going to break up.

We all sat down together and had a discussion. I had spoken to Ahmet Ertegun, and he had expressed to me and I'm sure to Stephen and to Neil that it would be very important to try to support the album as much as possible with a tour, otherwise the album would come out and be a flop. So, I really think, on his advice, and all of us sitting down and saying, "I'm willing to do it," we went out and toured and promoted that last album.

I had enjoyed being on the road with Buffalo Springfield. For me, it was a very positive trip, but I don't know what it was like for the other guys. I could feel the depression. What I tried to do all along in the group was to not get involved in any cliques or any one personality—although I did cater more to Richie because he and I just had a lot more in common as people. But I tried, wherever possible, to keep some kind of communiqué between all of us and, thus, our music. Trying to understand as much as possible about the group from the songs. Sitting down and playing with Stephen and trying to understand what he wanted out of his songs, and what Neil and the others wanted. And, as a musician, I could at least help to keep that part together.

POCO AND RICHIE FURAY

When Buffalo Springfield was still together, Richie and I were driving along one day in the back seat of a taxicab, and I asked him if he was interested in pursuing music, and he said he was. So I said, "Well, why don't we get a band together, a small band, part country and part rock and roll?" He said, "I'm willing to give it a try." So I said, "Why don't we start thinking about it now before this band busts up?" So during the process of the group slowly winding down, we were already thinking of something that we wanted to do.

We hadn't made any decisions yet because we were still out on the road, and Stephen was in one place and Neil was in another. We didn't know if they were going to like or hate each other.

During that time, we had gotten hold of Rusty Young through a friend of Richie's, and got him to come out, and I put him on some Buffalo Springfield tapes.[2] That was a lot earlier. So Rusty was in the back of our mind. That made three pieces. Then we got Randy Meisner after searching for a bass player for so long (I had decided to switch to guitar). He's now with the Eagles. We got a drummer friend of Rusty's[3] and started Poco.

We never thought about comparisons between Poco and Springfield. I never got into that shit. People would say we were in a Buffalo Springfield "flavor"—very positive comparisons. We just basically set out to get into something musically that we would enjoy with people who were going to be positive and just have some fun.

I had started writing when I was in high school, but I never really liked anything that I had done. I figured that when I had something to say, it would come out. It was just a question of having to live a little and experience something. When I was still in high school, I was really too young to write. It was too much engineering and too much running around to sit down and write. With Poco, I felt that I had to start writing more because I wanted to contribute a little more musically. I wrote a couple things with Richie, but I don't remember too much about those tunes.

I was with Poco for pretty much the whole trip—about two years. Randy Meisner had left, Tim Schmidt came in, and we had cut three albums. I just kind of got tired of the music. I didn't feel like we were progressing anymore. Or maybe *I* wasn't progressing anymore. I felt like I was beginning to stagnate. Richie and I weren't writing together. I was basically a guitar player in a band, and that's what started buzzing me out.

[2] It was *The Last Time Around* album.
[3] The drummer was George Grantham.

Richie and I have always been friendly, but I think our competitiveness and drive to be successful individually made us not be as close as we should have. That happens with everybody in bands, though. You really can't blame it on any individual. For the most part, it's good. Richie's really a great person—I think we're *both* great people—and I think it's a pity that we had to let things like that interfere with our relationship. We always maintained a good relationship in terms of our personal trip, but our work had a tendency to get in the way of that relationship going any further. I respected him too much to let the relationship go any further. So I decided it was time to leave Poco.

SO I LEFT POCO

I went to Clive Davis[4] and told him that I wanted to finish up touring to support the live album we had out at the time, but I wanted to leave the band, and I wanted to leave in a way that wouldn't hurt them. I went to Clive for advice because I also felt that if I left the band it might be misunderstood as to *why* and get bad-rapped for something I was trying to do in a good way.

So I went to Clive. I had never met him before, and I was totally petrified. Artie Garfunkel got me to do it. He told me that Clive was an understanding person, and that he could give me the insight to do what I needed to do, and that after I talked to him it would be easier for me to make a decision. So I made an appointment to see Clive, and it turned out that he had to go someplace, but he'd be willing to talk to me on the train. So we took a train from New York to Philadelphia, and he and I and Don Ellis[5] had a meeting. And the meeting is pretty much described accurately in his book[6] that he wrote with the exception of including my point of view. I was scared half to death, and I didn't want to smoke any cigarettes because it would make me appear to be more nervous than I really was. If I smoked I thought I wouldn't be able to think about what I wanted to talk to him about.

[4] Clive Davis was president of the CBS Record Group at the time, and he had jurisdiction over Messina's Poco contract on Epic.

[5] Don Ellis was, at the time, the East Coast director of A&R for Epic.

[6] *Clive: Inside the Record Business,* by Clive Davis with James Willworth, William Morrow & Co., New York, 1975.

It turned out that I really had a great talk with him. I talked about the fact that I wanted to leave the band and didn't know how to do it. I didn't want to hurt anybody by leaving. I would be willing to take the necessary time it would take to make the transition—finding somebody to replace me, finishing the album, going out and touring behind the album—whatever it took.

[Clive] tried to explain to me that I was on the verge of becoming successful with this band, and I was going to throw it all out the window—and all of that. But I explained to him that it was my personal happiness that was at stake right now. And I felt that if I wasn't happy, I was laying it onto other people and making them feel unhappy. The band needed to have a guitar player who wanted to be there and to make it work for them. [Clive] tried to convince me to stay, and I tried all I could to explain to him why it wouldn't work. In the final analysis, he said, "I think you're right. I think you shouldn't be there. But I want you to make sure you leave the situation in a good place. And if it's an independent producer you want to be, we'll discuss it at a later date. Just take care of this situation now, and we'll worry about the other one later."

After having spent two years with them, I left Poco. I had learned a lot. I wasn't involved as much as I thought I should have been—which was another reason that I left. You see, the group was very democratic. Everyone had their equal say. And there were some members who were capable of making equal decisions and some members who I felt were not. People who are willing to spend more time deserve to participate more. And I've learned that there's no equality in sharing these types of responsibilities. You can't equate it that way. I decided that if I wanted to make my own decisions, I'd have to write my own checks.

[After leaving Poco] I wanted to stay home and to be with my wife more and produce and approach that lifestyle. I didn't feel at all secure in the music echelon having been with Springfield and Poco. I had no reason to feel secure. Buffalo Springfield had never even gotten a gold album. The biggest album that Poco had had to that date was maybe 350,000 units with the live album. I've never gotten a gold album for any of the albums.[7] To me, in terms of

---

[7] To date, according to the Record Industry Association of America, even after reissues, Buffalo Springfield has not achieved gold status.

commercial success, there was very little. I felt very insecure after leaving Poco, but my position in the music business was in good standing.

I felt like I had to get away from what was a kind of communistic situation. I had to share equally and put out more. But I decided to try one more time when I met Kenny [Loggins], but still do something different—which was to produce and to make my own decisions.

I THINK YOU HAVE AN ACT

After leaving Poco, my lawyer, Abe Somer, and I negotiated a deal with CBS. I was an independent producer now. So I went back to Clive and told him that since there was a deal, I would be willing to produce anyone whom he might submit as an artist. Clive—as well as a lot of other people at Columbia, Don Ellis for one—had submitted ideas about acts I should consider producing, but I wasn't interested. They were acts that were already established. I can't remember who they were; they were acts I just threw out of my mind. It was getting kind of strange. It was like Clive was saying, "Well, what *do* you want to do? Make a decision." Because I had already been under the agreement for two or three months, and I hadn't done anything. What I was really looking for was a new artist. I wanted to produce somebody with whom I could start from scratch and be successful with and be proud of and not have to sell out my own creative energies. When I ran across Kenny, I saw the possibilities there to produce him.

Kenny first contacted me by phone. He said he was asked to call me, and he wanted to know if we could get together and he could show me some songs. And I said, "Sure, but why don't you just bring your guitar? We'll make some tapes at my house." So I set up a microphone in front of him, turned on the tape recorder, and sat and watched him—which is probably the most intimidating thing you can do to somebody. At the same time, I figured that if he could get through that, he could get through anything. And he sang his songs. I really liked them and asked him if I could keep them for a while. So I sat and studied whether or not there was an album there. There were a lot of ballads, and that kind of turned me off a bit. My impression of what he should evolve into was more from my point of view than from his. I also felt that having been out on the road and having seen what the competition was like that his music was going to have to become a lot harder—a lot more rock and roll—to really make an impression.

So time went on, and I started listening to more of his tunes, and he listened to mine and eventually we found another approach. Kenny wasn't signed to Columbia at the time. He signed with them a good six or seven months after I started working with him and began getting the musicians together for a band. Finally, Clive said, "What's happening?" And I said, "I think you have an act. I think he'll do it." And then they decided to sign him.

A "SITTIN' IN" APPROACH

Originally, my association with Kenny started out as a producer-artist relationship. He was my first artist, and I felt very personally attached to the project. I was afraid of working with Kenny in the beginning because he had never been on the road before, and the deal with Columbia involved thousands of dollars, my word to Clive Davis that this was going to work and be a success—he had nothing to worry about—and I felt that my reputation was being put on the line. I wanted to make *sure* that it worked.

I decided that if Kenny and I could do a tour together as two artists, it would give me a chance to get out on the road, help out in that sense. It helped my getting Todd (Schiffman) and Larry (Larson)[8] as managers for Kenny because I would be out there on the road knowing how they liked things done. So I decided what the hell—we'll do an album, a sittin'-in concept, make sure that Kenny has fifty per cent of the work and seventy-five per cent of the singing so that no one could say that he was hanging onto my apron strings. So we would do a tour and then I would jump off. The second album would be Kenny's *all by himself*. Having had a tour in and having had a taste for everything, he should then be able to handle his career by himself. If he couldn't, that was his problem. What happened is that it became a lot more successful than we ever thought it would be.

[8] Schiffman and Larson represented Poco.

I enjoyed performing much more than I had before. A lot more of myself was in it in terms of my songs and my music. We had to do it better than any other time I had been involved with a group because it had our names attached to it. It was really important to me to see that it was done to the best of my ability. And Kenny felt the same way about it too.

Clive didn't know, [that I would be part of the first album as an artist]. In fact, Clive was in some ways surprised, maybe even a little upset. He felt—and justifiably so—"What the hell are you making an album for when you're going to break up before the second album? Why do I want to spend money on a group that busts up after one album?" And I came back with the reasoning that there's nothing wrong with two artists doing an album together. The old jazz albums used to do that—they'd sit in on sessions. What's wrong with that? And Clive said, "What's wrong with that is that you're going to have to go out on the road and tour." I hadn't really wanted to, but I saw his point. It would be stupid *not* to go out and support the album.

A BUBBLE ON A BIG SEA

I first signed with Epic Records in 1968, and when the question arose of signing Kenny, it was decided to be Columbia Records. I then asked Epic to drop me so that I could be picked up by Columbia.

In the beginning, at Columbia, I felt like a bubble on a big sea. As time progressed, I started getting to know the people more politically: finding out who was running this department, who was doing that, how you get this job done, who's responsible—just studying the whole bureaucracy. And I suddenly realized that there are great tools there. There's a lot of people who are in the right position to get a lot of work done, and all they needed was the incentive, and that was showing them that I cared about what they were doing as much as I cared about what I was doing. It's just like me with Kenny. I wasn't sure that he could do it. And the record company could feel the same way. If they feel that you can do an interview without making a jackass out of yourself, then they'll set you up with interviews. If they know you're capable of doing a concert tour, they'll help in building your career in that

way. So Columbia Records, to me, has been very, very instrumental in our success as much as a manager and as much as our
agency. I think they're honest. I just performed an audit on them,
and I can see that they've really been straightforward. To me,
that's worth a lot to know that your record company's not trying
to rip you off. I feel a loyalty toward them because they've done a
good job for me. Loyalty [toward a record company] is not something artists have anymore—especially in a business that's as insecure as this one.

HIT SINGLES

The pressure is always there to have a hit single. I mean, we really feel bad about not having had recent hit singles. For the record company we feel bad. Those [promotion] guys go out there,
they walk into a station and say, "Hey, we got the new Loggins
and Messina single," and the disc jockey says, "So what?" And
those guys get a little discouraged after a while and they report
back and say, "Well, we're not getting any reaction." And the record company says, "Why aren't you getting any reaction? These
guys are selling out concerts and you mean to tell us you can't sell
a record?!" I mean, they're not coming down on them *that* heavy,
but that's what the promotion man is thinking in the back of his
mind. He's worrying about his job. It makes it really tough on the
guys out in the field. They lose their credibility; we lose *our* credibility. That happens not having singles.

Bruce Lundvall[9] called me on the phone the other day, and I
said, "I'm really sorry that Kenny and I haven't been able to give
you any singles. It's become very depressing to us." And he said,
"Hey, look, don't feel that way. First of all, you've got to realize
that we released a lot of singles on Paul Simon before we ever got
one. You can't think about those things. Just enjoy your career
and do it. If we get a hit single, we get a hit single." It sure made
me feel a lot better knowing the record company is understanding.
It also made me realize that Kenny and I weren't working as hard
as we used to, either. We had to get back out there and meet those
promo guys, do the interviews. But when you become a headliner,

9 President of Columbia Records.

you develop new problems. Not only do you have the responsibility of doing a great show that evening, but you get offstage
late, you can't get up as early, you don't travel as conveniently,
and you're moving a whole band around. It really makes it
difficult to organize all the things.

In the old days, the record company was there all the time
keeping an eye on us, helping and assisting—which, after you become a headliner, it becomes your responsibility. We were just
doing so many gigs—one-nighters—we got so tired and couldn't
do it anymore.

After "Mama Don't Dance," Kenny and I realized that some of
our better songs weren't given any AM (radio) attention, and we
felt that maybe we ought to start writing in that vein (of "Your
Mama Don't Dance") a little more, so, at least, the stations would
give us some kind of identity and we could expand a new identity
later. A slow building process. But we never were able to do it, so
we finally said, "Screw it!" Why beat yourself over the head to
write songs for somebody else that you don't have inside of you.
So, now, we just write songs for ourselves. If we're going to have a
flop, we'd have a flop with something we really liked.

After ("Mama Don't Dance") we released "Thinking of You,"
which was only a mild success and, after that, from the *Full Sail*
album, we released "My Music," which was a little more like the
"Mama Don't Dance" style, but more serious lyrically. We tried to
water it down a little to bring it back to reality. That's when we
realized that we didn't have to cater to the situation. It wasn't
doing us any good. "Thinking of You" and "My Music" were
more turntable hits[10] than sales hits.

ON MAKING AN ALBUM

The first thing that happens is that the song is written. Then the
song is shared between Kenny and me as to what it's going to
evolve into. We compare our songs and decide on the ones that
will work together in making a good album. Songs that are consis-

[10] Turntable hits are records which receive a lot of airplay, but don't generate sales. "The Wind," by Circus Maximus, or "Gilbert Street," by Sweet
Thursday, are good examples of turntable hits.

tent and somewhat conceptual, if possible. Once we've gotten
comfortable with the songs, we sit down with the band.

We throw the songs at [the band] and start rehearsing them.
First, we work with bass, drums, and guitar. Then we bring in the
horn section because they need to have a rhythm factor they can
work with. They create as they go, but we also dictate too. If
something in their creation doesn't sit well, or they're not getting
anywhere, we try to provoke a little thought by suggesting our
ideas. For the most part, Kenny and I leave everybody their own
space in which to work, but ultimately we have to make the final
decision.

Once the tunes are rehearsed, we set up a recording date. When
we get into the studio, we record everything at one time. We do
very little overdubs, only vocals. That, in itself, creates a spontaneous element that wasn't there when we were rehearsing. And we
can still be tight.

An album's usually cut in four days for the tracks. Then four or
five days for the vocals. And then, it takes me a week to mix it
down. If everything goes right and I don't have any negative input
along the way, I can get an album done in three weeks. In the beginning, I was bringing albums in for forty or fifty thousand dollars. *So Fine* and *Native Sons* cost a lot of money because of the
internal problems, which cause us to spend more money. You can
usually take a look at the cost of the musicians who played on the
date and at the cost of the studio time, and 99.9 per cent of the
time tell what the psychological makeup of the musicians was at
the time—whether they were confused about what they did and if
they were having problems.

THE L&M ALBUMS

Each of our albums has a different feel to it.

Sittin' In represents, to me, a whole lot of time before it was
ever recorded. We had to put a band together around music that
was already written, plus the group was together in rehearsals, and
that played an important part in what the identity of the music
would be. And then came time to perform. We had made our
album before we started performing. Because of that, what I knew
we had to do [in the future] was perform and then record an

album and then go out and perform [again]. *Sittin' In* had to be strong enough to create the concept about what we were going to do onstage. And when that album came out, it had to be credible, otherwise it was not going to happen. That was a lot of work and energy for me to keep all that in mind, trying to make the right grooves and the right steps. So when it came out and it worked, it was very fulfilling.

The second album [*Loggins and Messina*] also had a lot of time spent on it. At that point, the musicians had experienced a taste of success and were feeling pretty good about it and didn't want to spend as much time rehearsing. So we had a huge conflict because I wasn't going into the studio before I was satisfied, and neither was Kenny. Our dissatisfaction over mediocre parts started the deterioration of a situation that could have become great if everybody had just enjoyed being a musician. That was the first time we started experiencing negativity. I don't think it showed up in the album. Because when I started feeling [the negativity], I decided what I was going to do was to start taping everything and then let everybody sit down and listen. It was easy to see what wasn't working. Then they began to see what was happening and started making suggestions. And by the time the album was completed, I think everything was positive again.

If any negativity showed up [in the albums], it was in *Full Sail*. It came from Kenny and I wanting to expand musically and get into other things. I think you have to stay somewhat contemporary in terms of music styles. I've always tried to look for signs of new styles to use as a vehicle for what we're doing. Reggae was happening then. Since I love Latin and Jamaican musical feelings, that was a real nice thing to incorporate into the album. And reggae is also a mood which is a vehicle. So we said to ourselves: What could we do with it? And that started creating a lot of problems. A lot of the guys who we had originally were not into changing musical styles. But Kenny and I both liked it as a steppingstone. We finally went out and bought some reggae tapes and gave them to the guys and urged them to take them home and listen to them so that we could at least develop an understanding of the music. "Coming to You" had sort of a reggae influence, and "Lahaina." That was taking another mood of music and adapting it to our own to give us another depth of style. I think that *Full*

Sail had ushered in the peak of our career. Rather, *a* peak of our career.

On Stage came next. What I wanted to do with *On Stage* was to create a documentation of us as performers. Very few acts can really do a live album and I, of course, felt that we were one of the few that could. It gave us a chance to rest a little bit and get some more songs together. It also gave us a chance to give our 400,000 fans who kept coming to our shows a record, a chance to *hear* our concert. I got a lot of static on that album. [Columbia] didn't want to release it. They felt a live album could be a negative thing because live albums don't usually sell as well. I didn't have any proof that it would sell, but I *knew* it would. And I decided that it was going to be a double album. I knew I would lose money on this particular album, but I would create an incentive for people to buy it. My reasoning was: let's give them an album they would like to listen to in the form of a recorded concert. And, for added incentive, let's drop it from a $9.95 album to a $7.95 album. It would cost a dollar more than they're normally used to paying. It was a question of my sitting down with the record company and suggesting, "Here's an approach." So the album was released for $7.98, and it turned out to be one of our biggest selling albums. That made me feel good because it justified what I wanted to see happen anyway.

Then we made *Motherlode*—my favorite up to that point. I thought it was a good extension from *Full Sail,* but there were no singles on it and, therefore, the album didn't quite sell as much as the *Full Sail* album. Because we hadn't any singles, I believe AM radio stations began taking a lack of interest in Loggins and Messina.

So Fine was released because we wanted to have fun doing an album and do some of the songs we always used to warm up with. We were warned [in advance] by the record company that it wouldn't sell. They created a lot of negativity before the album came out—before they had even heard the music. My feeling was that sometimes you just had to take certain risks, gamble on certain things. I think that too many people took that album too seriously. For someone who wanted to do an album to show a lot of respect for a lot of great writers and a lot of great talent, our intention was to make an album which we could have some fun doing, not having to belabor coming up with new songs and new arrangements—shit! Just having some fun doing a summertime album. The radio people took it too seriously. The radio people are the ones that made that album not popular. The critics took it that way too. We do some of *So Fine* in our sets, and it's some of the best stuff we do. The audience loves it. [The radio people and the critics] should have listened to it as an album and had fun instead of trying to analyze it, determine what the ulterior motives were and all that bullshit. And, as it turned out, the album did not sell as well as I hoped. They shipped about four hundred thousand, and the sales probably leveled off at about three hundred thousand.

Right now, we're in the process of promoting *Native Sons* and, assuming we don't have a hit single, it will probably sell about 500,000 albums. Which is quite good when you're talking about album sales, but low when you're talking about superstar record sales, which are expected of us.

ON KENNY LOGGINS

Kenny Loggins is easy to work with in the studio. The only technical problem that I've had working with [him] is his enunciation. He doesn't enunciate very well, which results in his words becoming garbled. Since I'm around him pretty much, I pretty well know the lyrics [to his songs]. And my biggest problem is knowing whether I've asked him to enunciate enough. If we do a rough vocal, I'll usually bring in Jenny [Messina] or Kenny's girl friend Eva Ein.[11] And I'll ask them, "What is he saying?" On my songs, I'll let Eva listen to them; on his songs, I'll let Jenny listen to them—whoever doesn't know the material.

Kenny's musicianship is good. He really tries to compliment whatever I'm playing. And I try to compliment whatever he's into. Overall, though, he's really a great writer and a great singer. His musicianship is something that is getting better and better as time goes on.

Socially, Kenny and I remain pretty separate. I think we're more social now than we've ever been. We just had different types

[11] They were married in January 1977.

of lives. He had a different type of old lady than my old lady—so
the old ladies didn't work. That can be a very dividing force. And,
also, we did spend a lot of time together doing music, and when
you get home you've got to get away from each other. There's really not a lot of room for a lot of social life anyway when you're
traveling together. Rich [Furay] and I didn't have a strong social
life. Neither did I with Neil or Stephen. I've never had a strong
social life with anybody I've worked with because we've spent so
much time together making music—just music.

PARTING THOUGHTS

One of the things that led to the dissolving of [Kenny's and my]
creative relationship was when it became clear that Ken and I
were not spending the kind of time together that was needed in
writing and arranging our songs. Not singing and working out
vocal arrangements like we had done in the past before we went
into the recording studio. It was a big mistake. I believe we
worked harder in the beginning. I think, also, that this lack of attention to our musical relationship affected our band. They saw
that we were creating individually on the spot at rehearsals, and
we'd disagree, making it difficult because it actually put [the band]
in an awkward position of sometimes having to make a choice. All
of this could have been avoided by our mutual decision to work
musical ideas out before bringing the songs to the band.

The first thing Kenny and I did when we decided we weren't
going to work together [anymore] was to let our manager know.
Also my lawyer. I was of the opinion that before we told anybody
else, we should tell our record company and then everyone who
was actually involved in our career. So we brought all of the key
executives together—the presidents and most of the vice-
presidents—put them into a room with both of us there and told
them that we no longer had a strong creative relationship, we
didn't have any songs, we couldn't make another album, our
hearts weren't in it, and we were finishing our tour. We believed in
our album [*Native Sons*] and that was the one reason we were
going to finish our tour—because we wanted to support it. We
wanted their help as to how to effect the split. We were prepared
to deal with them saying, "You can't break up. We won't let you."

Instead they were very kind, very understanding and, of course, they didn't want us to discontinue our career, but they were appreciative that we had come to them before going to the press or anybody else and telling them that we were breaking up. They were helpful in helping us end a very long and very good relationship.

I'd like to take some time off because I have been touring and working for the last eight or nine years pretty steadily. I'd like to write some good songs. I enjoy being an artist more than anything —even more so than being a producer or an engineer or publisher or, one day, being a record executive. I enjoy being an artist most of all and I'd like to pursue that. In the meantime, I'd like to produce a couple of acts and help some new talent get going.

Don Kirshner

"You hear his voice above the roaring of
    the crowd
Dance while he goes through his charade
You see him standing there so tall and
    proud
And you know damn well the man has got
    it made."

N. SEDAKA AND P. CODY, *Your Favorite Entertainer*

*Intuition is perhaps the most curious of man's senses—a unique
marriage of imagination and spiritual intelligence incapable of
reasoning. Often it is mistaken for luck, but while time and place
interact compatibly, that inborn proclivity, that spontaneousness,
that instinctiveness marks the difference between talent and banal-
ity.*

*Don Kirshner has made a life's work staking his reputation on
intuition, committing himself and connecting. Fresh out of college,
he wagered his education on the plausible success of an infant
rock music business to evolve an omnific force in the multimedia
of modern-day entertainment. In slightly more than fifteen years,
he has developed more popular songwriting teams, song standards, and more musical sensations than almost any other industry
contemporary and has expanded that embryonic musical form on
which he gambled his career into a vast empire which includes
records, publishing, merchandising, television, and motion pictures.*

Kirshner's musical associations are legendary. Beginning with a "disheveled, young guy" named Robert Walden Cossotto (Bobby Darin), he soon associated himself with two unknown teenage songwriters named Neil Sedaka and Howard Greenfield. Their success soon attracted to him other writers such as Carole King and Gerry Goffin, Barry Mann and Cynthia Weil, and David Gates. As well as the entertainers: Tony Orlando, Connie Francis, Jan and Dean, Neil Diamond, Olivia Newton-John, and Kansas. And many others. He has brought respectability to rock music through the careful and tasteful televised presentation of his weekly program Don Kirshner's Rock Concert, *and other specials.*

While Kirshner's reputation has been in ascendance for more than fifteen years, he is still somewhat modest about his success, although he speaks of it confidently and easily. The thrust of that success has been his ability to do his own public relations, to come across and sell his personality—the wholesome Don Kirshner image—with relative ease. That image is ambiguous in the sense that it lends itself to both the youthfulness of the music and to the corporate starchiness which controls the entertainment media. But that is done intentionally, through Kirshner's decisive attack, to remain accessible to both factions and to succeed. Thus, Kirshner is the intermediary in the dichotomous rock music ensemble.

In contrast to his multiformity, Kirshner has remained true to musical diversification—universality—rather than specialization. He consciously appeals to the majority rather than limit himself to the "connoisseur." He has been criticized by the so-called rock elite for his unwillingness to regiment his perspective. This has always been Kirshner's way—delivering what he feels most people want to hear whether they are musical sophisticates or weekend enthusiasts. This is best illustrated by his scheduling of appearances on Rock Concert. *On any given show, there could be performances by the Eagles, Van Morrison, Linda Ronstadt, the Rolling Stones, or Barry Manilow. And yet certain of the rock press continues to criticize the shows for being too "soft," for being too "pop oriented." It is a characterization that Kirshner will find hard pressed to shake because of his long-standing dominance within the corporate establishment.*

He is methodical and relies heavily on his persuasiveness—an art which he has meticulously developed over the years. Don Kirshner is not a very loud man, nor is he dictatorial in his ap-

*proach to his business. Yet he is calculating and has definite ca-
reer objectives projected over the next few years which he will not
compromise. To hear him speak of becoming "as big as MCA
used to be" might lead one to believe the man has delusions of
grandeur, but with the extensive musical catalogue which he controls, the hours of network production already committed to his
organization, and the machinery in gear for feature film production, Don Kirshner is well on his way toward fulfilling all of his
ambitions.*

I WANTED TO PLAY PRO BALL

When I was much younger, I wasn't really into music. My family wasn't musical either except for my mother, who played concert piano and even played in Carnegie Hall once. But I was fairly
removed from it as a youngster. I can't even read or write music. I
do what I do by feel.

I never thought I'd even get into this business. I wanted to play
pro baseball and basketball when I was a kid growing up in the
Bronx and later Washington Heights. I even worked out with the
Brooklyn (Dodgers) farm team and had basketball and baseball
scholarships to Seton Hall University. I went there on a basketball
scholarship and later transferred to Upsala College in East Orange, New Jersey.

Before my senior year in college, and during summers I was a
busboy and played ball in the [Catskill] mountains. While working as a bellhop during my senior year, I wrote my first song. I
had no idea what I was doing, but I was having fun. I was swim-
ming in a pool, and there was a sixteen-year-old boy playing a
melody on the piano nearby. When I got out of the pool, I told
the boy that I liked it and said, "Why don't you put some words
to it?" He said, "I don't know how. Why don't you try?" So I gave
it a try, and I wrote my first song as a result of that meeting.
Frankie Laine was playing at the Surf Club on Long Island at the
time—that's where I was working. He was very hot in those days
with songs like "Mule Train" and "Ride the Wild Goose." And I
was his bellhop. So I played the song for him, and he said, "It's
great! Make a demonstration record, and I'll help you push it in

New York." I said, "What's a demonstration record?" And Frankie told me how I had to go into the studio and put it down.

My mom and dad gave me the money, and I went to a studio in New York and got a young kid, who was a bartender, to sing it. It was very exciting. You didn't have to be brilliant to make a good demo: just bring the voice out higher than the piano. And that's exactly what I did.

That was my entrance into the music business.

WHY DON'T WE TEAM UP?

After that demo session, I pushed around for five or six months and nothing really happened. I finally got the song published, but it didn't mean anything because it was never recorded by anyone. But in my neighborhood that year I was kind of a big deal—I had just published a song, I was captain of the basketball team.

One day, while I was having an egg cream in a local candy store, a girl friend of mine walked in with a kid whose hair was kind of disheveled. She introduced me to him as Robert Walden Cossotto. This was, of course, Bobby Darin. She had introduced me to him because I had just published a song. So we went up to her house, which was close by, and Bobby played four or five things for me. Well, I just thought he was an incredible talent. I sat with him for a while and said, "Why don't we team up? We'll be the biggest thing in the business." I didn't know anybody in the business at the time. I couldn't even get in a door. But Bobby had nothing to lose. We got along as friends, so we teamed up. I wrote lyrics and Bobby wrote melody.

It really was tough trying to land a deal for him. I was still in college. I was still captain of the basketball team and sometimes had to cut practice, which was really embarrassing. I didn't drive, so I had to take the bus from New Jersey to New York City. And if I had a twelve-thirty appointment with a record company to play Bobby's material—songs that Bobby and I wrote—they usually kept me waiting until two-thirty or three and I'd come back and the coach would be mad. Here I was the captain of the team, and I couldn't even make practice. I had gotten the music bug. We struggled for a year before we got our first deal.

Herb Abramson[1] was at Atlantic Records at the time, and we
convinced him to get us in to see Ahmet [Ertegun] and Jerry
[Wexler]. Jerry signed Bobby right away. That was in 1959. Ertegun and Wexler believed in him from the start. We had a couple
of things that didn't hit right away—a couple of things that Bobby
and I wrote. Then he recorded "Splish Splash," "Mack the
Knife," and followed it with "Dreamlover," which broke everything wide open. After that, Bobby wanted me to manage him, but
I didn't want to carry his bags all over the country. So we parted
ways professionally, but we always remained friends.

Bobby Darin was probably one of the most underrated talents
in the business. He could do everything: he wrote, he could play
eight or nine instruments, he was an actor (he was nominated for
an Academy Award for his performance in *Captain Newman,
M.D.*), he was a songwriter—he was brilliant.

Bobby was moody. He was introverted at times and egocentric
like most performers are. Everything had to revolve around him.
He only had one or two close friends. He had a driving ambition
to be a legend before he was twenty-nine, and that consumed him.
His idol was Frank Sinatra. In the early days we had a problem
finding an identity for him because he emulated Sinatra so much.
He was a great imitator. When we were walking the street (before
getting a record deal), he would imitate Pat Boone, Little Richard, or Fats Domino. And until "Splish Splash" hit—which was a
novelty song—he had no identity of his own.

I HAD A GOOD SONG SENSE

After Bobby and I broke up, I really had to decide what I
wanted to do. My idols at the time were Max and Louie Dreyfuss,
who had built Chappell Music. I had watched some of the old
movies they were in, like *Night and Day* and *Rhapsody in Blue*
and had observed them molding the greats like Gershwin, Rodgers
and Hammerstein and Lerner and Loewe. And my philosophy—
my dream—while I walked from office to office with Darin, was
that we were approaching a new era in the music business with
room for new people to accomplish what the Dreyfusses had. And

[1] An original partner in the early days of Atlantic Records.

I believed that if I got the chance to sit behind a desk in the music business, I'd be the guy to accomplish that. I felt I had a good song sense. I could discover and work with new talent. When you're a kid—I was only twenty-one years old then—you believe you're the guy, that you can do anything.

So I started my own publishing company. In 1958, I had met a guy named Al Nevins, who believed in me. I met him through a friend. Al had been with the Three Suns musical group. I kept telling him how much I believed in music publishing. I kept nagging him and telling him we should get together. Then I introduced Al to Bobby Darin and told him, "He's going to be a star." Al thought I was a little nuts. But I bothered him enough so that one day—he had a little office with an answering service—he put two desks in the office. I put up fifty dollars for my first stock certificate, and I began drawing fifty dollars a week for salary. We formed a company called Aldon Music and our concept was to build new writers. From that company we formed the first independent production company, which brought Tony Orlando to CBS, Sedaka to RCA and Barry Mann, with whom we had a number-one hit ("Who Put the Bomp"), to ABC.

THE OFFICE GANG

I met Neil Sedaka at the time I had just opened the office with Al. We had just been open a week or two. The office was a big closet. Al had a small desk, I don't know what I used.

One afternoon, while I was sweeping the floor with a short-sleeve shirt on, getting ready to start business, Neil and Howie Greenfield knocked on the door. They had just been turned down by Hill and Range [Publishing] upstairs. They asked to see me. I said, "I'm the guy!" They said, "C'mon, you're kidding us." But they figured they had nothing to lose, they proceeded to play six incredible songs: "Stupid Cupid," "The Diary," "Calendar Girl," and a few others. I thought they were putting me on. I couldn't believe that anyone could turn down songs like those.

I wanted Neil and Howie to meet Connie Francis, who was a dear friend of mine. I knew her from Jersey when I was going to Upsala College. She was a nice girl who always knew what she wanted to do, very definite. We had been doing commercials with her and Bobby Darin for local furniture stores. And Connie had just had a number-one hit with "Who's Sorry Now?" So I took Neil and Howie over to her house and had them play "Stupid Cupid" for her. She loved it. It was the first song I did with Sedaka and Greenfield. We did a couple more with Connie that were all hits, songs like "Where the Boys Are," "Everybody's Somebody's Fool," and "Frankie."

Even Neil was dubious at the time about his singing ability. I felt that he could sing. He was only doing the writing then. So we went over to RCA, set up a deal, and all the hits which I produced with Al Nevins just started coming. Neil was brilliant in the studio. He knew what he wanted right away, did all his own overdubbing, and got the job done. Producing a record then wasn't much different from what it is today. Today, people make much more of a big deal about it and have to spend hundreds of thousands of dollars in the studio to make it more artistic. But if you rehearse before you go into the studio, there's no need to spend that kind of money. In a three-hour day in the studio, we came out with "Calendar Girl," "Happy Birthday Sweet Sixteen," and "Breaking Up Is Hard to Do." In those days we used to cut ten or twelve hits in a row. Today, if a recording artist has three hits, there's a national party for him. Neil and I are still associated as writer and publisher. We formed a new deal a few years ago. I teamed him with Phil Cody, who was a writer in my office, and together they produced "Laughter in the Rain." After that, Neil struck again with Howie Greenfield with "Love Will Keep Us Together," which was named Song of the Year. I also publish it.

After he had "The Diary" I wanted Neil to write something uptempo like "Little Darlin'." And he came in with "Oh Carole." I went to a recording date, and Carole King was doing an answer record to "Oh Carole," called "Oh Neil." I saw her seated at the piano and heard her sound, and I thought she was magic. We became friendly.

Gerry Goffin, at the time, was working in a chemistry lab downtown. One day, I went down to Brooklyn, got him out of that chemistry lab—he was in a white robe and everything—and said, "Look, I'll give you and Carole fifty dollars a week each. Sign with me, and I'll make you the biggest writers in the country."

They did, and for years they only took that fifty-dollar-a-week check—even though I was giving them six figure royalty checks.[2]

Another team, Barry Mann and Cynthia Weil were with us from the beginning. Cynthia had been writing for me at the time, and I put her together with Barry. We were terrific with husband-and-wife teams. We used to have playpens in our office and the secretaries would change the babies. Barry and Cynthia wrote "You've Lost That Loving Feeling" and "I Love How You Love Me" for me and a stack of other hits which we had. Afterward, I urged Barry to record "Who Put the Bomp." He wasn't sure he could do it, but it turned out sensational. I produced it, and we had a number-one hit. Then, they wrote "On Boadway," with Lecker and Stotler and had another string of hits which still hasn't stopped. They were nice young kids, very intense as writers, concerned about everything they did. I really valued our association.[3]

I remember taking Tony Orlando to see Bobby Darin at the Copa. Bobby was his idol, and I took him there when he was only sixteen. Tony just walked into my office one day—I don't remember how he got there. He was exceptionally heavy. But what I liked about him was that he had that kind of ethnic quality and warmth which has won him his popularity today. He's one of the nicest people this world has ever seen. Recently, my son Ricky had a bar mitzvah, and Tony showed up to entertain with a full orchestra which he completely paid for. I couldn't believe it. But that's the type of man he is. The best. I really thought that the market was ready for another Ritchie Valens, and Tony reminded me very much of Ritchie. You didn't know if he was Puerto Rican or Greek or Italian. He just had that universal quality and a soul sound like a white Ray Charles. And I felt that it was just right. So I put him with Carole [King] and Gerry [Goffin] and they did "Bless You" and "Halfway to Paradise" with Tony.

Even the people who worked for me read like a history of the record business. Allen Klein[4] was a college classmate of mine who

---

[2] Salary advances were deducted from royalties, and therefore receiving more as a salary accomplished little. They always wanted to remember the days they were getting a fifty-dollar check.

[3] Today Barry Mann records as a solo artist and still writes with Cynthia.

[4] Former mentor of the Beatles and the Rolling Stones, Klein now is president of ABKCO Industries—a multimedia corporation.

FERNALD LIBRARY
COLBY-SAWYER COLLEGE
NEW LONDON, N. H. 03257

I brought into the business as an accountant. He had a different style from mine, so we eventually parted ways. I brought in Lou Adler[5] and gave him a job running my West Coast office. Jerry Moss[6] was my promotion man. And the people who ran in and out of the office were producers like Snuffy Garrett and Phil Spector—just hanging in and hanging around and doing our songs.

It was a whole creative environment. We had offices with six or seven pianos going all the time with the kids writing and competing, working together, working against each other. But it was a family. Everybody was friendly in our office, but the competition was fierce. I'm sure that Carole King would rather have gotten a record [from her writings] than [allow] Neil Sedaka to get it instead. Somebody had to win. And if they didn't, we'd lose it to another publisher. I've always believed that competition is healthy in any environment—especially in one where everybody gets along.

THE EARLY DAYS OF ROCK MUSIC PUBLISHING

We were a breakthrough publisher in the Fifties. A lot of the old line publishers like Leeds Music or Sheldon Music with Goldie Goldmark were going along undauntedly, and I think they were becoming a little staid. There was no new thinking or new blood, and here we were involved with a new music. Al and I were just a different breed of ballplayer—we may have looked a little different or unorthodox—but the ball went in the basket the same way, and that was what mattered.

I started the era of the demo record. The demos we used to make were absolutely terrific. Imagine Bobby Darin or Carole King or Neil Sedaka or Barry Mann doing demos. Our demos were just like masters. In fact, one day Carole and Gerry brought in a demo of their baby-sitter doing a song they had written called "Locomotion." It had originally been written for Chubby Checker and Dee Dee Sharp, but they turned it down for sounding too much like "The Twist," so I put the demo of the baby-sitter out as a master, and the singer was, of course, Little Eva. So most of the

5 President of Ode Records.

6 Co-owner and Chairman of the Board of A&M Records with Herb Alpert.

time, the demos were so professional that we had to low-key them —otherwise the A&R men wouldn't have any depth of imagination. It would turn them off. They'd never be able to top our demos with their record. But we really conceived the demonstration record and, at that time, even though it was all done in-house and they would do five overdubs and all the instruments, they all sounded like masters. That's one of the reasons it was easier to come home with the hits. If Darin or Goffin or King or Mann or Sedaka walked in with a song, how were these A&R men going to turn it down?

It was almost impossible to get songs played in the beginning. That's why we started the independent production of masters with the majors [record companies]. The only outlet when I started was getting the songs recorded by other independent producers or A&R men, or recording it yourself and selling the record to a major label as is.

The A&R man was very big, and two men controlled the industry: Mitch Miller (at Columbia Records), and Milt Gabler at the Decca Group. If Mitch or Milt turned down a song, you were in trouble. I brought Mitch "Will You Still Love Me Tomorrow," which Carole and Gerry had written, for Johnny Mathis and he turned it down. But finally, I took it over to Florence Greenberg and Marv Schlacter for a group they had called The Shirelles, and that record virtually started Scepter.

I used to schlep all over with the songs. I was a little bit of a renegade. I didn't believe in the principles they had about how you had to go about getting a record for your song. We tried every method in the book to get our material recorded. It was a lot of fun in those days. Much easier than it is today.

Today, the artists get greedy. They insist on doing their own material which blocks out publishers and blocks out their discovering good outside songs.

ON BEING A PUBLISHER

I've always been the champion of music publishing. To me, a song is like real estate, like gold. Publishing is one of the most lucrative businesses in the world. On a balance sheet, it may not show, but when it comes down to people in the [music] industry,

then the true value shows. On a balance sheet, if you show that
you've just invested three hundred grand in Sedaka and
Greenfield, most people would think that money is gone. But people in the music business assume that the same three hundred
grand has been well spent and is working for you. People never
understand the worth in a specialized field until they see the sale
of interests in that field.

It was difficult for young writers in the Fifties to understand
their own talent. Most of them were struggling, they had to make
a living; they had to pay the bills. My job was to nurture and
develop their talent and to build the writers' confidence.

A publisher is really a teammate on a song. He shares the income. And he must exploit and promote the material, get the record to the right group, be it the Rolling Stones or Captain and
Tenille. A creative publisher should help to shape the song. If the
title is "Take Good Care of Her," and he thinks a better title
would be "Take Good Care of My Baby," then the publisher
should have the creative input to suggest the change be made. He
should help with the rhyme pattern, the hook, *anything* to get that
song recorded. Carole and Gerry brought me "Will You Still Love
Me Tomorrow," and it was four and a half minutes long. I shaved
it, changed a hook on it; they were brilliant, talented people, but
I had to condense it to the right thing.

A publisher's job is being a father, mother, lawyer, psychiatrist,
writer, as well as someone who enhances songwriters' creative
juices, picks them up when they're down; takes their phone calls
at three in the morning and enhances the copyright for them—by
encouraging other artists to record the song even after it becomes
a major hit. In other words, when we have a record like "Love
Will Keep Us Together" recorded by the Captain and Tenille, we
don't settle. We still get it to Shirley Bassey or Stevie Wonder[7] and
extend the life of the copyright.

A good publisher also has to be able to spot the song. When I
think about all the songs I've published that have become standards, I also think about how incredible it is that they've lasted so
long, that people still hum them today. That's what I look for in a
song—longevity. And a writer's got to have it to be a success. I

---

[7] He recorded "We Can Work It Out," published by ATV/Kirshner.

don't know what it takes to spot a good song or a songwriter. It's an innate thing. It's something I know, I can feel inside of me. It's like what Mantle and Ruth had inside of them that made them great ballplayers. You can't describe why or how you know—you just do.

Sometimes, if a writer comes in to see me and I know he's got the potential but his songs aren't up to the level they should be, I have to make an investment. I have to spend a year or two shaping the writer, working with him until he develops. You have to stick with a writer you think is going to make it. In the early days, I gave my writers fifty dollars a week. Fifty then was like $150 or $200 a week now. You'd invest a salary in them so they could exist, so you could do demos with them and get them around. For example, I stayed with Phil Cody for four years paying him big money. It's a big investment, time and money, but you don't push. Phil stayed in our back room working and doing, getting himself together, and I just had to have patience because I really believed in his talent. You commit yourself to your beliefs and ride them out.

In addition, you've got to know how to bring the writer over to the American public. It's knowing the market, knowing how the trends will be shaping up—like we did with the Monkees and the Archies. A feeling that the market is ready—the awareness of the psychological and sociological impact of the marketplace. Knowing when the country is ready to laugh or to cry or to dance and disco should be the result. It's a combination of all these things. You really try to keep aware of the needs of the market and to create a trend. When I did the Monkees, the Beatles were getting married, they weren't touchable to the public anymore; they lost their innocence. I knew that if a group like the Monkees came on TV, it would take all the marbles.

SCREEN GEMS/COLUMBIA MUSIC

In 1963, we sold Aldon Music to Columbia Pictures and I named the new company Screen Gems/Columbia.[8] After that, I had offers to work for a lot of companies, including ABC and Co-

---

[8] Screen Gems/Columbia was sold to EMI for $23.5 million in 1976.

lumbia Pictures. I became president of Columbia Pictures/Screen Gems Television Music Division, where I was president of their publishing company and president of their record company.[9] I was also the music supervisor receiving screen credit on shows like "Bewitched" (whose theme was written by Howie Greenfield), "I Dream of Genie," and "The Farmer's Daughter" (theme: Mann and Weil). I also won the Academy Award as publisher of *Born Free,* and did *Baby the Rain Must Fall* and *To Sir, with Love*— most of their successful motion pictures. I brought all my writers there, too, and signed people like David Gates and Neil Diamond for them.

I had a percentage of the profits at Screen Gems/Columbia. I was earning about $1,300,000 a year as a company employee, and I was earning four times more than Abe Schneider[10] after the Monkees hit. Before they hit, I earned 30 per cent of nothing (on a percentage of the profits), but when they started outselling the Beatles by two million albums, my 30 per cent became worth an incredible amount of money. They had just resigned me to a ten-year deal and probably felt threatened by my earning so much. So, instead of being a *mensch* and calling me in and settling it (by renegotiating my contract) which I would have been happy to do —I had just resigned Mann and Weil, Sedaka and Greenfield, and Goffin and King to ten-year deals at Screen Gems/Columbia— they fired me. Just like that.

I hired Edward Bennett Williams as my attorney and got the biggest settlement in the history of Columbia Pictures. It was such a large settlement that I was not allowed to disclose the amount at the time. So I set out to build my own entertainment complex because my concept was: Why shouldn't I build my own Columbia Pictures? Why shouldn't I be as big as MCA used to be? And that's what I'm attempting to do now, only bigger and stronger.

HEY! HEY! WE'RE THE MONKEES!

Columbia Pictures had a concept for a music show. It was based upon a group called the Monkees, and it was to be produced by Burt Schneider and Bob Rafelson. The group had never

---

[9] Including the Colgems and Colpix labels.
[10] President of Columbia Pictures

sung together, had never done *anything* together. Burt called me up and said, "Donnie, I want you to come out to Hollywood and perform a miracle. I need singers, I need songs." I didn't like to fly in those days, but I schleped out my wife Sheila and two children, and they got me a home there for two months. I brought in Goffin and King, Mann and Weil, Sedaka and Greenfield, the Tokens, and Neil Diamond and created songs for the group. On most of the records I did with the Monkees, Carole King and Neil Diamond would sing background.

I had heard that Snuffy Garrett had tried to do some records with the Monkees and the boys had given him a hard time. So the first time I went to a Monkees record date, I came prepared. We were all real nervous about it; they were prestars and were a little frightened about being on TV. I was there to do business because I had records to get out. So I walked in with four ringers—four studio men—because I assumed [the Monkees] would give me a hard time. And after they clowned around for the first ten minutes, I said, "All right, fellas—out!" And I brought in the four ringers. I put them on the mikes, and the boys came back right away and we made some great records together.

The Monkees were very temperamental guys. I had given them royalty checks for over a million dollars at a time—kids who [previously] had nothing. After the first two hits, Mike [Nesmith] said he didn't like the way the records had been produced. I was out at the Beverly Hills Hotel with my wife and mother-in-law and friend, Herb Moelis,[11] and we were all pretty happy, what with the success of the Monkees. And, in front of everybody, Mike gave me a hard time and proceeded to put his fist through the wall.

I was fired soon after the first couple Monkees successes, and their sales went from eight million right down to practically nothing.

HOW DO I TOP THE MONKEES?

After I was fired at Screen Gems/Columbia, I said to myself, "How do I top the Monkees?" I came home that day, and my son Ricky was reading an Archie comic book, and I got the idea from

[11] Herb was presently executive vice-president of Kirshner Entertainment Corp.

that. I suggested that Filmation do a show on the Archies. I felt the Archies represented a lot of wholesomeness. We had grown up with Archie, Jughead, and Veronica, and I felt that what I wanted to do would be similar to what Ross Bagdasarian had done with the Chipmunks a few years prior. We would be substituting Archie, Jughead, and Veronica for his Alvin, Theodore, and Simon. John Goldwater's property was put on the air as a 10:30 A.M. cartoon show, and most people thought I was crazy. They said, "They'll never sell records." But I thought that if I gave the characters a sound like Bagdasarian did and it was good music and it had television exposure, it could work.

"Sugar, Sugar" became one of the biggest international hits selling ten million singles and becoming one of the biggest singles in the history of the record business without even having a live group. I signed Jeff Barry and Andy Kim to do the song for me. Ron Dante, who produces Barry Manilow and is still a writer for me, was the lead singer of the group. That same year Ronnie did Tracy and the Cufflinks too.

ROCK CONCERT

One night, I was sitting at home watching Johnny Carson. He had a rock group on, and when it came time for the guitar riff, the camera was on the piano. I said to myself, "That's ridiculous." No wonder they weren't doing rock on television. Nobody understood it. I thought that as I was a music man, there wasn't anybody more qualified to do it. I had paid my dues for years as a music supervisor for television shows, I had links with the major television producers, and what was it to being a producer other than having concerts, having faith and getting the gig?

I went to ABC-TV and I said, "Look, put me on late night TV, and I think I can beat out a Dick Cavett or a Jack Paar and get bigger ratings." I think they thought I was a little crazy, but they called me back and asked, "Who do you think you could bring in?" I said, "I don't know. Give me the gig and I'll get them." So they gave it to me.

I got a break because ABC had the appetite to put rock on the air. They were about to experiment with late night programming and they didn't know what to put on. They were going to try some comedy, some horror, some music. I said, "Give me a few shows. Where are you going to get hurt? I'll bring it in on budget, I'll do what you want me to do," and we did it. We put the only per- formance of the Allman Brothers Band on the air, we did Alice Cooper, we did Grand Funk Railroad from Madison Square Gar- den, and then, two weeks later, I put four unknowns on the air and ABC got mad at me for doing that. The four unknowns were: the Doobies (Brothers), War, the Edgar Winter group, and Jim Croce.

Dick Clark got a little annoyed that after a twenty-year rela- tionship with ABC they gave a music show to me. So he called up one of the heads at ABC-TV and said, "How about giving me a couple?" So they did. And I tried to help Dick by getting people like Loggins and Messina and other acts for him. Pretty soon, they were starting to give a lot of shows to Dick and I said, "Hey look, this is not for me. I'm going to go out and do my own thing."

Mike Douglas, who is a friend of mine, started telling me about syndication and how it affected shows like his and "Hee Haw" and "Lawrence Welk." This was a whole new field for me. So I pitched an idea to a former high-school buddy, Merril Grant,[12] at Viacom, and they said, "Let's try to clear some stations." So they started clearing fifteen or twenty stations. Then I made a deal to get the Rolling Stones—their first appearance in ten years since [their being on] the [Ed] Sullivan show. And when I did that, all of a sudden [Viacom] cleared fifty or sixty stations and I wound up on the air. I said to myself, *"In Concert*[13]—for that I'm getting very little credit. I'll call the show 'Don Kirshner's Rock Con- cert.' If it doesn't happen, nobody will know the difference. If it happens, *terrific!*" All these things seemed very simple to me, and they *were*. They were practical. The show has done very well, and we've had on all the top groups as well as breaking the new- comers.

There are a lot of complaints that my show has hurt the concert business. First of all, the people in the concert business don't re- ally care about my television show, so I can't concern myself with the concert business. All those kids who can't get a ticket to a cer-

---

[12] Currently president of Don Kirshner Productions.
[13] The title used for Kirshner's original concept which opened late eve- ning TV for rock music.

tain show can't economically afford to go to all of the concerts—
they can finally get a chance to see their favorite groups right on
television with excellent fidelity and good camera work. And if
they do go to the shows, most of the time, these kids have to either sit up in the green[14] seats or pay scalpers' prices. Hell, I feel
as though I'm doing them a service. And, in all due respects, if
I'm a parent and these parents see what happens at a Z Z Top
concert or at Altamont or wherever something like that happens,
I'm much happier if my kid is at home watching [these same
groups] in the confines of the home.

DON'T MAKE ME DO THAT

One Wednesday, I had made a deal for Jim Croce to be on my
show. He was also to appear on a Wednesday. That next Thursday, after doing my show, he went up in a plane, and that was it.
He was gone, and it destroyed me emotionally. I called up his
family, and they said, "We want you to talk about Jim." I said,
"There's no way in the world I'm getting up in front of a camera.
I'm terrified."

Two weeks later, I didn't get any footage from them, and they
said, "We're not giving you the rest of the show." I said, "Look,
I'd love to talk about Jim, but don't make me do that." Anyway, I
went on, all nervous, sweaty, terrified, and I did my little minute.
All of a sudden, I started getting very nice fan mail about what a
nice piece it was—and why don't I do more talking on camera.
They said that I wasn't Dick Clark, I wasn't Wolfman Jack, I was
refreshing. And I was personally pleased.

We got picked up by the stations for another year, and I said to
myself, "What I'm going to do is like what *People* magazine does,
like *Rolling Stone*'s "Random Notes" does, I'm going to get up
there and talk about people in our business who have shaped the
industry—the managers, the agents, the Ahmet Erteguns, the
Jerry Wexlers, the John Hammonds—and give them credit. These
people are the Thalbergs and De Milles of the future. And there
are a lot of young people out there who might not be able to be-

---

[14] In Madison Square Garden, the quality of the seats is graded according
to the color of the fabric, and the color of the cheapest seats is green.

come a manager or an agent, but they can become a roadie or a singer like Jagger, and I wanted to open up a lot of new horizons.

I also wanted to let the kids know interesting facts about the groups they like—how the Hues Corporation made their own clothes or how one artist was a Baptist minister's son—how they came about, who they were, it could happen to you.

So, my being a host on the show began working, and now I'm going on my third year being on camera. And I thoroughly enjoy it.

WHY DON'T I DO THAT TYPE OF SHOW?

Tony Orlando and I have gone to the last three Grammy Awards years together. The year he was up for "Tie a Yellow Ribbon" I was there with him. Well, I just sat back when I heard the nominations, and I said, "It's really incredible—Dylan, Led Zeppelin, the Stones, Joni Mitchell, none of them are nominated!" I turned to my wife and said, "Why don't I do that type of show, a rock awards type of show?"

Well, I framed the idea and took it to the heads of CBS-TV. I didn't think they would do it because they had the Grammies. They knew about my "Rock Concert," and they had been getting a lot of protest mail about the same things I had thought about earlier: why is it that year after year there is no mention of Bob Dylan on the Grammy Show, no Zeppelin or Stones? They didn't like getting mail like that. It was almost as if they were being un- fair to a segment of the audience. Once again, they said to me, "Who do you think you can get?" I said, "I can't get anyone until you tell me I've got the gig. Give me the show. I've delivered in the past." A little later, they called me back and said I had the gig. I couldn't believe it.

We felt that since the American Music Awards represented the public voicing their opinion and the Grammies represented our own industry association (NARAS),[15] a panel of judges who shift every year made up of the rock press and disc jockeys who are in the streets and in the trenches writing about the music should be

[15] The National Academy of Recording Arts and Sciences; the Grammy is their award of achievement.

the ones who voice their opinion for the Rock Awards. They live
with it all the time. I thought that was the logical choice.

We got Elton [John] and Diana [Ross] and structured the categories so that all aspects of the rock business would be represented. It felt really good. It wasn't too hard convincing the artists
to appear. Once I had Elton and Diana, everybody wanted to do
it. But then, that's been the story of my life: creating the vehicle
and enticing people to want to be a part of my organization.
That's the best way. That's the *only* way.

Barry Manilow

> "And when I heard all the words about
> passion
> Singin to me about love of fashion
> that I never heard anywhere else
> That's when I said, 'gotta get some of
> that for myself.'"

B. MANILOW and M. PANZER, *Beautiful Music*

It would take a master makeup artist to disguise the amusing look of bewilderment on Barry Manilow's face these past few years. It is as if he has been riding along on this buoyant cloud of fulfilled dreams, expecting it to burst into reality at any moment, yet appreciative of the one-in-a-million chance he has been given to be professionally recognized as a musician on an international scale.

Shortly after we had concluded this interview, Barry invited me to a combined press conference and free concert to benefit deprived and disabled children on the day before New Year's at New York's Beacon Theatre. He had just come off an intensive and financially rewarding tour and wanted to share a little of the pleasure he felt with these kids who, ordinarily, would not be able to see him perform. It was a dank, winter morning, and as I moved through the throng of lively children assembled in the unheated, Gothic lobby of the theater, I noticed Barry milling among them unobserved as if he, too, was waiting for the star to make his entrance. He looked healthier (he is extremely lean) and was flawlessly coiffured as befitting a successful man returning home. He was still wearing blue jeans, but now they were tailored and stiff. We talked briefly, and I could tell he was having the time of his life playing out his new image. It might end tomorrow and it might continue on forever, but no matter what, he intended to consciously equalize the give and the take to maintain a perspective on what was an otherwise exaggerated lifestyle.

As we talked, I noticed that traces of a rough childhood spent in the slums of Brooklyn crept into his speech. He had traveled a long road since those days, struggling through the bureaucracy of CBS (where he started in the mailroom) and the any-rules-go empire of commercial advertising, to emerge as a contemporary alongside other pop music celebrities like Neil Sedaka, Carole King, Paul Anka, and Paul Simon. This period of apprenticeship, I think, helped him keep his perspective, since he was not rushed into stardom and was able to view the entertainment industry from another side. He learned that stardom was a manufactured euphemism for mass-media success, and he knew how easily it could be manipulated by the corporate powers. This accounts for his acute business sense, which gives him an edge in his work. Moreover, Barry realizes the varied extent of the pop music business in conjunction with his talent and knows that, should it all end tomorrow, he could always be successful as an arranger, accompanist, composer, or any number of related possibilities.

Manilow's eager manner never minimizes his total confidence in his talent, yet he realizes his own limitations and has no demur about collaborating with strong-minded colleagues. He is a musician and finds it difficult to put into words what he senses easily in rhythms. Almost all of his material is lyricized by collaborators or drawn from outside catalogues. This leaves him completely free to create within his self-reliant capabilities and to encourage equally capable, albeit diversely talented, people to complement him in the finished product. This elucidates the varied styles which comprise his repertoire and, in his own words, "keeps the critics from stamping me with a certain style."

Yet, it is just that—his style—on which he is most calculating and vocal. The cognoscenti of rock music critics have usually conveniently managed to ignore the caste of performers whose musical language is less complex than the so-called aesthetes dominating the pop charts, the performers whose styles lean more toward hard-driving electric or self-indulgent music than pop. And Barry Manilow's style of music has been catagorized and filed, by these critics, under the dubious title of M-O-R—a generalized abbreviation signifying "middle-of-the-road." Ironically, there is nothing demeaning about being an M-O-R artist. Hardly—his music reaches far more listeners in a wider range than the more progressive artists; his talent has managed to transcend the parameters of rock music, still retaining its recognizable origins. Because of this, Manilow has had to patiently learn that the value and acceptance of his music are far more supportive than written evaluations—there is an ardent demand for what he does. And it is because of his insistence of maintaining a balanced outlook on his work and his life that he is able to shrug off the egotistical snags that seem to discomfit so many of his peers—and this ultimately pervades his live performance. It is light, fanciful, and full of the precision and professionalism which have followed him throughout his career.

As I sat in the audience of the Beacon Theatre watching Barry talk to and, later, perform for a grateful house, I couldn't help thinking that he was a genuine example of the integrity that is so often overlooked when talking about the rock music industry. Here he was, on a morning when any normal person should have been in bed preparing for a night's celebration, working furiously as if his reputation hinged on this very show. He was certainly inspiring to those kids both as a performer and a human being. His enthusiasm overwhelmed them, and as he told them about how he had come off the streets to hit records and stages around the world, I got the feeling that for a flickering moment they saw that success was not out of reach for them.

GROWING UP

I grew up on Division Street in Brooklyn, which is comparable to a white Harlem, slums and danger being the best words to describe it. It was in Williamsburg—*oh God*, it's so painful. Roots are really an incredible thing, especially when you've been able to pull yourself out of an awful situation and can look back on it fondly. I mean, I wouldn't have traded it for the suburbs any day.

It was New York, it was exciting and you never knew what was going to happen next. I may be a slum kid by definition, but I lived in a very nice house and was treated terrifically by my parents and grandparents, and I never knew, at the time, I was a slum kid.

But my father got tired of it early. He took off when I was two and left us there to fend for ourselves. It was rough being a skinny kid on the streets. I was the kid they always beat up, but . . . well, it was fun in a strange kind of way.

When I was seven, I was encouraged—got saddled with taking accordion lessons. It was *the* instrument *everyone* learned in the Fifties. I don't know why, but any kid who learned to play a musical instrument in the Fifties learned the accordion. It was a hell of a lot cheaper than buying a piano. There must be hundreds of thousands of dusty accordions packed away in storage closets all over Brooklyn today because, except in ethnic areas like Little Italy, none of the younger kids are playing [it]. Anyway, for five long years, I squeezed out versions of "Lady of Spain," "Tico Tico," "Carnival of Venice" and "Hava Nagila" to the delight of my relatives.

I came from a musical household, heavy on the pop stuff of the day. We had an old record player which continuously played the Andrews Sisters and all the big band music. But my greatest musical incentive was when I got Willie Murphy as a gift for my bar mitzvah. He became my stepfather, and he drove a beer truck and was a jazz nut. He took me to my first jazz concert—Gerry Mulligan at Town Hall. I didn't know that kind of music existed. Willie also threw out my accordion and got me a piano and started turning me on to Ted Heath and Chris Connor and shows like *The King and I* and *Carousel,* and *The Most Happy Fella.* That really got me into music on my own.

THAT'S WHAT I WANT TO BE WHEN I GROW UP

I got through high school pretty easily, but when I got out, I had no idea what I wanted to do. Music as a profession never crossed my mind. Nobody I knew considered it at the time. It was just a hobby.

I enrolled in an advertising course at City College nights and clipped ads in an ad agency during the day. That got to me quick, and I switched to the New York College of Music and, then, Juilliard, and I worked in the mailroom at CBS to get by.

At the time, I never really paid attention to rock or commercial radio. I was into jazz. But the first time pop/rock music really knocked me out was when I heard the Beatles. And it wasn't really the Beatles that knocked me out—it was what was happening behind them. It was the arrangements and the production, because it was the first time (with rock music) that I heard somebody back there thinking about what they were doing. It wasn't just four guys getting up and making music. Somebody else had put it together. And I said, "That's what I want to be when I grow up." I wasn't in the music business yet, per se. But I now knew what I wanted to do. I was going to be Henry Mancini. I was going to be Nelson Riddle or George Martin.

I knocked around at CBS for about eight years doing various assignments. I was a musical director of an amateur series they had called "Callback," which won a number of awards. I did a number of Ed Sullivan TV specials and worked on a musical adaptation of *The Drunkard,* which played off-off Broadway for six years, and off Broadway for two.

I even had my own little act with a girl singer named Jeanne Lucas for about two years. I was basically her arranger and accompanist, but the first out-of-town job we got, they wanted a duo. "We're a duo," we said. It was at the Holiday Inn in Richmond, Virginia. We packed up, had goodbye parties and everything, and on the plane we learned "Georgie Girl" and "Something Stupid." Well, we got there and opened with "Georgie Girl" and then Jeanne sang her entire act, and we closed with "Something Stupid"—and emptied the whole place in five minutes. We were doing New York arrangements, and these farmers were yelling, "Hey, sing 'My Bucket's Got a Hole in It.'" We were fired in three days. We couldn't go back home because of all those goodbye parties and everything, so we went to Jeanne's mother's house in Detroit and tried to put an act together. We played Upstairs at the Downstairs in New York for about two years after that, then decided to go our separate ways.

THE DIVINE MISS M.

I met Bette Midler in the spring of 1972 under the most unusual circumstances which would follow us both for some time to come. I got a call one night from a friend who was the house piano player at the Continental Baths. He asked me to sub for him for a while, which evolved into a couple of weeks. Well, I needed the money real bad and jumped at the chance.

About a week and a half later, Bette walked in. I wasn't really impressed with her all that much during rehearsal. She kind of walked through it. But that night—well, it was as if she was lip-synching, because she knocked me out. I mean, to hear Bette for the first time is a surprise to anyone with any musical taste. She was marvelous. I knew she was going to be a big, big singer once a few more people got to hear her. After the show, I walked backstage and said, "Hey, kid—where did this incredible voice of yours come from?" And, as they say in the movies, that was the start of a beautiful relationship.

I became Bette's arranger, conductor, and pianist, and her career just took off. We had the time of our lives doing it.

I also became her producer and album arranger, and we worked on the act a lot. Her "image" was intact when I met her. That was something she had worked out a long time before I met her. But the act—the music—it was nowhere. She knew what she wanted to do, but she didn't know how to put it all together. I helped her with that. It was a lot of fun, but it was also a lot of utter chaos.

My being with Bette—I don't know if it made me a more successful musician, but it gave me a better idea of how to put on an interesting, lively show and make a better record. I know that Bette has been working on a record album for the past year,[1] and I know that she's only got five cuts done. She's a stickler for it—it has to be absolutely perfect. But by her not playing an instrument, it's going to take her longer to get it down. Once I get it down on paper, I know exactly what I'm going to do. I can communicate it very easily to the other musicians and to myself in terms of spon-

[1] This portion of the interview was completed before the release of *Songs for the New Depression,* and it is this album to which he makes reference.

taneity. I play the piano exactly to what I want to hear. It used to take Bette a long time to communicate it to me what she wanted to hear and what she wanted the song to sound like. She'd say to me, "Make it purple." Purple—what does that mean? Slow, or fast or what? And, so, it takes nonmusicians longer to communicate their music and express themselves musically, even though their music may be brilliant.

ON DOING COMMERCIALS

Before I worked with Bette, I did a lot of jingle singing. It's a very difficult field to break into—very tight, very closed.

I was playing piano for a singer, and she was making demo tapes of jingles to show around to various agencies. She asked me if I could do a song that she had written. She took it around and got hired, and one of the ad agencies asked her, "Who wrote that song?" They called me and asked me if I wanted to submit a Dodge commercial. And so I wrote one for submission and they bought it. It wasn't supposed to happen like that. There were about a hundred people up for that Dodge commercial who had been in the industry for a lot of years, and I got the first one that I went out for. And I said, "Oh my God!" And they gave me another one! And for the next one, I was doing some of the singing, too. You get paid umpteen times more for performing on commercials than writing them. So, little by little, I began to work my way into jingle singing. I could sing, I could read music, and I could do what they wanted me to do. So they started calling me more often.

But it's a very tight field, and anyone desiring to go into it should know in advance that there are only about ten or fifteen singers that do *all* the commercials, and you can't compete with them.

I sang on the MacDonald's commercial, "You Deserve a Break Today." I also did the Dr. Pepper commercial and the Pepsi People spot. I also did the Kentucky Fried Chicken jingles and the one for State Farm Insurance. I'm still involved with commercials a little bit, but I've been on the road so much that I really don't have time to be there when the agencies call.

SO ONE NIGHT I FOUND MYSELF
ON THE STAGE OF THE PALACE!

I loved being in the studio with Bette. It was a unique experience, and I felt as though it was the pediatric ward in a hospital, where something special was created and preserved. It's a totally artistic environment, and people are generally happy when recording.

It was during the time we were working on the first album, *The Divine Miss M.,* that I was introduced to Larry Uttal and Irv Biegel, the president and vice-president of Bell Records. They had heard some of the music that I had written and sung, and suggested that I give it a try on my own. They would be glad to have me as one of Bell's artists. Well, this was a big decision, but it was something that I had always dreamed of doing, and I was not about to pass up the chance. So I signed a contract with Bell.

But they said, "You cannot make an album for us unless you go out on the road with it and perform the music." From a record company's point of view, this is the only way of promoting their interests. A record album costs on the average of $35,000 to $100,000 to produce, and nobody will know that it's there after it's finished unless the artist performs it in public. It's not like ten years ago when record prices were much lower and consumers might speculate and pick up an album because of word-of-mouth or because they like the cover. Today, it's five bucks a shot, and record buyers are going to be damned sure that it's quality material before they make the investment.

Well, Bell figured I had a good opportunity to break out by my association with Bette Midler, and they felt that if audiences could get a chance to hear me live, they might pick up the record.

So I said, "Okay." And I worked out a deal with Bette so I could perform a few numbers right in the middle of her act and I could still continue to be her conductor.

The first gig I did my numbers with Bette was in front of eight thousand people in Columbia, Maryland, after she had driven them absolutely crazy with the first half of her show. I was sitting at the piano conducting "Do You Wanna Dance?" and I knew, as I finished the last note, with people screaming and yelling as Bette went off, that after the intermission the first one they were going to see was me. I wasn't on the bill. I was just listed on the program as musical director. So nobody knew that I was going to come out and sing three of my original numbers in the middle of this bedlam. It was outdoors, and you could not see the end of the heads. So what did I do? What any other red-blooded American boy would do—*I threw up!* Really!

But the worst part was toward the end of the tour. We were playing New York City—home. And I practically knew everybody in the audience. All my friends. And this colossal theater. Judy Garland played there—all the greats. And so, one night I found myself singing on the stage of the Palace Theatre. It was an awesome experience for me. And my career took off from there. It's been like a dream ever since.

WINDS OF CHANGE

(*In 1974, Larry Uttal resigned as the president of Bell Records, and he was replaced by Clive Davis, the former president of the Columbia Records' Group, who had been responsible for the signing of artists like Janis Joplin, Santana, Blood, Sweat & Tears, Chicago and Laura Nyro, to name a few. Clive felt that the label needed a new image along with its new leadership and, as a first step, changed the name from Bell to Arista. Barry tells the rest.*)

I was very nervous when Clive came in, because they had just released my first album on Bell Records and it did: Zip! It sold thirty thousand copies, which sounds nice, but it's not. It's what's known in the business as a "stiff" because it didn't make back its initial production outlay. And the only strength I had in my corner at Bell Records was Larry Uttal and Irv Biegel. They believed in what I did. They were there from the start. They heard me making my first album and saw that there was some talent there. They saw I had potential. And suddenly, this was all taken away, and I had no track record. Nothing to justify my reputation. And this stranger who was followed in by press and blaring trumpets and red carpet came in, and he couldn't even pronounce my name. And so, he found my face laying on his desk and said,

"What's that?" So I was in a very tense situation because I had a two-year contract.

Clive didn't see what Irv and Larry saw. I was signed at the label, though, and if he wanted me to stay I was going to have to stay—and if he wanted me to go, I would go. At that point, I had hoped he would say, "Go," because I really didn't feel like having to prove myself all over again. I'd been doing it for a year and a half.

And so, Clive started to toss out artists. He said, "Nope—I won't take that one with me," and "Nope—that one goes too." And he got to me and, I guess, I was on the borderline. I did a concert in Central Park—it just happened to be during the same month he made his evaluations—and he came down just to check it out because he had heard some rumor that the live act was okay and that some people had gotten into the first album that he hadn't cared for very much. He came to check it out, and people were screaming and yelling, and he really enjoyed it. And I think, at that point, he said, "Oh, I see, it's *Manilow,* not *Man-ni-now!*" And so, he decided to keep me on the label. Then I made the second album, and that led into it. He changed his opinion right away.

CLIVE AND "MANDY"

We were just finishing up production on the second album when Clive called me into his office and showed me a demo of a song called "Brandy," which had been written by two young New York musicians: Scott English and Richard Kerr. He was very enthusiastic about it, and assured me that a hit single at this point in my career would be a key factor.

I listened to it, and it was a very raunchy rock and roll song, not really my forte. And Clive said, "I think you could do something with it. It has a good melody." I said, "Whatever you want." And I went back to the piano and thought about it and, sure enough, it *was* a real pretty song. And if you listened to it closely, the words were real nice.

And so, I went into the studio—and Clive helped[2]—and we

_____
[2] Clive Davis receives co-producer's credit on "Mandy."

made this very raunchy rock and roll song into a ballad and we changed the name from "Brandy" to "Mandy" because there had been a record out named "Brandy"[3] and we didn't want to get in its way. It was a part of my second album, and we decided to release it as a single.

ON COLLABORATION

I have not been opposed to doing outside material.[4] I'm not that paranoid about the writing because there's a lot of great material waiting out there to be discovered and a lot of people who don't get a chance to be heard. I wanted a record on my material for a long time, and nobody wanted to do my songs until I finally did them myself. The problem is, that's the chain of events most of the time, and nowadays there are so few recording contracts to be had for songwriters. And, you know, there are a lot of people out there who may not be able to sing well, and I just keep hearing too much good music that I didn't write that I would like to perform.

I don't specialize in lyrics. I'm a musician, and the music comes very easy to me. Lyrics don't, and I know that. Sometimes I come up with something that, at least, makes sense and I'm not too embarrassed about. But most of the time, I'm totally moronic when I write my own lyric. And I will call somebody and say, "Listen, I got this terrific idea. Will you please put it down right?" Most of the time it's like that. Or I'll get lyrics in the mail from friends or from people with whom I've collaborated, and I will write music for the lyrics. I'm just not secure enough to do it all by myself.

I like to write by myself. I don't think there are many established collaborators who can work in tandem in the same room. It's too personal a thing, and it's inhibitive. I make a million mistakes musically and vocally when I try to compose, and it's just something I have to go through by myself. I like to sit at the piano with the lyric in front of me, and either I sing something, or . . .

[3] The record was a hit by The Looking Glass and, by coincidence, it was released on Epic Records while Clive Davis was director of operations for that label at CBS.

[4] Outside material is that which is recorded, but not written, by the artist.

"COULD IT BE MAGIC?"

I bet everything that this song wouldn't make it. I mean, I am totally amazed that it was a success right in the middle of "Kung Fu Fighting" and all the other disco stuff. It's not a single record. In fact, it's patterned after Chopin's Prelude in C Minor, not exactly your run-of-the-mill Top Forty song.

We had a lot of trouble getting it on the air. The promotion men would run around to the radio stations and hand them the record, and [the disc jockeys] would say, "Are you joking? We aren't going to play that. It's too soft. It doesn't start until three minutes into the song." So we edited it down to a respectable length and reissued it. And, sure enough, they would finally play it, and the phones light right up (with requests) and people would call in for it, and the DJs would have to "go" on it. That happened across the country. But had I not had two hit singles out before that, and had the promotion men not threatened their families with instant death,[5] nobody would have played the song. Originally, it was seven minutes long. We released it in its full length as the flip side of "Cloudburst." And even now, it runs pretty long.

THE BUSINESS SIDE

Now, I'm getting involved with my daily business activities more and more these days. I want to know where I am booked, how much I'm making for the date, and how well the record is selling.

In the beginning, things happened to me so quickly that my head was continuously spinning for eight months, and I really had to concentrate on the live performance and making the music. Luckily, I had people around me that I could trust and could handle all the rest of it. Now that I'm settled into it a little bit more and I've had a lot of hit records and we are pretty sure that people will be showing up at the concerts, I'm trying to find out what I own and what I don't own, about the publishing and investments that were made for me which I never really got into before. I

---

[5] Barry's obvious sarcasm.

think it's healthy for a performer to become involved in the administrative mechanism of his career. It's not very difficult to understand, and it keeps things in perspective.

It's difficult to find the right people to work for you. My attorney became my manager, and I was just lucky. I had worked with Miles Lourie, my attorney, for five years, and he handled all my legal matters. So it was natural for him to become my manager. I kept asking him, "What do I do now? How do I do this?" And I continuously asked him advice that really didn't pertain to law anymore. And he said, "Barry, I think it's time we got married." When you get a manager, you couldn't be more married.

M-O-R

I don't know how you'd really peg my style. I hated the term "M-O-R" (middle-of-the-road) in the beginning because M-O-R, for all these years, all the years I had grown up, typified all the music I *didn't* want to be associated with. When the reviews came back saying, "M-O-R," saying "easy listening," saying, "pop," I kept cringing and saying, "No! That's not it!" My music had a sound different from Andy Williams or Vicki Carr. It has more of a street sound, more of a city sound.

Well, I'm still doing the same music, and they still call it M-O-R, but there are other people who are joining me, and I'm not embarrassed anymore. In fact, I think my audience has grown because of the label. A lot of older people with an aversion to listening to anything called rock will listen to me and enjoy what I'm doing. I think of what I do first as making music, but I also think of myself as a rock singer.

The last place I ever expected to find my music was on commercial radio. But Clive just insisted that I come up with that hit single for the album. Now, I'm happy with my sound. I don't have any plans to change my style—whatever they may be calling it today.

ON PERFORMING

I know that if I just went out on the stage and sang for an hour and a half, I'd be boring. That's why we worked so hard on putting some kind of show together before we began our first tour.

Other performers get caught up in their acclaim and forget that they have to keep up the interest during their performance. Singing straight is just not enough anymore—not for eight or ten bucks a ticket. You have to be damned good. Getting up there being able to talk to your audience throughout your performance is a serious part of putting on a concert. My forte is, of course, making music, but I had to force myself to learn how to get up there and talk a little, not sounding too slick, like a Vic Damone. I'm always on edge doing that because I have to know exactly what to say. I'm no good as an ad libber. I want the audience to get to know me, I want them to get to know the band and the girls. I think that if they get to know me—whether they are into the music or not—the music will mean more to them.

I saw Frankie Valli and the Four Seasons the other week, who I really like. I've seen him on TV and he's a good performer. But this was the first time I had ever seen him live, and that's when your cards are really on the table. You'd better be able to duplicate your records or television appearances. Well, Frankie came out at the beginning of the show and said, "Thank you, thank you, everybody. You're beautiful. We've been doing this material for thirteen years and . . ." and it really *looked* like it! He had his eyes closed, he was doing it by rote and, if I were a reviewer, I would have given him a bad review. I just couldn't feel it, he wasn't convincing. But then he got to the new stuff, and you could see that he was a little nervous about it. He was concerned about his timing, and he came alive. He did it great. That was the difference—*he* was bored for the first thirty minutes. The audience was bored.

I haven't been doing this long enough for things to get to that stage yet. I sure hope it never does. But now, every performance is my life or death. And every time I walk onto that stage, it's critical. I just have to give them my best, and then a little more.

Janis Ian

"Some make it when they're young before
the world has done its dirty job
and later on someone will say, 'You've
had your day, you must make way'
But they'll never know the pain of living
with a name you've never owned
or the many years forgetting what you
know too well."

J. IAN, *Stars*

*Introspection has always been an essential element of songwriting,
the ability of the writer to step back from himself and reflect ob-
jectively on his own life. A good writer is able to communicate
that introspection as oneness to the listener, to create an affinity,
to seal a philosophical bond. And, at that point, what might have
become a self-indulgent ode on the writer's part translates musically to the listener. It is that quality—the communication of a
universal feeling (or the creating of a universal feeling)—which
differentiates the successful singer/songwriter and an undistin-
guished egotist. In the commercial music market, there is not even
a niche for the latter. While there are many artistic musicians who
don't engage in talent prostitution, who do not allow their music
to be sold down the throats of fans, who refuse to assist the record
company in promoting their careers—they still attract an audience. And that audience understands them in a manner that is
self-serving and still commercial.*

*For Janis Ian, musical introspection has been a long, painful ex-
perience which has been happening throughout her adult life. Be-*

cause of her enormously successful album on which she sang the
controversial "Society's Child," Janis was at fourteen awarded a
recording contract and immediately thrust into a world of managers, agents, lawyers, accountants, and producers. Soon Janis
was on the road, touring to promote her career and the new
album, working day and night. Then, back into the studio for a
company-encouraged repeat of the social protest song—which
never materialized. Janis wanted to grow professionally, but her
career never fully developed; too many "creative" people saw it
too many different ways and, by the time she was nineteen, Janis
Ian was show-biz history.

In 1973, after four years of sitting it out professionally, contem-
plating her future, a slightly older Janis returned to the musical
fold much smarter and more developed as a songwriter. She had
worked diligently at her craft and had entrusted her business decisions to the right people. This time things were done properly. Columbia Records signed her, applied their star-making expertise,
and, by the end of 1975, Janis had been awarded a Grammy for
the Best Female Performance of the Year and a well-deserved
reputation which she knew she could live up to.

Ian's musical style is sober and spiritually meditative. She writes
thoughtfully about life from a defensive standpoint—almost as if
it were a psychological exercise—assessing her emotions and her
reactions, working in concise, tightly worded images. At times, her
imagery is deeply personal, at times obscure; however she manages to connect with the wavelength of her audience and convey a
sharing of those feelings no matter how autobiographical they may
be. She rarely disguises her own role in her lyrics, choosing to expose her most vulnerable emotions rather than holding them at
bay. And it may be that aspect of her personality with which her
audience chooses to identify.

Janis is not the easiest of people to relate to. She is abruptly
cynical and, often, succinctly indignant. She has been compelled
to prove herself publicly—not the most comfortable of terrains—
fighting her past reputation as an "arrogant little brat," she has
developed a defensive callousness to others' expectations of her.
Because of this, she has not had the best of relationships with the
rock press and has fared poorly in interviews. She has a history of

being misquoted and misrepresented and thinks well ahead of her statements in defense of her public image. On stage, Janis is the same way: obviously uncomfortable, not overly engaging, humorless. But her material and musical delivery shine through.

Meanwhile, Janis Ian continues to write relevant songs about Seventies people, songs of today and songs about life's ups and downs. Her introspection is severe but human, she is a good singer/songwriter, and, these days, one tends to believe that Janis Ian has had to prove herself for the last time.

HOW IT ALL STARTED

I learned how to play guitar by listening to Joan Baez records slowed down. I just kept playing them over and over and over again lifting the needle until I got it right. Every young girl who played guitar back then wanted to be Joan Baez—or maybe Buffy Sainte-Marie. They were the only women we could identify with at the time. The choices weren't that great.

Basically, my other musical influences were Odetta, Ledbelly, and Billie Holiday. When I was about twelve or thirteen, I started getting into the Beatles. That was a very delicate transition for a folk music enthusiast to make at that time, like selling out. But it was such great music that I couldn't restrict myself. I would have to say that the Beach Boys and the Beatles and the Stones were as big an influence in my music as the folk artists.

When I was in school, I played all the time. I loved to sing, and I began to write around that time too. My songs weren't that complex then—simple statements about how I felt at the time.

When I was fourteen, I met the Reverend Gary Davis, who was one of the most incredible guitarists of all time. His wife liked what I was doing, and they took me down to the Gaslight Cafe (in Greenwich Village) to do a guest set. And while I was playing, a music industry guy saw me and became interested. He hustled me over to a lawyer who took me over to a producer who turned out to be Shadow Morton and before I knew it I was in the business. That's how it all got started.

I didn't get a chance to hang out in the Village folk scene like so many of the other performers who came out of that era. I was only fourteen at the time—highly underage—so I couldn't go into the bars to play or drink. It wasn't like it is now where if you're fifteen or sixteen you go on in anyway. So I really didn't have time to pay the club dues and settle into that creative type of culture, but, even so, the Village really came alive to me.

WE CAN'T PUT THIS OUT

Shadow and I went into the studio and cut "Society's Child," a song I had sketched out in school one afternoon. We did it for Atlantic [Records] because Shadow had an existing deal with them —he had the Rascals or somebody.[1] And after we cut it, they gave it back to us, which, to think of it today, is understandable. They were a black-oriented company at the time and it undoubtedly would have created problems for them. They were cool about it, though, because they didn't ask for their money back or anything. They just said, "We're sorry, we can't put this out—so take it." And I thought that was a very decent way for a record company to act. But that's Jerry Wexler.[2] I've always found him to be very straight—at least, with me.

Then, we took the record and went through twenty-two companies, but no one would buy it. They were all afraid to touch it with the straightforward lyric. It was a little too relevant. And people began to look at me like I was a little weird. Finally, Verve/Folkways bought it on the third time around. They had passed on it twice before but got a sudden burst of inspiration or social conscience. And then, a lot of people [on radio stations] wouldn't play it. They said the lyrics would alienate their listening audience, which [I thought] was pretty stupid. But that's how it went down.

All of a sudden, Leonard Bernstein invited me to appear on this television special he was doing. It was that April, right after the record was released for the third time and we were having trouble getting airplay. And then, everybody apologized and played it.

[1] Actually, it was the Shangri-Las on Atlantic's subsidiary label, Red Bird. He produced their hit, "Leader of the Pack."

[2] Vice-president and partner in Atlantic Records at that time.

That show sort of legitimized what I was doing. It also told people that if their kids were going to be recording artists, they weren't going to die in the gutter, because there I was on their screen right in front of them.

WITH VERVE/FOLKWAYS

(*During the Sixties, Verve/Folkways Records, a subsidiary label of MGM Records, introduced some of the most eclectic recording artists of that day including Richie Havens, Laura Nyro, Tim Hardin and, of course, Janis Ian.*)

Jerry Schoenbaum, the president of the label, was the man who signed me at Verve. When I first went there, it was a very nice company straight ahead. But then they got very weird after a while and were rude to a lot of artists. Maybe unintentionally— you never know whose hand is washing whose. But they treated me very much like a piece of meat.

As soon as I started selling, they immediately wanted to repeat it. If Verve really had their shit together toward me, they would have noticed that I had a producer who was having a lot of problems. He was not there most of the time when we were recording. They might have either suggested someone else [to produce me] or given me some backing to go in and do it myself.

They did nothing to treat me as a human being. They went through five presidents in three years—I mean, how much could they do in all that turmoil? Finally, Charlie Callello[3] and I cut a real good album—I still like that album—but it seems that [Verve/ Folkways] used it as a tax write-off. They seemed to be using everyone's albums as tax write-offs for MGM, but I didn't find out about that until a lot later on. Somebody from the company told me that they apparently didn't care if they dropped sixty grand. It's incredible.

There were parts of my other [Verve/Folkways] albums that are defendable, but there were so many problems with them in the studio. It was very hard because I was very young. I couldn't run the session because it was my producer's job—which I now know

[3] A very successful record producer and arranger most noted for his work with Laura Nyro.

is a crock of shit. As a guy, I wouldn't have had to deal with it, I think. But at that time, I didn't know that. I had little or no musical support, because no one knew what I was trying to do. I was trying to do *Stars*—that kind of album but, Jesus, everyone else was just stuck in this goddamn rut. I couldn't make them understand that I was listening to the Beatles and I wanted to be doing *that*. And they wanted me to be doing Judy Collins.

Mike Curb was the last president of the label, and he wanted me to go over to Jerry Ross and be produced by him. He had done things like "I'm Your Venus" and Jay and the Techniques stuff. He was a very weird guy. So I went to see him, and he sat in his office and opened his mail while he talked to me for a half hour. Finally, he looked at me and I said, "Well, did you listen to my tape?" And he said, "Yes." So I asked him, "Do you want to produce me?" And he said, "Well, here's some records. Go home and listen to them because then you'll learn how to write." He didn't even know what I did. That's what I mean by "a meat rack." They shoved you around having no conception of what you were trying to do. Instead, they figured that as long as we had made it with "Society's Child," we should hang on as long as we could. There was no way out of that. I went through four albums, and after that I had a nervous breakdown.

I COULD HAVE USED SOMEONE

As soon as "Society's Child" hit, I went right out on the road. It was real different then. Promoters didn't have it together—it was still mostly fly-by-night promotions. I traveled alone or with a friend. That was real hard on me because I didn't have a band. It was very lonely. Nor did I have a road manager. I was taken care of in so much as I was insulated, but there wasn't really anyone my age or close to my age who had any idea of what I was going through. I could have really used someone like that.

I'm sure that there were record company people who could have helped me. Like a place like Columbia [Records] might have known what to do, or *more* of what to do. You see, my manager had managed Peter and Gordon and was new to the United States. I don't fault her for that, but . . . It's just very difficult to understand what it's like when you're sixteen. In retrospect it's difficult for me now to understand.

I didn't even have an accountant to advise me on what to do. I was making a lot of money, more than I ever dreamed of making. More than anyone in my family had ever known. I think my parents were combined making something like $20,000 a year, so they really didn't know what to tell me to do. I didn't have a good accountant until I was eighteen and discovered that I owed a lot in back taxes. So I lost about $200,000. I thought I was rich, but that was all I had and there it went. And I was in debt to the government until 1972.

I TOOK OFF FOR FOUR YEARS

After I left Verve, I was really crazy. I just couldn't function at all. By the end of the fourth album for them, I was really out there, really crazed. So I took four years off, and in between, I made an album for Capitol [Records]. That was really not a good album at all. I had gone away and left the album uncompleted in the middle. When I resumed work on it, it was just unsalvageable. But it went out on the market anyway.

During those four years, I just lived in Philadelphia and then Los Angeles, staying close to home. It gave me a lot of time to get my head together, to think about what I had just gone through and to grow up normally a little. I did a lot of reading—learned a lot—and wrote all the time. I worked real hard at my writing, and I think that that's where I really matured as a writer. Pretty soon afterward, I ran out of money and I moved back in with my mother. That was just before we got *Stars* together.

I DECIDED I WANTED
TO RECORD AGAIN

About 1973, I began to get edgy, and I decided I wanted to record again. I had written "Stars" and this whole batch of songs, and I really wanted to make a record. It wasn't that I felt I had to prove myself to anybody. It's just that I *knew* my material was good, that it deserved to be heard. If I want to do something, I

will. If I don't, I won't. Beyond that, I don't have to prove anything to anybody.

Jean Powell[4] and I had been looking for a recording contract
for months and months. A lot of companies said they would give
me a deal for one single. If it was a hit, they had me, and if it
wasn't a hit they didn't have me. That was really my first taste of
what it was like [trying to negotiate a recording contract] because I had never been involved in that end of it before. Jean and
I decided that we would rather wait and be hungry than to bank
my career on just a single. It wasn't worth that. Roberta Flack
had just recorded my "Jesse," which turned out to be a hit, but
the companies insisted that I didn't write commercial songs.

And then, Herb Gart called and said that Festival Records, in
Australia, would back an album. That was what got me back in
the business as a recording artist. So I cut *Stars* for Festival. My
producer, Brooks Arthur, knew Charlie Koppelman, who had just
become the head of A&R for Columbia Records. Columbia had
already passed on me when Clive Davis was doing all the signing
there. Clive originally turned me down probably because he has
no ears—for *my* kind of music. Clive didn't believe in albums that
were personal statements unless it had a single in it. But Charles
liked the record, and he signed me. I went down to play at (CBS
Records') Nashville convention, and I was real good. The Columbia people got faith in me from that appearance. And that was
a new start.

ON COLUMBIA RECORDS

I'm glad I'm with Columbia—they're terrific. Personally, there's
no place I'd rather be. Except Atlantic—but that would only be to
talk to Jerry Wexler. But Columbia's very straight. They don't
bullshit you at all—that *I've* been able to see. They also trust *me*.
They trust me in the studio by not sending someone around to
check up on me all the time. They trust me not to mess up on the
road. The promotion men are always there to meet me in each
city I perform in. And that's important to me.

Between *Stars* and *Aftertones,* which was the first time we were

4 Janis' manager.

ready to go out on the road by ourselves, they picked up all the band's air fares, hotel fares, part of the salaries. They really supported the first album and *Between the Lines*. *Between the Lines* didn't start making any money for us for a long, long time. I plowed back money [into the group] about eighty per cent of what I made and kept [only] my rent, and Columbia paid for everything else. They spent thirty to forty thousand dollars on us on the road over a two-year period. Which they made back after "At Seventeen" was a big hit, but still, that's a lot of faith.

Their promotion men always work fairly with me. If I say, "I'll work with you from ten to one and from two until six—we'll do all the radio stations and get them done," they don't pick me up at nine o'clock and work me until eight at night. They understand you have to eat once in a while. They also do a really hip thing, which is after they've worked you really hard, they take me to a very nice place for dinner. Which is great. You look forward to it. It's like a kid with candy, and it works. They also don't lie to you. They don't tell you it's going great when it's not. They tell you what you have to do in each territory, and then they get it done.

But I'm learning something I didn't know as a kid, which is: whoever I meet from Columbia is probably more scared of me than I am of them. That's something I'm only beginning to understand again. It's their asses if they mess up. They're not going to get fired if it's some whim of mine, but if they mess up they are going to get into trouble. You see, not only is it my career at stake, but it's Columbia's money. We work together, which is the really good thing about them. And, they're class. They're not tacky. They don't say they're going to throw you a party and bring frankfurters. If they throw you a party, they do it because you need to have a party in a particular town and they invite the right people. They don't jive around. It's an amazing machine. Except, as an artist, you don't feel like it's a machine.

WORKING WITH A BAND

I tried establishing a democracy. But that didn't work. So now it's gone back to an aristocracy. I figure that I know best; next to me, the guys in the band know best, and then comes the rest of the world. The reason I trust the guys in the band is because we play together so much. We're all teaching each other what we know constantly. So none of us are ever too far behind. We were all playing reggae eight months ago. Now we're all sick to death of reggae. Also, they do so many sessions that they're up on everything immediately. I love a band situation. It's great. On the road, it brings a stability that you cannot get [without it].

I have an unusual situation in that I'm a female artist, and it's very unusual for a female artist to have a band she works with constantly, all the time over the years. Very unusual. Because most female artists don't know anything about playing. And the ones that do usually aren't in a position to carry a band. I've been working with Barry (Lazarowitz—drums) since I was seventeen, Claire (Bay—vocals and percussion) since *Stars,* and Stu (Woods —bass) and Jeff (Layton—guitar) since just after *Between the Lines* so (the band) is at least three years old. And we've done maybe five hundred dates together. There's a consistency that you get. Also, if I'm down, they can sense it and they'll pull me up, and vice versa. We cover for each other to the point where the audience never knows that there's anybody off. The thing is, most female artists have a *back-up* band, and I have a *band*. Those are two very different things.

We run into problems sometimes—like when we go to London. CBS will want to take me out to dinner. And they're not going to want to take all five of us out to dinner, plus our manager and the road manager, so I'll go alone. But everybody understands that. And I always get the fun of doing interviews and picture sessions and shit like that. But when it comes to hanging out, *who else am I going to hang out with?*

It's not hard asserting myself with the band because they're professionals. They're basically studio musicians—not studio musicians like your old-guard studio musicians who are so tired that they give you their standard, tired studio licks and then leave. My band *knows* how to create, and they bust their asses putting everything forth when we record. It took them a while, but they now understand that not only do I genuinely care about them, but it's important to me that they get credit. Their names are always on the back of the album, they're all over the songbooks. You see, we're also buddies. We've all learned to separate business from pleasure and music. In the end, if one of them wants something and I want something, there's five of us. Usually four of us will feel one way and one of us will feel the other way, so it's easy. Except if I hate it and the other four love it, I have veto power. But I've rarely used it, and usually they're right or I'm right and it's perceptible to the others. Our taste usually runs along the same lines. I'm really happy with the situation. It's a great band.

THIS IS MY PART

If I have three or four months off, I can usually write twenty or thirty songs toward a new album, but I'm never gonna get time off like that. There are so *many* other little things that creep into my schedule that I have to do, that trying to imagine getting away for that long is ridiculous. And I definitely have to be alone when I write.

After I have enough songs so that I know I've got a big enough choice, I decide which of the songs will work best [in an album context], what keys are best for my performance, and then I write the basic charts. Next, I decide what musicians will enhance the band, book them, and then I make a deal with the studio for the time and amount of money it's going to cost. I do all of this by myself. I have to. This is *my part*. I don't enjoy it, but then nobody else but me can decide these things.

Then I'll sit down with the band and make a really rough demo tape of about fifteen songs. We'll later narrow them down to ten or twelve. Then I do the sheets [arrangements], and if there's going to be strings or things, I decide whether or not I should do [the string charts] or somebody else should. Naturally, I argue with everyone else about all those things. That's where gems come out of—creative arguing. And then we're ready for the studio.

IN THE STUDIO

I love recording and being in the studio. It's probably one of the most creative things in my life. Watching it piece together is absolutely fascinating. Unlike other recording artists claim, it's not painful for me to record. It depends on how much arguing is going on. And it's taken me a while to learn not to sing songs for people before going into the studio because they don't understand what you're trying to do. Like, "Watercolors" everybody thought sounded like something of Dylan's and, you know, it didn't come out sounding like Dylan. But it's weird when people closest to you think that. Then you begin to question your own perspective, and that's when failure begins. So I've learned to avoid all that by being most secretive.

I'm looking to change the way I record because it's getting so damn expensive. The Columbia albums (to and including *Aftertones*) cost about $55,000 to $65,000 to make. That's fairly average. But the kind of stuff that we want to do now—we're not going to be able to do it for the same price if we're going to spend six hours a day just testing for different sounds. So what we're talking about now is rehearsing outside the studio to a point. We're also trying to find a studio where we can buy twenty-four hours a day for a change instead of working for a few hours, being interrupted by another group who has booked the intermediate time, and then having to come back in and try to pick up where we were. It never sounds the same, and that's not good. So we'd like to find someplace like the Caribou Ranch or Le Studio in Montreal where we could just go in and cut the whole thing without interruption. 'Cause everybody's getting tired of having to go in later and overdub.

It's a lot of work, but of everything I do, next to writing, I like being in the studio best. But there are so many things I'd like to do there that I don't have time to do there right now. Like trying string things. If I could have a studio twenty-four hours a day, it would add a lot to my knowledge, and the albums would benefit from it. You can afford to write a forty-stanza song and then go in and cut it. But with an album, you can't labor over your work like you do with writing a song. Unless you're going to spend a quarter of a million dollars, and I can't justify that kind of money.

ON THE ROCK PRESS

Doing interviews is one of the parts of the business that could really be a fun thing. But, over the past few years, I've had to deal with so many different egos of the people interviewing me that it's become a very difficult thing. Sometimes, I feel that I should be interviewing the interviewer—they seem to think that their opinions are more interesting to their readers than the person they're doing the profile on.

The rock and legitimate press are really weird. I'm quoted honestly only about thirty per cent of the time. It's not usually distorted too heavily. It only occurs when the person [writing the story] decided: I'll combine those three sentences into one. Then you really don't sound like yourself.

But a lot of the time, the press wants to grab hold of something sensational to give their story more importance. Because of that, they tend to make me uncomfortable when I'm speaking to them. Because I know they're just waiting for me to make a slip that they can pounce on. Then my words don't belong to me anymore. Like, I just did a major piece with the *Village Voice* and I talked with them for about six hours. Five and a half of those hours were spent discussing music. About ten minutes was spent discussing my being bisexual. And wouldn't you know that half of the article was devoted to that. That's what I mean when I say that my words don't belong to me. Things are taken out of context, and then I resent having said anything at all. The press tends to see what they want to see. *I* don't mind doing interviews at all. I could sit and talk about myself all day!

Publicity is about the same way. I was reading some of Bruce Springsteen's statements about how he'd like to find the guy who started all the hype [about him]. That's so jive. Those cats at Columbia—I've never seen them do anything the artist didn't ask them to do or the manager didn't go along with. I mean, some of the things they come up with are a little weird. Like, they wanted to compare me to Judy Garland. But we stopped it. We said, "This whole thing won't work because . . ." So, they're very straight. And they stand by a commitment.

I DON'T CONSIDER MYSELF A STAR

I *think* I cope well with success today. I *think* so. I don't think of myself as a star, you see. Stars are people who are skinny and have perfect makeup and crazy clothes. Mick Jagger's a star. I mean, it's too weird for me to consider myself in the same class.

Sometimes it's weird coping with my popularity. There are things I do, like signing autographs after my shows, that I didn't used to do. At a Carnegie Hall show, there were three hundred screaming people waiting for me afterward, and I had no idea what to do because it happened so fast. Now I have our truck driver stand by me so that if anybody gets weird, he just *suggests* that they move back.

People tend to get overzealous. We were at a concert once where we were trying to get to the car, and *we couldn't get to that car!* That's really scary when you're in the middle of a bunch of people who are grabbing for you. When people are shoving pens in your face, they could poke your eye out. But they don't realize that. Or they try to get the scarf that you're wearing, and it's possible you can choke. Since then, I always knot my scarves *twice*. Those type of things can really make you paranoid.

I REALLY WANTED IT!

For me [winning the Grammy] meant acceptance by the Old Guard. There's a whole lot of stuff going on now about the Grammies which is really weird. I vote, and I know a lot of other people who do. But a lot of people suggest I won because Brooks Arthur, my former producer, was president of the New York chapter of NARAS, and that's a crock of shit. For the record, you can belong to NARAS and you don't have to do anything. But to vote, you have to have a certain amount of credits on albums in specific categories. The people who were making all the flack, I think, just don't understand how it works.

I'm proud of winning. I'm proud of any award I get. Hey listen, I worked hard for it. I fuckin' voted for myself. Even Barry voted for me. I *know* he did. I worked very hard to get to the point where the people in the industry were aware of my existence. Best female vocalist is . . . well, Ella Fitzgerald was best female vocalist! That kind of company is fine with me. And the recognition is from the people you work with. So if it's not from the heart rock and roll people—okay. You see them in the bars and they say, "Hi." I think it's terrific that I won it. I really wanted it.

I didn't know what to do [when I accepted the award]. I walked up there in a daze, and when I finally looked out at the crowd, everybody was standing up and expecting me to say something. That was real nice. And I was at a loss for words. I think those were the people who know what I've been through.

I'm real happy now as a performer. It's a good job and I have a good time doing it. But I could always stop. I've stopped before, and I could always do it again.

John Hammond, Sr.

"Well I got a harmonica job, begun
to play,
Blowin' my lungs out for a dollar
a day.
I blowed inside out and upside down,
The man there said he loved m'sound."

BOB DYLAN, *Talkin' New York*

No one will ever be able to assess the magnitude of John Hammond's contribution to popular music. It is incalculable, priceless, and such an overwhelming gift to the spectrum of modern music that one wonders where the state of the recording arts might be today without his discoveries. They read like the lead page out of "Who's Who in Music": Bessie Smith, Billie Holiday, Benny Goodman, Red Norvo, Bob Dylan, Aretha Franklin, Bruce Springsteen—all of these extraordinary artists have, at one formulative time in their careers, come under Hammond's sculpting hand. In addition, he was instrumental in desegregating the big bands of the 1930s and 1940s and, today, conscientiously devotes much of his tightly scheduled time to the advancement of racial equality in all phases of the performing arts. So much of John Hammond's achievements have gone uncredited to him because of his selfless desire to credit others where they have only lent assistance to his accomplishments. He is not one to call attention to his merits. Instead, he regales in recollections of the music business evasively acquiescing his involvement as a method of giving credence to what would otherwise sound like colorful lore, and to entice his audience to come to him, to unassumingly uncover his contributions which he knows are there.

John Hammond sees himself as a catalyst, sparking the creativity and assisting in bringing it to the attention of the public. He is a true patron of the arts. This is one reason why his "discoveries" invariably make a quick transition from his sponsorship into the record company to independent management and production; he is more interested in keeping the flow of creativity constant than imposing his own original conceptions on a productive artist. However, in almost every case, the recording artist has found success on the very principles which Hammond intrinsically conceived and for which they sought outside help. This is due largely to his desire to record the artists in their most fundamental sense, with the least amount of accompaniment by others, focusing primarily on their genius, a result of his love of the music and the aesthetics of true talent. In Aretha Franklin, he heard the church influence, the soulfulness of the black existence and fought hard to capture that on record. In Bob Dylan, John Hammond found that rare genius capable of painting pictures with words that one is fortunate to come into contact with once in a lifetime—and he heard it again in Leonard Cohen and again in Bruce Springsteen. This accounts for the primitive surfaces of his work, its lack of ornamentation. He represents an old-fashioned way of getting it down on record (he continues to refer to it as "wax") and allowing the public to hear for themselves what he heard. It's as if he's asking for an appraisal of his own inherent talents. Yet John is too devoted, too immersed in his love of music to be aware of his own critical needs. When he is not listening to auditions of performing hopefuls, he devotedly spends his time supervising the reissuing of legendary sessions of jazz, blues, gospel, and traditional music from amassed archives. He is an incessant reader of all music and trade journals, frequently a contributor, and, more likely than not sounding back at a piece he has read in one of his numerous letters to the editor. I cannot ever remember walking into John's office without noticing the stacks of current reading matter occupying every available space. It is not unusual for John to page through a magazine while he talks to his appointments, not out of disrespect or boredom, but out of a self-imposed zeal to read everything he can.

Although some record executives have accused him of indulging himself in musical capriciousness (most probably because they are only businessmen), John has outsmarted them all by delivering the goods. He is an extremely shrewd businessman who has spearheaded Columbia Records and his discovered artists to infinite commercial success. Bruce Springsteen had just signed a multiyear contract at Columbia when John suggested that he would like to see Bruce perform that same evening. In a matter of minutes, he arranged for Bruce to be included on the program at the Gaslight, a reputable showcase club in Greenwich Village. Immediately upon entering the club, John took things into his hands. He told the proprietor exactly when Bruce should be introduced onto the program, how he should be lit and engineered, and what to say as a means of introduction. After Bruce was just about into his set, John told his manager to "get him off—now." He had initiated the mystique and preferred to let it spread gradually before the first album was released. Which, of course, it did.

John and I discussed my idea for a college course on rock music in March of 1975. About six months before I was slated to begin the opening session, I asked him if he would be a guest. Genuinely surprised, he responded, "Why me? I don't know much about rock music. I've had a little to do with jazz and R&B, but I don't think I can help you out where rock is concerned." I assured him that my class would be elated to spend an evening hearing about his experiences. As far as rock being the subject, I explained that we were more interested in hearing about the pioneering of the record industry. And he was more than welcome to discuss his struggle against racism within the performing arts.

For years I had been hypnotized by his recollections of "the old days." What's more, there are few people in the business today who delight in storytelling as much as John Hammond, and even fewer who have the rare ability to do so with the warmth and verve that foreshadow his accounts. He weaves rare bits of history about Billie Holiday, Benny Goodman and Aretha Franklin with such effervescence, such feeling, that it is easy to understand his

*unyielding dedication to good music for over forty-five years. I
wanted my class to see that. I wanted them to know how it was
possible for a dreamy young man who had dropped out of Yale
University, fighting against all social standards of the day, to provide mankind with a gift more valuable than all the record royalties combined.*

I WAS GOING INTO RECORDS

In 1931, I left Yale. I had to. I had a couple bouts with jaun-
dice, which is now called hepatitis. I just didn't feel I had the energy to stay at Yale because the music I was getting in New York
every weekend was so much better than anything I could get at
Yale. My family happened to be well-off, so I could afford to say
to my father, who was a lawyer and a banker, "No, I'm not going
to be a lawyer. No, I'm not going to be a banker. No, I'm not going
into real estate." I was going into records. So my father looked at
me and said, "You're crazy." He said that the record businesses
were all going bankrupt—and he was right! But I believed in my
decision.

I actually broke into the business in 1931, because I became the
American correspondent for an English magazine called the
Gramophone, a very high-class magazine. I was playing by mistake one day. You see, I had sort of a double musical life—the
world's lousiest viola player. I played the viola because they
needed viola players then and I could play with musicians better
than I. The cellist in my string quartet was a guy called Arthur
Bernstein. Artie later became Benny Goodman's bass player and,
at the time, he was Ben Farr's bass player. He knew all the white
musicians that I was too shy to get to meet, but I knew all the
black musicians because I had been going to Harlem for years—I
mean, to the Alhambra Theatre on 126th Street, to the Lincoln
Theatre, where Fats Waller played organ, to the Lafayette Theatre,
where many more great stars played. And the Club Saratoga,
where Louis Russell would drum up a band with Henry "Red"
Allen, J. C. Higginbotham, Albert Nicholas, Charlie Holmes, Pops
Foster, Paul Barber, and other great musicians in jazz. There

was no cover charge, there was no minimum at these clubs.
I didn't smoke, I didn't drink. If the shows were boring, I would
read the trades or *New Republic* or *Nation.* But as soon as the
band started, I'd perk up. I knew the Harlem team fairly well.

THE GOLDEN DAYS OF BURLESQUE

I happened to be a burlesque aficionado, too, in those days. I
subscribed to anything, what in those days were called Negro
papers. I got the Baltimore *Afro American,* the Norfolk *Journal
and Guide,* the New York *Age,* the New York *Amsterdam News.*
And there was a fantastic paper in Philadelphia, which actually
had better black show business than New York did. They had
three live theaters with black stage shows: the Lincoln, the Standard—where I saw Sammy Davis, Jr., God help me, when he was
three years old—and the Ford. Black shows were playing houses
in Philadelphia before they ended up in New York. There were
black and white [integrated] shows, but only in burlesque. Sliding Billy Watson's Black and White Review. Minsky's Republique
Theatre had black and white performers, had one half of Fletcher
Henderson's band in the pit for the black part of the show. But
Fletcher Henderson's band would play one half of the show, and
then the regular Minsky bands—which were the worst bands in
the world—would play the white show. On Forty-second Street, in
those days, it was strictly segregated. Blacks were in the second
balcony—only one balcony for blacks. From the Twenties to the
late Thirties the scene in New York was absolutely disgraceful.

THE EARLY YEARS

So, I was an American correspondent for the British *Gramophone,* and then for *Melody Maker,* the same *Melody Maker* that
exists today. It was better then because it was mostly about jazz.
Now, it's mostly about the current teeny-bop stars.

I had gotten into the record business, and I was terribly lucky.
Actually, I bought my way into the record business because I
sponsored, for the first time, a recording date by a pianist named
Garland Wilson. He wasn't all that great a pianist, but he had
come to me and I paid for a session. And, because records were

only three minutes in those days, I had to make twelve-inch sides so they could stretch out a little.

But this way, I got to meet Frank Walker, who was the man who had introduced me to Bessie Smith and supervised all her recording sessions.

The next year, I had made a recording with my favorite band of all jazz bands—Fletcher Henderson's orchestra. And Fletcher Henderson's band was in terrible trouble all the time because of bad management. We made a wonderful session, just one.

During this time, I used to go to England every year or so and stay with my sister, although most times I tried to stay in a hotel so I could hang around and listen to whatever music there was. The music wasn't that good in England in those days. But because I had been writing so much for the *Gramophone* and *Melody Maker,* I was sort of a celebrity, to my great surprise, in England. 'Cause nobody else had any idea about the music coming out of Harlem. They didn't care. *Metronome* was as square as you could be. *Downbeat* hadn't even started yet. *Orchestra World*—I don't think they had ever been north of Ninety-sixth Street. It was crazy.

Well, in 1933, I was over in England that summer, and I found out that English Columbia and Parlophone had run out of American jazz to put out because American Columbia was in bankruptcy, which meant Okeh (Records) was in bankruptcy, which meant Harmony was in bankruptcy, and these were the only three record companies with which they had an affiliation at this time. So they hired me to make something like a hundred and sixty sides of whatever I wanted to make. I had carte blanche, because I wasn't going to get paid anything. But the musicians would get paid by English Columbia because American Columbia was broke, and if the American company ever wanted to put out the records, they could pay a small royalty for the rights. Which they later did.

The first band I got together was formed around an obscure clarinet player called Benny Goodman. People forget that when Benny finally made it as a star, he was just as big as anybody today, as an Elton John or a Dylan or as anybody else. I mean, he was not just the biggest thing only in the country but practically in the world. I recorded Benny Goodman, which led to a Columbia contract for him, and then led to a Victor contract.

And I was also able to record Fletcher Henderson's band, calling it Fletcher Henderson on one label and Horace Henderson on another. Then I got the smaller bands together to form big bands. I got everybody I could think of. And then I got out to Chicago and recorded people I'd always worshiped like Jimmy Noonan and Albert Ammons, a boogie-woogie pianist, and all those people.

It wasn't that I had better ears than anybody else. It's just that I was lucky to be around, you know.

THE RACE PROBLEM

I got so involved in the race problem—always. I covered the Scottsboro Case for *Nation* in 1933 at the age of eighteen. I felt deflated. I had done all those things for the music magazines and I always got censored. I was writing, in those days—from 1933 to 1935—on the staff of the Brooklyn *Eagle*. It had the best cultural coverage of any paper in New York. It was fantastic. I was a third-string newspaperman, but I had my own column on Sunday. And when I told my audience that black people couldn't go to the Cotton Club, which was in Harlem, because it was run by the mobsters, they wouldn't print it. So, finally, I was reduced to writing for a magazine called *The New Masses* because they were the only ones who would print me. This was in the days, you see, when there was a big romance going on between the Communist Party and the black people. But when I started criticizing trade union policies and the discrimination by Local 802 [American Federation of Musicians] against blacks, they started censoring me again. So I had nobody to write for.

REMEMBERING BILLIE

I went actively to all the joints in Harlem, obviously for the very best in music, and I had been doing that since 1929. And, on this very night, Garland Wilson was playing at a place called Copan's Morocco Club, which was behind the Lafayette Theatre.

There was a singer called Monette Moore. She was a very famous blues singer on her own, and she had finally left Copan's for Broadway and was working in a show with Clifton Webb downtown at that time. She had all sorts of celebrities out there that night to see her. And so, she was being a hostess at the door and hired, sort of to fill in for her, a seventeen-year-old girl. And that girl was Billie Holiday.

This was the most miserable little room. It was in a basement on 133rd Street between Lenox and Seventh. This was long before she worked at Pod & Jerry's. In fact, she had just gotten out of jail when I first heard her.

There was a wonderful pianist in the back, a fellow called Don Hill. And Billie was different from the other singers around. There were about twelve or fourteen ringside tables, and she'd go around and sing the same song to each table. Not one of the dirty songs. All the other singers in the Harlem cabarets always sang "Hot Nuts" or the 1930 equivalent of "Rock Around the Clock." But Billie, well—Billie would sing the standards. And she sang them differently to each table. She was the complete improvising vocalist. I mean, Bessie Smith had a pretty set routine. But Billie was like an instrumentalist. Like what was later Lester Young, whom she hadn't heard at that time. She worshiped Louis Armstrong, she worshiped Joe Smith. She had a wonderful sense of jazz in those days. Billie was unique.

It took me six months to get Billie to do a record for England, because in England they didn't think any female vocalist was jazz. It just hadn't been done. The first records she ever made were with Benny Goodman. That was the first time Benny had ever worked with a race singer. This was in 1933, and it was an incredible thing to do. 'Cause when I first recorded Benny, he said, "I don't dare, John. If I record with those [black] musicians, I'll be blacklisted. I'll be boycotted. I'll never get another radio job in my life." And that [recording of Billie Holiday with Benny Goodman] was within a week of when I recorded Bessie Smith's last recording date. Nineteen thirty-three was probably the biggest year of my life because that was when I really got started in the record business.

Billie was never a superstar. She should have been a superstar, but she wasn't. When Billie recorded "Strange Fruit," made in 1939, and "God Bless the Child," and some of her other great songs, she was only making about a hundred bucks a week. And when she was with Basie's band—I mean, Basie's band wasn't making any dough in those days. 'Cause in those days, black bands, except for Duke Ellington and Cab Calloway, didn't make any money. The most these bands ever got paid was seventy or eighty bucks, and maybe twenty-five dollars a side a record. And they weren't getting royalties on their records.

After 1933, when Billie recorded with Benny Goodman, it took me a year and a half to get her back in the studio. Well, to explain that, I have to tell you about the circumstances [surrounding getting her back in the studio].

At that time, there was no such thing as BMI.[1] There was only one publishing society, and that was ASCAP (The American Society of Composers, Authors and Publishers). So the publisher had the complete power to dictate exactly how a song would be performed on record. The melody had to be predominant. Benny Goodman was the first man who was ever able to get around this because Benny had Fletcher Henderson in his band and Fletcher was a competent musician, and he knew how to play a very melodic, not too straight but straight enough first chorus which satisfied the publishers, after which anything could happen. And Benny's records sold like mad despite what the publishers tried to do. Essentially, they were presenting the vocalist. The songs were written in script.

I was able to persuade Harry Graves at the American Record Company that with jukeboxes coming in they should record all the straight tunes with people like Kay Kaiser, Eddie Duchin, Ben Berney, every Mickey Mouse band they could get. And I said, "Jukeboxes are capital, and you'll have something that will live for a long time. Your publishers can't squawk if the bands take pop tunes and let the guys have a good time. There'll be no arrangements. You won't have to pay for orchestrations. It'll be seven musicians and a vocalist. That's all." So that's how I was able to get Billie Holiday back on record as a vocalist at twenty-five dollars a side.

Until about six months after she recorded the first session, she recorded "I Cry for You," and suddenly got them a hit that sold twenty thousand copies. The earlier records might have sold five,

[1] Broadcast Music, Inc., was founded in 1940 as a performing rights society.

six, or seven thousand copies. These figures are incredible, compared with business today. The record business was that broke in those days.

On the first session we made [for the American Record Company], we had four tunes. One was, "I Wished on the Moon." That was the plug tune for *The Big Broadcast of 1935*.[2] That was introduced in the movie by Bing Crosby. If you listen to Bing Crosby's version and listen to Billie Holiday's, you won't know they're the same tune—I'm happy to say.

And in the band were Teddy Wilson on piano, Cozy Cole on drums, Don Trueheart, Benny Goodman, Roy Eldridge, and Ben Webster. It was an incredible band. I think the entire cost of the session, including Billie Holiday and the band and Teddy Wilson getting double scale, was three hundred dollars. It's incredible.

And then they did an awful tune—a Mickey Mouse tune—called "What a Little Moonlight Can Do," which was a two-step. It was absolutely the funniest melody, and they made a masterpiece out of it. There was a tune that nobody ever heard of—I don't know where they ever found it, or who found it—called "Miss Brown to You." We always made it a point of getting some guys together who had never played with the other guys before so there could always be that element of surprise in the recording session. And those records really stood up over the years.

"STRANGE FRUIT"

(In 1938, Billie Holiday briefly recorded for Commodore Records, a small New York-based company on which label this classic was recorded. John wasn't too clear about the specifics, but what he did say bears repeating.)

As I remember the Commodore thing, Billie was recording for us at the American Record Company, and the American Record Company pressed records for Commodore, which was owned by Milt Gabler of the Commodore Music Shop. And I'm pretty sure that this was right. I guess it was Columbia who refused to record "Strange Fruit" because of their Southern distributors. I called up

2 Actually, it was *The Big Broadcast of 1936*, made for Paramount by director Norman Taurog in 1935.

Milt and said, "Listen, Milt, about this session. Why don't we just take it and put it out on Commodore?" Now, Milt doesn't remember it this way, and Milt may be right. But he got it and, of course, what he got was "Fine and Mellow" on the other side. "Strange Fruit" was one of the really great hits that Billie ever had. And I was just so delighted that the American Record Company, by their shortsightedness, should miss one of the greatest hits of all time.

SPIRITUAL TO SWING

In 1938 and 1939, I did a couple concerts called "Spiritual to Swing," which were done at Carnegie Hall. And they introduced the great black artists to an American audience, a sophisticated New York audience. And my assistant and stage manager on that was a guy called Goddard Lieberson.[3] When I joined Columbia in January of 1939, there was an opening in the classical department, and the president of Columbia came and said, "Do you know any bright young guys, John, who could work here? 'Cause the man we have isn't making it." So I said that I knew a guy who was the vice-president of the American Composers' Alliance who, I said, is a wit, is a scholar, and is a delight to work with. So I introduced Goddard to Ted Wallerstein immediately. Wallerstein, the Little Napoleon of the record business, later became president of Columbia. Wallerstein and Lieberson both had a feeling that for every Johnny Mathis tune they made, they [also] had to do something for American culture. I mean, they knew culture wouldn't sell, but it would bring glory to the music business and to Columbia.

I did another "Spiritual to Swing" concert in 1967 at Carnegie Hall with Lieberson as my master of ceremonies. And I felt I was too close to it to supervise the cutting down of it to recording. Columbia botched it, and that 1967 album is being remastered [and rereleased], and a whole lot of great stuff from Joe Turner, Big Mama Thornton, Edmund Hall, Count Basie, and Marion Williams that was not used [on the original record] for some reason is going to be on the new album.

[3] Goddard Lieberson served as president of the Columbia Records Group from 1956 to 1966, and again from 1974 to 1975.

RHYTHM AND BLUES

Without blues, there wouldn't be R&B. I don't think there would be rock and, I think, that to call the blues out of style is positively the most shortsighted thing that anybody could say. I have all my Bessie Smith records and all my Billie Holiday records and all my Aretha Franklin records and all the other R&B records I made. But there will always be somebody who will call it sinful music.

Middle-class black people hated it. It reminded them of everything they always wanted to forget. I'll never forget, I was on the board of the NAACP for about thirty-one years until I couldn't take a lot of their policies anymore. They threatened to expel any cranks who criticized the Vietnam War, and I figured that was time for me to get off the board, cause I did [criticize the war]. But in 1938 I brought to the NAACP the idea of a spiritual concert. And Laurel White, who was a nice guy and also was the executive secretary of the NAACP, said, "John, our people would never go for that. They don't like gospel. They don't approve of gospel. They *hate* jazz. And, as far as blues is concerned—forget it!" And I'm quoting verbatim.

And when I was on the board of Legal Defense in 1948 and I suggested to aid Legal Defense that they put on a concert with Mahalia Jackson, the head of Legal Defense said, "Whaddya mean, John? All that whooping and hollering?" So I said to him —he was also my friend—I said, "What are you, Episcopalian? 'Cause you have the narrowest mind I ever saw." You see, the whole middle-class black reaction to anything as earthy as blues or gospel was murder in New York.

LADY SOUL

You know, this is the most embarrassing story of my life, and I didn't find out how embarrassing it was until four months ago. I had worked for various record companies in my life, and one of the record companies I'd been vice-president of was Mercury Records back in 1947. And they had a wonderful singer named Helen

Hume. And Helen Hume sang a record by a man called Curtis
Lewis called "Today I Sing the Blues." Now, this was a record I
had completely forgotten about. In 1960, the same Curtis Lewis
brought in a demo record of his blues tunes, and the fourth tune
of the first side was "Today I Sing the Blues." I didn't recognize it
at all. Nor did I remember doing it thirteen years earlier. Well, I
heard this singer on this demo—which was just a girl playing a
piano and singing—and, I mean, as soon as you hear it you *know*.
I knew that this was the greatest blues singer since Billie Holiday.
Curtis Lewis told me that she was a seventeen-year-old girl from
Detroit named Aretha Franklin, who was a gospel singer and sang
with Sam Cooke in her father's choir. Well, that was all I had to
hear. I didn't want RCA to get wind of her.[4]

So I screamed and I yelled loud enough to Goddard Lieberson
at Columbia, who was impressed, and to Mitch Miller,[5] who was
also impressed. They signed her. I did the first album with her.
And the first thing I recorded was "Today I Sing the Blues" with
Aretha wailing away on piano. We also used Ray Bryant on piano
for a couple of tunes.

I had wanted to keep Aretha strictly as a soul singer, but Columbia, of course, thought they could make her big as a Top
Forty star. I did about one and a half albums with Aretha. And
then, Dave Kapralik, who had become the A&R co-ordinator at
Columbia, signed up Aretha's sister, Erma, and her father, the
Reverend C.L., and everything became so confused that I happily
bowed out. Aretha is still a very good friend of mine.

HAMMOND'S FOLLY

I had goofed [passed] on Joan Baez. Joan Baez had wanted
more money than I thought she was worth and—boy!—was I
wrong! Vanguard signed her. And here I was, new [again] with
Columbia, and I wanted to do something to change the image of
"Sing Along with Mitch." And I had just left [working for] Van-

---

[4] Sam Cooke was recording for RCA at the time.
[5] Mitch Miller, the same man who later did "Sing Along with Mitch,"
was the director of Artists and Repertoire (A&R) for Columbia Records,
the department responsible for signing new artists.

guard a year or so before. I had goofed on Joan Baez, but I signed a girl from Texas, Carolyn Hester, who was married to a very great writer called Richard Farina, who a lot of people forget. And Dick was one of the real reasons I signed Carolyn. And poor Carolyn has had such terrible luck because it's always been—well, first it was Joan who was in the way, and then Dick divorced her and married Joan's sister, Mimi.

I went down to Carolyn's rehearsal because I wanted to be sure that this was going to be good, this was going to be an exciting record. And there, at this rehearsal, was this strange kid who had just gotten into town the day before. And he had a little cap and, you know, a holder for a harmonica around his neck. And I started talking to him, and I couldn't believe that he was for real.

This was Bob Dylan.

So we made the first session with Carolyn, and it was pretty good. She had a lovely voice—not quite as pure as Joan's—but good.

So I got Bobby aside and I said, "Bobby, would you be willing to do an audition up here?" And he said, "Sure." So I made an audition [tape] with him and I signed him. And he was incredible. And then the Robert Shelton review came out in the New York Times[6] about his debut at Folk City, and that was the end. Except until the company brass heard Bob Dylan, and then they called it Hammond's Folly.

The first album didn't sell. But there were about five or six of us at Columbia who absolutely sensed that Bobby was going to make it. And, luckily, Columbia is one big company that will stick with an artist even after two or three albums. If they think there's enough originality there. Most companies don't. Most companies will try a second album if the first one's a stiff, but after two albums, that's it, because albums are too expensive to make.

Bobby's first album cost $408 to make. In those days, we didn't charge for editing time, we didn't charge for studio time. All we had was Bobby accompanying himself on guitar. I would let him come up to do as many sessions as he wanted. We must have sixty or seventy unreleased Bob Dylan things from those early days. And, historically, they're going to be wonderful for the Library of

[6] It was an unabashed rave.

Congress. Whether they'll be sold to the general public, I don't
know. Only if Bobby permits. If he doesn't, they won't.

I had always wanted Bobby to record in Nashville. I thought
this was the logical place for him to record. And the head of our
national operation was a guy called Don Lloyd, who was really an
Englishman, but in the record business longer than I. And he had
lived in Nashville long enough, so he was familiar with the culture
there. Nashville culture in the sixties was quite unlike the mad
Nashville culture today. And, as luck would have it, I said,
"You've got to get Dylan a recording there. Come up to Studio
A." And what do you think Bob was recording at the moment
when Don Lloyd arrived? "Oxford Town"—about the murders in
Mississippi. And Don said, "John, you're crazy. We couldn't
touch this in Nashville." And that is what kept Bob from recording in Nashville for four important years. I didn't feel that New
York musicians interpreted Bob correctly. Bob was really so much
into the whole Woody Guthrie scene that I felt that, in the first
place, Bob would be a wonderful influence on Nashville. And the
studio musicians are so superb in Nashville that there would be a
natural affinity. And that is exactly what happened—but it happened three years later.

The reason I stopped producing Bob Dylan can be summed up
in two words: Albert Grossman. This is probably the most tactless
speech ever going to be made, but . . .

When Bobby first came to me, he had no manager. As a matter
of fact, he told me he didn't have a mother and father and that his
uncle was a dealer in Las Vegas. And I was in a terrible spot because Bobby was underage, and I knew that without another signature of a close relative, he didn't have a valid contract with us.
But Bob said, "Don't worry about that. Trust me."

Anyway, Grossman came onto the scene and tried to break the
Columbia contract, but he didn't succeed. Clive Davis asked me if
Bobby had been in the studio [recording] for Columbia since he
had turned twenty-one, and I said, "Sure. Lots of times." So Clive
said, "Well, you can tear up that letter from Dylan's lawyer. If
he's been in the studio for us on his own free will since he's been
twenty-one, then that supersedes anything else."

Grossman and I have never been able to work together. We

were both on the board of the Newport Folk Festival for a couple of years together, and Albert is a man of "some" ability and "some" taste too. Actually, he was somewhat of a tiny hero of mine because he had given work to Big Bill Broonzy in Chicago when nobody else would employ him.

THE KID FROM ASBURY PARK

I was in on the Bruce Springsteen thing from the very beginning. Mike Appel[7] came into my office with Bruce about three and a half years ago. Appel I did not like very much. He let Springsteen play about three numbers. And I was just convinced that this was . . . that he was forever. He was one of the greatest new talents that I had ever heard. And so, I had met him that day and put him down in the Gaslight that night 'cause Bruce told me that he had never appeared solo in New York City. He had been in various rock groups in South Jersey. But you know, he had not had a chance to play alone in front of an audience. So I put him down in the Gaslight—about 8:30 P.M. before their regular show began—and, of course, the magic was just as great with the twenty-odd people who were there as it was with just me in the office.

And so, the next day I got him into the studio, and in about two and a half hours, we lay down fourteen songs. Now, we did it with just Bruce on guitar or Bruce playing piano—not very good piano —but lovely guitar and some of the things on this demo were absolutely masterpieces.[8]

Now, I don't know, I hadn't conceived of Bruce as a rock music player. Bruce, to me, was just plain "an artist." He was a wonderful musician. He was a sensitive, witty guy, and I didn't anticipate what would happen. After all, Appel had come in with all kinds of comparisons to Dylan which, except for looks, I didn't see at all. Bruce could sing.

[7] Mike Appel is the former manager & producer of Bruce Springsteen.
[8] The demo tape included acoustic versions of "It's Hard to Be a Saint in the City" and "Does This Bus Stop at 84th Street" and two unreleased Springsteen songs: "Arabian Night" and "If I Was the Priest," the latter of which was John Hammond's favorite.

(John has told a story elsewhere that when Appel came into his office for the first time with Bruce Springsteen, Appel looked John in the eye and said, "Well, you're supposed to have the best ears in the business, and I wanted to see if that's true or it's all a hype. This here is Bruce Springsteen, and he's going to make Dylan look like . . ." Here, Appel pantomimes snoring.)

Bruce was far more advanced than Bob Dylan when I met him. When I first heard Bob, he was playing that harmonica for Carolyn Hester. It wasn't until a couple weeks later that I got Bob into the studio for an audition alone. After that, I heard him at the old Folk City. But Bruce—I mean, Bruce had already paid all the dues. Bruce was three years older than Bob was. When I first heard Bob, he was twenty. Bob was already traveling in the footsteps of Woodie Guthrie, and he resembled him physically.

I didn't realize that Bruce had Dr. Zoom & The Sonic Boom and his various other rock groups behind him. And he fancied himself as . . . as hopefully the ultimate rock artist.

Well, I found out soon enough when I went up to this recording session out at Brooks Arthur's[9] studio (914 Recording Studio), and I was horrified at what I saw. Because here was Bruce—probably as natural and instinctive a guitarist as I had ever seen—here was Bruce with headphones on, in a soundproof booth, listening and trying to sing to the [rhythm] track with his band. The band wasn't all that great at the time. It was a good band, but it wasn't all that great. I thought some [studio] musicians were going to be there, but I didn't know that he had a band. But I saw Bruce needed direction so badly. And he wasn't getting any—nor would he take any.

Just to think about it, in 1932, when I celebrated my first record at the old Columbia Phonograph Company at 55 Fifth Avenue, there were two studios and three mikes for those two studios. And we didn't have any money to throw around. I used to do all my recording with a fifteen- or sixteen-piece band on one mike. And I knew from watching Bruce that he could do the same thing. I mean, Bruce sparked his band and the band sparked Bruce. And if you separated them with headphones, then there would never be

[9] Brooks Arthur has produced records for Janis Ian and other artists.

a really great record. I still don't think there's been a really great record.[10] Bruce had two albums out before, and I think *Greetings from Asbury Park* was perhaps the slowest starter in the history of Columbia Records. He had people having trouble understanding him when all the lyrics *were* printed on the sleeve inside the record. And they still couldn't understand the lyrics. And on the second album,[11] we didn't print the lyrics at all. And that was ghastly!

I hate to say this in comparison with Bruce's impact in person, but I don't think that Bruce has found a way to transmit his personal excitement onto tape as yet.

HAMMOND "FAILURES"

I think that George Benson is one of the greatest artists ever, and he hasn't made it with the general public as he should have.[12] To me, he's the best guitar player alive and a hell of a singer. He's making a lot of records right now with Benny Goodman. We may surprise everyone yet. It's really quite exciting.

ON CLIVE DAVIS

Clive would make stupid statements like: "I'm against any album that won't sell 100,000 copies." That would kill jazz, you know. But fortunately, he didn't kill it. He supported jazz, as far as that was concerned. I always continued to record jazz throughout Clive's regime.

He is a very much misunderstood and very much maligned human being. I know that's not the fashionable thing to say, but Clive was not a crook. And Clive was put in a very unfortunate position. Look, Clive made mistakes. Everybody makes mistakes. He probably had to leave Columbia Records, but he never should have left with the kind of stigma that was attached to him.

[10] This interview was completed a month before the *Born to Run* album was released to critical acclaim and achieved gold record status.

[11] *The Wild, the Innocent and the E Street Shuffle.*

[12] Another Hammond prediction comes to fruition as George Benson is today enjoying commercial success as a Warner Bros. Records recording artist.

THEY'LL NEVER LEARN

A marvelous thing happened to me at Columbia today. I came across a girl a few weeks ago who plays marvelous blues on guitar. And she sings mostly traditional blues, although she writes a little. And, I assure you, her voice is better than Janis Joplin and the guitar playing is not too far from Jimi Hendrix. And so, she had an audition this afternoon, and one of the Columbia vice-presidents said, "All right John, you can audition her [make a demo tape], as long as you keep it cheap. But . . ." he said, ". . . there's really not any market left for traditional blues."

Famous last words.

Arif Mardin: The Producer

The crystallization of any concept has always been the most difficult task of the artist—the ability to accurately transmit one's inner feelings in carrying out a resolve. The process of extricating the musical seed from the inspiration and forming it is left to the record producer, whose job is to augment the artist's intentions in a reflective manner. The producer is the creative catalyst—the person responsible for exhibiting the artist's talent in an imaginative way, a complimentary way, so that in the end there seems to have been no other way to have done it.

The producer is essentially an artist who paints with sound. He works in expressions of mood, rhythm, symmetry, perception, and originality as well as content. He must be freethinking and willing to incorporate a variance of influences and alternatives into the project. He must be able to regulate the complexities that go into a recording session—creating a musical dialogue, preproduction, selecting tunes, cutting the tracks—without becoming too meticulous, too elusive, or too self-indulgent in his approach to shaping the music.

There are few record producers around today who can success-fully handle such a task. Too often, they are not able to separate their artistic ideals from the over-all viability of the finished prod-uct, thus condemning the recording artist to uncommercial obliv-ion. Others are technicians who have no understanding (love may be a more appropriate word) of the music they are producing. And still others lack that basic feel necessary to convey the talents of the artist. In addition, the versatile producer must be able to convey those talents for many different types of artists.

Arif Mardin is the quintessence of the studio mentors, a musical chameleon who adapts easily to any artist fortunate enough to benefit from his guidance. Since joining Atlantic Records in 1963, he has worked closely with Aretha Franklin, the Rascals, Roberta Flack, Bette Midler, Hall and Oates, the Bee Gees, Stephen Stills, Laura Nyro, John Prine, and Wilson Pickett, as well as with jazz luminaries Dizzy Gillespie, Herbie Mann, David (Fathead) New-man, Les McCann, and Elvin Jones. He is the recipient of an abundance of gold records (I would mention the number but it becomes obsolete almost monthly) and in 1975 was awarded a Grammy as the Producer of the Year.

The diversity of artists alone tells one something about the per-sonality of the man: Arif Mardin is a person who is sympathetic to and capable of understanding the problems of the human psyche. He can relate to the pressures of creativity and can allay those problems in a positive manner. Moreover, he is a person ca-pable of assimilating into many modes of music; therefore, it would be plausible to assume that he is well versed in the intrin-sics of music theory. He is. A student of jazz, Mardin has been awarded the BMI scholarship to the School of Jazz in Lenox, Massachusetts, and was a recipient of the Quincy Jones Scholar-ship for Music while attending Berklee College.

Upon listening to a sampling of the records on which he has worked, one can readily perceive an Arif Mardin style of produc-tion. His records are technically precise and clean. They emit the painstakingly crisp sound of the studio, carefully calculated and rather unspontaneous; the tracks are extremely tight and cohesive in their movements from measure to measure. One can almost predict what he is going to do next. Because of that, he is more so a listener's producer opting for a familiarity in the sound by

choosing to record the artist in his most fundamental sense, uncomplicated and unpretentious; he rarely takes risks when recording an artist. Although his arrangements are not considered "too
sweet," Mardin takes full advantage of multitrack recording by
working with many instruments on his sessions. He uses string and
woodwind sections freely as a supplement to the basic rhythm
track—not vice versa, which leads to overproduction—giving a
more distinct definition to the artist's sound. He provides depth to
the over-all production by melding a counterpoint of song, artist,
and arrangement and by restraining any one of those ingredients
from overpowering the other.

Arif works swiftly and concisely, thinks in terms of a total package, and strives toward commercial acceptance for his artist. He is
a realist and depends on the rock establishment to properly
market his completed record as he moves to his next assignment
without becoming involved in sales and promotion. He understands and accepts his role in the development process and
chooses to work in a totally creative atmosphere—one where the
decisions and directions rest wholly upon his shoulders, where he
is undoubtedly one of America's consummate music producers.

I BEGAN TO MAKE A NAME FOR MYSELF

I was born in Istanbul. My family wasn't very musical, but
when I was eleven years old I began collecting jazz records and
that's what did it. I really started with the mainstreamers back
then. I used to listen to Lionel Hampton, Coleman Hawkins, people like that. Their records were easily accessible [in Turkey]. In
fact, I had to get them by way of London. But there was a lot of
breakage: five out of ten arrived in pieces. All my nice Charlie
Parkers would come in broken! I was a real bee-bopper in the beginning.

When I was fourteen, I began to dabble in writing and orchestrating and started to write for local bands. The Dizzy Gillespie
orchestra came to Turkey in '56. Through the help of some
friends associated with the Voice of America, I was introduced to
Quincy Jones, who was with Dizzy. I presented my compositions

to Quincy, who was interested. Quincy had an all-star band with
Hank Jones, Art Farmer, Phil Woods, *everybody*. For the Voice
of America, they made a transcription of three orchestrations I
had written, and on the strength of those I got a scholarship to
Berklee College in Massachusetts in 1958. So I was really only
self-taught before I got to Berklee. I got my formal education in
music there.

When I first arrived in the United States, I got a job as a music
instructor. I had gone through all the classes at Berklee so fast—
in a year and a half—that I stayed on another semester and
taught. Then I came to New York and began free-lancing. I wrote
fast orchestrations for publishing houses—really struggling, trying
to push my own themes. I also wrote for the Herb Pomeroy band,
an excellent workshop band who were recorded; Marshall Brown,
who was very active in international music; Billy Taylor; Dizzy
Gillespie, and some of the other bands. During that time, I was
also awarded the first jazz scholarship given by BMI to the Lenox
School of Jazz, which was a very cream-of-the-crop affair. Three
weeks in the Berkshires with an incredible faculty including Max
Roach, Lee Connors, and George Russell.

So little by little I began to make a name for myself. I starved a
little. Then, one day Neshui [Ertegun] called me and asked,
"Would you like to work for Atlantic in the album department?"
And I said, "Great!" I had known Neshui for a long time. My father knew his father [who was a very well-known man in the foreign service] from Turkey. So when I arrived in the United States,
I saw him and reintroduced myself and we always remained in
contact.

With my background in orchestration, jazz, and harmony, I
came into Atlantic and learned album production, mixing, and everything else.

THE RASCALS CAME BY

When I first came to Atlantic Records, they were almost completely involved in R&B and jazz. The company had been built on
it. But Ahmet and Neshui are very smart men, and they could
foresee a diversification coming for Atlantic, so they began to consider other types of groups.

Well, the Rascals came by, and they gave them to Tom Dowd and me to produce. That was my first assignment for Atlantic Records. Not a bad way to start my career as a producer! I listened to them carefully, and I had this feeling that this was the group that was going to open up other areas for Atlantic. They were fantastic singers and musicians and I loved the songs.

The Rascals were fantastic, a lot of fun to record. Very easy—in fact, too easy. I spent a lot of long hours with them playing basketball, ordering food—they loved to eat—and just having a good time. And even once, I said to myself, "Is this what producing is *really* like?" Because I was enjoying myself so much. But I knew it was a job, and I knew it was going to be successful. That happens with certain groups—you just know. Well, we all knew. And luckily it was with Tom Dowd who I got to work with on the Rascals. He had had so many years of experience recording. So I just watched him and learned. And we turned out to be a very good team.

THE PRODUCER'S ROLE

The producer's role can be paralleled to that of a director of a film. In films, producers put up the money and run the business. In records, even though you may be an independent producer and put up the money yourself, or you're under contract like me, you are in charge artistically. And you take control without putting too much of yourself in the record and crushing the artist. You are a relay person. You take the talent, place it, and then maybe enhance it. Maybe you help and advise to make it more commercial or more artistic. But while doing all these things, the producer also has to order the sandwiches and keep the floor clean.

Today, in producing the record, the song is still the most important thing. Of course, the dressing up has become more complicated as the technology has advanced. When I started, we recorded in mono. Then we gradually had two, three, four, eight, sixteen, and now twenty-four tracks to work with. So today, the producer must be more careful, more technology-minded. He has to learn to avoid things like hiss. Overdubbing and sweetening also have become more complicated, offering more choices. You might find yourself with eight tracks left over after basic recording

to do many things with. In the old days we had maybe one. So
you had to combine the tambourine with the harmony vocals—
strange combinations were needed to free a track. So now, more
than ever, a producer *must* make sure that the song comes
through without being obscured and still manage to keep a tab of
the echo and eq's and things like that. It's just *so* much more
complicated today.

YOU REARRANGE YOUR LIFE

Before I establish the criteria for selecting a new act to produce,
my main concern is the availability of my time. At this point, I
have commitments for five albums and that's enough to keep me
going for a year and a half. So it becomes impossible for me to
take on any other act. Unless somebody with a shining voice
comes along—then you rearrange your life!

After the matter of time has been solved, my major criterion for
selecting an act has to do with getting along with that person or
group. I meet them, and there has to be good vibrations right
away. If there isn't, it's a waste of time because you're going to be
with them so much. I spend a lot of time with an artist before I go
into the studio—a *lot* of time. We go through hundreds of songs;
either the artist writes his or her own songs or I find them or they
find them. So there must be conferences about songs and procedures and musicians and studios—a big preparation period.

I just finished the new Judy Collins album (*Bread and Roses*)
with her, and Judy did her homework in such a way that she was
prepared for recording: songs, lyrics, *everything*. When she came
in with her songs, she had already gone through maybe a hundred,
and then she and I only had to go through maybe about twenty
(to narrow down her repertoire for inclusion on the album). She
made my work much easier. She also went through an enormous
amount of rehearsal. She came to my house, we played the songs
on the piano, then we cassetted them and listened to the form. If
we didn't like what we heard, we tried a new form. Of course, my
being a musician helps. There are certain producers who cannot
play the piano and they have to hire somebody. So a combination
of talent and selectivity is essential to good record production.

I DO ASSUME CONTROL

People assume that acts have more of an ego today than in days past, but I don't find that necessarily true. Not with me, at least. It may look like I am extremely loose in the studio, but there is a lot of discipline involved. I dictate certain things so as not to waste any time, like what stage of the production will come first, who should come in and sing, and who should go home. For instance, when I work with a group like AWB (the Average White Band), there may be many phases of operation. One day I may set aside completely for guitar work and we therefore don't want to bother the other people [in the group]. But we *do* want to have everybody else nearby so that if it finishes quickly you can call them.

Actually, it's a fantastic way of orchestrating people—like being a stage director. I don't do anything with a militaristic attitude, but I *do* assume control, at times, through diplomacy and friendship. All the people I work with are my friends—they have to be. That's a secret to good production. It has to be like that because I live with the artist in the studio for a long time—approximately two to three months—and if we don't get along, we might as well get a divorce early on to save us both the time and energy.

You see, recording is painful as a growth process for all artists. It's fun, but at the same time, you're creating something and responsible to a lot of people, including yourself, for coming up with results. Some artists don't show the pressure and some do, but there's *always* pressure on the artist. Always! There is also a lot of pressure on me and on the musicians. But more on the artist. There are days when we'll end up a session much earlier than expected because an artist is tired or frustrated. At that point, we just scrap the day. It doesn't pay to continue. Or, at least, I'll find something to do so that if the musicians are hired for more time it doesn't go to waste.

I DEFEND THE ARTIST'S CREDIBILITY

New material usually gets to me either in the mail or through publishers—but what they send is what they send routinely. They don't sit down and analyze the artist's style who I am about to produce. So I listen to other people's albums, go to clubs, check out new acts—anything that can lead me to a good song. The best thing, of course, is to have some friends who are writers and beg them to write a song for the act I am going to produce. So far, I've gone to friends like Steve Goodman, John Prine, and Danny O'Keefe for material. I've worked with them all before, so I can always call them up and say, "Please come up with a song for me."

I still always look for a single when I'm doing an album. Sometimes, in the course of sessions, inspirations may be great and solos may tend to be longer than they should, so it's up to me to shorten them so that we could have a single from it. I wouldn't produce an album that didn't have a single in it. It's not for money for me or anything. I have to do my job. It's like if you call a lawyer, he has to defend you. He doesn't say, "I've read the civil code, don't worry," and then the man goes to jail. So, in the same respect, I have to do what I've been called in for, even though the artist may sometimes lose perspective and say, "My songs are great and I don't need a single." That's not right. So I have to impose direction. I have to say, "Look, this is good, but let's try it in a three-minute version." Of course, there are groups that do not need a single; they have a massive FM audience. But having that single sure wouldn't hurt even them. So by producing something with a single in mind, I defend the artist's credibility. I have to think, How can the artist be heard by more people? Well, the album will sell more if there's a hit single in it. It's a simple answer.

Ringo always picks songs with a very definite chorus line—always. The same with the Bee Gees. If you look at all the songs they have on albums, they're all potential singles, but one is always better than the rest and *that's* the one we go with. The same with the Average White Band. Some of their songs are long, though, and we have to make them shorter. Even with someone as talented and respected as Judy Collins we look for singles. By doing that, we secure the artist's future.

You know, sometimes I hear people say, "You're so singles-oriented." That's okay. It doesn't mean I'm selling my soul. I'm actually trying to come up with a three-minute commercial to sell the album. Something that's more energy-packed, more edited.

So that people who don't have time to listen to a whole album or long song when they're driving can become interested quickly in the artist and, subsequently, the album. In the old days, the single *was* the record. Then, if that happened, an album would result. That's because we used to make 78s, and it was only one song on a record. So the three-minute art form is a leftover from the 78 days.

ON ARETHA

I was driving the other day—on my way to the studio to work with Ringo—and I turned on the radio, heard one note, and almost hit a tree. It was Aretha, *her!* with that "oooh" she does unlike anybody else, that wavy note. She does that *all the time* in the studio, and each time it's a delight and a surprise. I wish I had a private collection of cassettes to capture all those outtakes she discards. Just incredible notes.

Aretha's very easy to work with in the studio because, if she's pleased [with her performance], she really sails through the rest of the recording. If she's not, she tells you. But she doesn't come to the studio with preconceived ideas. Most artists do. They say, "My song starts here, ends here, and that's exactly how I want to do it." And you try to say, "How about a deviation here?" And they say, "Nope! It will ruin my song." Not with Aretha. She's always open to suggestions, and if she likes them, she goes with the changes, which allows for improvisation and chance. Often I'll say, "Aretha, since you just gave such a beautiful performance I'd like to erase the previous take because there's an extra note which crept into it." Then she'll listen to that previous take and say, "I like it, it's great. It's a harmony note and we'll leave it in." What can you do? That's her inner ear working, and she usually hears herself better than anyone else. It's a pleasure working with such a great talent.

EVERYTHING'S UNDER CONTROL

The engineer physically sets up the studio for me, and I lend suggestions to this layout. If you work with one engineer all the time, all these things are done automatically.

In the session, an engineer brings confidence—that's the most important thing for me. He does it in such a way that the artist should not be aware that there is a million dollars' worth of gadgetry in the studio like a complicated cockpit. He helps to humanize things, rather than allow us to see the studio as only being mechanical. And a good engineer should always give the impression—not just the impression, but the *reality*—that everything's under control so that the artist can sing or perform at ease without wondering, "Am I distorted or am I being recorded badly?" I imagine that, in theory, there could be an incredible engineer who is a wiz at the board, but who would be so cold or so demanding or even allowing his worrying to show through that he could actually ruin a session. Luckily, I've never worked with anybody like that. For example, I've worked with Gene Paul, Lou Hahn, Tom Dowd—who unfortunately doesn't do much engineering anymore—and Phil Ramone. All of those people, especially Phil, use their fingers like part of the equipment and their recording is incredible. But that's taken for granted. Almost all of the engineers I've worked with are good.

But there's an extra dimension which has to be projected into the room which I look for. I look for as much creativity in the engineer as the artist looks for in me. It's all a give and take, like a play where the actors come in and exit. So if the engineer wants to try a new echo on the spur of the moment, he does it. That's it! He doesn't ask me, he does it. Without creativity the producer cannot function.

SOME WARM MOMENTS

Joel Dorn produced Bette's first album, *The Divine Miss M*. He asked me to write three of the arrangements for it; only one was used, and the remaining two are on her third album, (*Songs for the New Depression*—"Cape Cod" and "Marahuana." For whatever reasons, on the second album Joel didn't work with her, so they called in Barry Manilow and me to produce.

Bette is very sweet and fun to be with in the studio. In the first few weeks of recording [her second album], we all had to sense each other out. She was thinking, Can they handle it? And we were thinking, What is she like to work with? After that initial phase, everything was fine. She's just very picky with her vocals. She would come into the studio, sing her vocals, and we'd think they were great. Then she'd come back and do it again, and next week she'd come back and do it *again*. And again and again until she was satisfied. So the album took a long time because she really worked hard on those vocals.

I look forward to being with her in the studio because she's a creative person. She sings very well—especially on her third album. That's the type of performer every producer needs. If we do this for a living—for the art, for the money—at least we should have some warm moments in the studio. Bette has definitely created some of those for me. That's the payoff to keep you going.

ON MIXING

Mixing an album used to be fun, but now it's extremely tedious. The more choices you have with twenty-four tracks, the more paranoia sets in. It takes me a long, long time to be satisfied with the final mix. Sometimes I wish I had a magic wand to touch and turn the work into the final mix.

I try to mix a song a day in the course of six hours. I only work twelve hours a day if I'm *really* under pressure. So it takes about ten days for me to mix an entire album. Then I allow for a 25 per cent remake. A remix is much faster because you've already gone through all the hand-to-mind computer process, and you tend to remember all the cues.

STUDIO MUSICIANS

Today, the level of studio musicianship is just incredible, compared to fifteen years ago. Everybody can play fast runs and read very well. Studio musicians are like businessmen: they have a time slot in which they have to play and then they go to the next job. So I try to create an atmosphere in which they won't look at their watches. And if we need them for three hours, I book them for six. I don't push them. It's not a strict union hour where the last ten minutes of each hour belongs to them. If they want to go out for sandwiches or take twenty minutes for something personal, it's fine as long as it's in my schedule and they don't disrupt the session.

I work with a number of great studio musicians: Steve Gadd, Tony Levin, Will Lee, Hugh McCracken, David Spinoza, Richard Tee, Cornell DuPree—the New York Connection. I heard a lot of things about studio musicians in California before going out there. I heard that they never show up, they're slow, a number of similar things. But I just finished Ringo's album there, and the co-operation was incredible. They played *so* hard just to please us. I think it's the same on both coasts. I also think a producer's job is just that: to create a certain atmosphere in the studio where people work very hard no matter what, and where there is also a good time being had. The idea is to work hard, though, not to have a good time, and if, in the meantime, both happen, then I've done my job.

IT'S A DIFFICULT PROFESSION

Producing is very time-consuming. I'd like to work near my family as much as possible. But five months of nights in the studio is just too much for anybody to take. And you know, every act says the same thing: "Just for me—three weeks of your life, and that's all." But it happens with the others, too. This way I don't get to see my family. My children worry, "Where's Daddy?" I am badly in need of a civilized program where I work until seven o'clock for a week and then a week of evenings—something to even out my life.

Living with a producer is like living with a doctor. I get called on Sundays to do things. Even though my wife is unhappy with that, she accepts it. It's a difficult profession, and the family just has to accept the crazy schedule. But it causes a lot of problems for musicians. Their children and their wives don't understand why they're not home all the time. It is a strain on family life. New formulas *must* be found. I had two projects going when I started Ringo's album. He had time commitments—he can only be in this country a certain length of time. AWB has to be on the road, Judy Collins has to do this or that. All of a sudden, everything was finished and I had to start a new project. That kind of situation harms my perspective and places a great deal of strain on me. Then, while I'm preparing singles for AWB, I have to begin work on something *else*. I don't know—it's a hectic business, a lot of worrying, a lot of pressure. But I love it and it never ends.

Dion DiMucci

"You know, there was a time I was so low
I had to look up at the street,
I was only a shell of a man walkin'
   'round
I couldn't get up on my own two feet."

DION DiMUCCI, *Sunshine Lady*

Some kids grow up with pennants of sports teams or colleges on their bedroom walls. My room was decorated with one 5×7 photo of an angelic, sleepy-eyed young man which, for ten years, was tucked securely under a metal prong that held my mirror in place. Scrawled across the bottom of it in ballpoint pen (which I smudged when I received it to authenticate the signature wasn't machine-signed) were the words: "Yours, Dion." And, as Dion would say, that was heaven.

Dion and the Belmonts were anything but angelic. Looking like they stepped right off the set of Blackboard Jungle, *they were from the real jungle—the streets of New York's south Bronx— where zip guns and drugs were the accessible props and nobody was around to give them the right answers. Only the right tune. And it was their ability to make music—their own type of music —which ultimately pulled them through the frustrations of urban poverty and crime.*

Dion DiMucci is a rock and roll authentic, a street corner singer who, during the late 1950s, hunched over pinball machines and

*pool tables while instinctively working out counterpoint harmonies
to the latest songs written by neighborhood friends. It was all fun,
a part of his everyday existence which slowly crept out of the
candy stores to the hallways and subways and school gymnasiums,
and, finally, to the recording studios where the music became permanent—forever. Little did Dion realize that his music, as well as
his environment, would become a romanticized legend. We still
know, by heart, the lyrics to "I Wonder Why" and "Teenager in
Love" and "Runaround Sue" and "The Wanderer." They roll off
our tongues like old friends, twenty years later—old friends with
whom we associate happy times and carefree memories. There's a
lot being written today about the power of rock and roll. And if
there is any metaphorical truth to it all, then it is certainly the
power to be able to recall those good times through song.*

*People frequently walk up to Dion today and say, "You haven't
changed a bit." They couldn't be further from the truth. Aside
from the obvious corporeal distinctions—he's no longer seventeen, a receding hairline, a few grays, etc.,—Dion has undergone
an intense spiritual catharsis, a long and painful process of coming
to grips with his consciousness and being able to look himself in
the eye. He's proud of it, and he'll let you know it. He understands himself—the way he is now and the way it was when he
was on the road with the Belmonts—and there's no bitterness.*

*Unlike many of the other artists represented in this book, Dion's
artistic success relies heavily on trusted contributions from assorted people. He is from the old school of the recording artists,
which accentuates the performer as opposed to the auteur, and he
places himself freely in the hands of his producer, his record company, and his manager for positive decisions. Dion is essentially a
singer/interpreter, and in that context he was and still is exceptional. His vocalizations contain a stylized scat type of singing
mixed expertly throughout his choruses. They propel his songs, allowing his renditions a constant energy, a constant enthusiasm.
Additionally, they provide much of his older material with a
timelessness, not evident in the songs of his contemporaries. If
one listens to "The Wanderer" and "Lovers Who Wander," there
is a feeling that they could easily meld into today's Top Forty list
without need of rerecording. "Runaround Sue" is a classic but not
in the sense that is out of place when played in succession with*

recordings of newer artists. His choice of material, today, follows
the same pattern: fresh, uncomplicated, and spirited.

The "new, improved" Dion is more individual than musical. He
is relaxed, contemplative, and confident. He reflects casually over
what he refers to as his "overstated importance" in musical his-
tory, more concerned with how people will accept him today as a
contemporary musical artist. But the "old" Dion, the streetheart
of the Bronx, continues to shine through. A little cocky, a little
sentimental, a little tongue-in-cheek, and a lot of talent.

MY IMPRESSIONABLE YEARS

I don't really come from a musical family. My father is tone-
deaf; he has no rhythm at all, but he has the soul of an artist and
the body of an athlete. All my uncles would go to the race track,
and he would go along and sketch everybody. He never put a bet
down, though. My dad was always into the music, but he couldn't
sing. But my mother was musical, and there are people who are
musical on her side of the family going all the way back to Italy.
Her father was a conductor of symphonies in Naples.

I always liked hearing music around the house. It put me in a
mood. It always stirred me. If it was opera, it would just take me
away. If it was Al Jolson or Buddy Clark, it was heaven. My father loved Al Jolson and played his records all the time. Jolson
had so much impact on me. Jesus, I was a toddler then, but I can
still remember hearing him sing all the time. And I would sing
along with a lot of those records. And the radio. I grew up listening to that all the time, too.

There was a country station that I found by accident. It was
playing "Honky Tonk Blues," by Hank Williams, one day, and I
didn't know what the hell I was hearing. In the city during the Fifties—my impressionable years—honky-tonk was unheard of. You
went to Roosevelt High School or P.S. 32 and nobody had *ever*
heard of honky-tonk there. You don't hear anybody talking about
honky-tonk on "Happy Days." So it was odd hearing it by somebody who was raised on the street corners and living in the city.
But I got into "Cold Cold Heart" and "Your Cheatin' Heart," and
"Moanin' the Blues." It was almost prerock and roll and served

as a link for me. R&B was happening too and, all of a sudden, rock and roll came at me out of nowhere. The street corner sound. I remember the first record that I heard was "Gee." For me, it was kind of basic. I didn't have a formal musical education. I was raised on records. *That* was my education. Then, later, I cut my teeth on Bo Diddley, Chuck Berry, and early Elvis Presley records. Between the group sound and the rockabilly of Elvis and maybe the rolling piano playing and the Cajun accent of Fats Domino playing things New Orleans style. It offered a different sound to my ear to mesh with the Hank Williams influence I already had. I just put it all together.

MUSIC GOT ME THROUGH IT

I got my first guitar when I was about eight years old. My parents wanted me to take guitar lessons. I had come from a relatively poor neighborhood in the Bronx. And my mother would get that three dollars up every week (for lessons), but I'd spend it in the poolroom. And I'd feel guilty. Then I'd rush home and work on some Hank Williams records just to please her out of guilt. I wanted to learn those Hank Williams songs rather than sitting and learning "Yankee Doodle."

Kids really *did* sing on the street corners then. There were no instruments. Guitars were associated with country singers. In the city, the f-hole guitars were popular. But the guitar players used to sit in the back of the band and play rhythm. That was pre-electric. Basically, nobody ever hung out with instruments on the street corners.

There were a lot of gang wars. It was a real frustrating time because everybody's emotions were suppressed. You had to be cool —that was the only thing expected of you. Jesus, I used to see a lot of my friends drop over in those street wars. It was hell and it was *real* scary. I was a member of one of the gangs—the Fordham Baldies—and I took it real seriously, too. I had a lot of fun with them, but I wouldn't want to see my kid involved in something like that. It would seem insane. Yet, for then, it was the norm. It was recognition within my own little group. Music got me through it. It helped me come into contact with my feelings, and I could at least let them out. I remember the first time I took a plane, I got so detached from all that. I remember looking down and picturing those few square blocks as they got smaller and smaller. I thought, the problems and the troubles that I take so seriously in that little square area are so insignificant. And that was when my goals started changing.

When I was hanging out with the Fordham Baldies, there was a little songwriter in the neighborhood who knew somebody who was opening up a record company. And he brought that guy a demo record which I had made for my parents as a Christmas gift. I sang a Fats Domino song, "Rosalie," and "Boppin' the Blues," by Carl Perkins. My mother played it for anybody who had two seconds, who could stand in one place long enough for her to get it onto the record player. And she played it for this songwriter who really didn't have anything going for himself except that he *did* know these people who were opening up a small record company. That was Laurie Records, and they offered me a record contract. It overtook me. It wasn't that I made any kind of great business decisions at the time. I had quit school. I was a restless kid and had been to seven high schools. I was having troubles. My parents didn't know whether to send me to an uncle who lived in the sticks or to keep me at home. They were real concerned. They did the best they could. So I wasn't a businessman who said to himself, I think I'll look for a record contract. It found me.

THE BELMONTS

The Belmonts were the best of the street corner singers. There were little candy stores in the Bronx, and each of [the Belmonts] hung out in a different candy store. If you walked into one of those candy stores, either Freddie Milano or Angelo DeLeo or Carlo were leaning against the jukebox singing along with Robin or Johnny or the Flamingoes or the Cadillacs. I gathered them together when I lucked into a record contract.

In those days, if we rehearsed, we rehearsed in the subway or just walking down the street. We'd get it on anywhere. We used to really practice in the hallways and let our girlfriends listen. And our friends were our biggest fans, but they always thought we sounded better when we were practicing in front of them than the way it came out on the records. But we could sing anywhere. We didn't need the equipment. We didn't need a cellar to rehearse in. No amplifiers, no mixing boards. Who gave a shit? We didn't care.

The Belmonts and I were considered real characters. We were always up to something. People thought I sang with the Belmonts because they *sang* good. Hell no—they used to *protect* me. And they used to protect the whole tour when we went on the road. Fabian and Frankie Avalon and all the pretty boys from Philadelphia. We used to find that funny. Frankie Avalon used to have a little scar over his eye and even *that* looked just perfect. We *hated* him for looking so good; I say that with love, of course. But the Belmonts and I used to talk about it all the time. We used to say, "That son of a bitch even has a scar that looks good!"

If we'd go into a town or some diner where a bunch of local boys would start up with us, the Belmonts and I would kick their asses. We would drag the street with people. We were crazy. We didn't know how to talk or get ourselves out of anything. We'd say, "Whaddya mean?"—POW! "You let 'em say that to you?"—POW! It was just cut and dry. We got a problem?—Punch it! We never used any reasoning. We were just dumb kids from New York City who thought we were the toughest—and coolest—guys on earth.

BEING THE COOLEST

That whole attitude—the Fonzie attitude of being cool—it originated with us. We were the *coolest*. Of *course* it was a cover-up, but it worked and we needed it. We worked at being cool. Are you kidding? I was so fucking cool nobody would have believed it —hah! That was it—*cool*. We always had to maintain that. It was in our attitudes and in the way we approached our music. We used to buy jackets that we thought would knock everybody out, would make them think we were cool. It mattered. It mattered to us and to the kids. How do you think they would have felt if they knew we weren't cool? It was the most important aspect of our image. Sometimes, I couldn't figure out whether being cool meant more than our music.

You know, we were crazy then. We were never able to see ourselves from a different perspective. Images—musical images never made sense, they just gave off a good feeling. We never hurt anybody by having a cool image. It was fun. We weren't playing to twenty-five- and thirty-year-olds like I'm doing today. We were playing to kids. Fourteen- and fifteen-year-olds. And it mattered to them—really mattered—how their stars looked to their friends. These were the kids who got rock and roll off the ground and spread it. These are the same kids who are still listening to it today. They may have a couple kids now, but they also have memories—real good memories—and to them we're still the coolest.

ON THE ROAD

Being on the road in the Fifties was rough. And that's what they called paying dues. But it was fun. We were kids and had a lot of energy. At that time, I used to sing myself hoarse every night. I was never spoiled by the fantastic monitors, which groups use on stage today. I didn't know [any different way].

If I would walk into a session, I could just sing from my inner soul. But in a public appearance, there was no sound system, and I'd sing with my outer ear and I'd be yelling—not really expressing myself. We were never able to reproduce live what we really felt when recording a record. And that's bullshit.

My first tour lasted for six weeks, and the Belmonts and I traveled with Bobby Darin, Jimmy Clanton, and Sam Cooke. We traveled by some planes, but mostly by bus, which is really tiring. Bobby Darin and I got really close. He was a warm guy, very positive—*very* positive. The first day I met him, the Army had turned him down because of the heart ailment he had from when he had rheumatic fever when he was a kid. He was twenty-four years old at the time. Most people would feel sorry for themselves or get into some kind of negative trip, but I don't think that ever dawned on Bobby. He always stayed on the positive side. And he had no fear about anything happening to him physically. That was an inspiration to me. He was grateful for the things he did have, and he stayed with those things. I think he did an awful lot. He was tough on himself, really a perfectionist.

Darin taught me about taxes. I came from a poor section of the Bronx, and my father—and I say this, not as a put-down, but out of respect—he never made the kind of money to have to pay taxes, so I had no idea what they were. Well, on that first tour of mine, Darin had already had some years in the business, and he taught me all about taxes. He told me about all the things you could deduct, about ledgers and how to keep records. For me, that was a novelty. It became a road game to me—keeping records. The Belmonts and I had two separate contracts. They got half the royalties, and I got the other half. And they ended up individually paying two thousand dollars more apiece than I did on their income, and I had made a considerable amount more than the Belmonts. I said. "There's something to this tax thing." They never kept receipts or anything. Today I still do it like a hawk.

Sam Cooke was also an out-of-sight guy, and I loved listening to him sing before it was our turn to go on. He was an easygoing guy who mostly kept to himself. Most of the black performers did. Things weren't easy for the black performers then. There was still a color bar, and they took a lot of bullshit quietly. Today I think back and say to myself, "How did those things happen? How could we have let them happen?" But that's no excuse. They *did* happen, and all we can do now is to make things right *today*. But we didn't know these things. For us being on the road then was great fun, we got to see the country and make money doing it.

I was on that Buddy Holly tour. I'll never forget it as long as I live. I just couldn't make the plane. I don't remember the exact circumstances, but I didn't get to it on time. When I heard the plane had gone down, well—it was probably one of the scariest feelings I've ever experienced.

DICK CLARK AND ALAN FREED

I thanked Dick Clark on my new album (*Streetheart*) because he's been in this business a long time, and whether people agree with me or not, he's been a hundred per cent honest with me and the rest of the acts who I've talked to about him.

On those tours I did for him, there were a few sleazy promoters and opportunists—people who tried to pull off backseat deals— Dick always cut them off from us right away. Nobody ever *not* got paid by him or not get treated fairly. He always spelled out the terms for us right out in the open: this is the way it is. And that's always the way it was. He was a man of his word. If you were working for Dick Clark, you always knew it would be a professional show. He didn't take any bullshit either. He never put up with it. If somebody on the tour wasn't "with it," he'd say, "Get with it, and maybe next time we can use you. You're beautiful. We love you." But he'd get to that guy's agent and get somebody else. The man insisted on seeing things work properly. You could never be in the business as long as Dick and not have people feel about you the way I feel about him. He *is* the business. He's been our spokesman and he's fought for us to be represented properly. Christ—where would we be without Dick Clark? Where would I be?

I didn't know Alan Freed too well, but I did work for him a few times. Alan believed in the music more than anybody else involved with rock and roll; he *was* the music. He was very close to the birth of rock and roll. If you walked into his studio, he never turned the music down. When he played music over the air, it was always at a peak, and people would always be dancing in his studio. Today, nobody could believe that was possible, but he always had kids up there dancing away. He loved all the kids and related to them. They were his world. He put out a lot of energy and did an awful lot for the kids. When he got blown away by the bad publicity, we lost an awful good friend of rock and roll. Actually, I don't think we ever lost him as a friend. The guy loved music until the day he died. But it was never the same.

IT WASN'T MY CUP OF TEA

We recorded a song called "Where or When" on our first album for one of the executives of Laurie Records—a beautiful man named Allen Sussel. It was his favorite song, and he asked us if we'd do it. It wasn't my cup of tea; it wasn't a street corner sound. But we did it in block harmony. A lot of people thought we were trying to imitate the Four Freshmen, but we didn't do any fancy harmonies. We did street corner harmonies. Hell, it was his favorite song and a Rodgers and Hart tune—we couldn't say no. We sang the song and put it on an album for him. The song became number-one overnight and sold a million copies. After that, I always used to ask Allen, "Got any more favorite songs?"

But the Belmonts got on this thing that they wanted to do more stuff like the Four Freshmen. They started getting into this straight group-type sound. It wasn't my cup of tea, so I just left and I kept the group sound the way I wanted it as I continued working. I kept it in "The Wanderer" and "Runaround Sue" and "Ruby Baby"—all of which I recorded with a group called the Del Satins who became the Brooklyn Bridge. They were a group of five kids who were really good.

The Belmonts also felt very strongly about what they wanted to pursue. It was a mutual kind of split. We both needed our own sounds—different sounds. I was too excited about doing my music —what I wanted to do—to be concerned about being without the Belmonts. I was too young to be scared or afraid. Hell, I never felt fear then; I used to walk through walls at that age. Even though we were scared, we didn't show it. Sure, I was probably nervous about going on my own, but I was too excited about what I was going to create to knock people out.

"ABRAHAM, MARTIN AND JOHN"

In 1963, I really became influenced by John Hammond, Sr., at Columbia Records. He saw me in the hall and called me into his office one day because he was familiar with things I recorded like "The Wanderer" and "Ruby Baby." He felt the primitive kind of approach to music I had, the grass-roots-blues approach. He said, "You like this kind of stuff. *Now* listen to *this*." And he played me some Delta Mississippi blues by Robert Johnson and Lightnin' Hopkins. Well, I felt inspired and I felt resentful. I felt resentful like: Who's been hiding this stuff from me all these years? Why haven't I ever heard of this? Why didn't anybody ever play this music for me before? Where's it been? I was singing rock and roll, but I never knew what the roots of it were. I thought I had heard it in Fats Domino, but that was it. That's probably why I had a passion for the Al Jolson music. Because when the rural blues got to the cities, he turned it into his type of Dixieland style of delivery.

So John Hammond turned me on to this kind of music, and I just took home a bunch of albums. Everybody was calling me up to do sessions, and I'd just say, "Wait a second, huh. I've got something to do here." And I kind of got carried away with it.

Then, after I'd heard the records, I'd go down to Greenwich Village and breathe down Lightnin' Hopkins' back, and I ran out and got a set of finger picks. I started picking and hearing things I'd never heard before. Great music. To the point of getting hung up in it, really hung up. I tried to get out physically this flowing sound that I kept hearing in my head.

"Abraham, Martin and John" was a result of being influenced by the blues, becoming a better songwriter, and getting close to the roots. I got called a folkie because I had picks in my hand, but, to me, I was just moving forward. Laurie Records really put that one together for me. They cared about it. Gene Schwartz[1] and I really sat and talked about that song for a week. We didn't quite know how to approach it. It was sort of a protest song, but it brought people in the back door instead of hitting them in the face. That song was God-sent.

A friend of mine wrote it, and Phil Gernhard[2] brought it down to me in Miami. I listened to it for three weeks and discovered that the simplicity of the song had passed me by completely. Originally, I thought that whoever recorded the song was an opportunist trying to cash in on assassinations. But the tune stuck in my mind.

It was written in an entirely different way, a shuffle. And my wife said, "Dion, that song is the gospel. It's the truth." And then I started listening to it and realized that the song had nothing to do with assassinations. It was about *now*. It was about how men live to see their dreams fulfilled while they're here; some work like mad to see their dreams fulfilled, and they die short of that. A lot of great men through history never lived to see their accomplishments come to fruition. And they'd freak if they knew it happened after they're gone.

LAURIE RECORDS; BEING WITH WARNER'S

Warner Bros. Records has been great to me. They care about building you as an artist, bringing you out, and tapping the source of where you're coming from. They've given me a lot of positive

[1] Gene Schwartz was the president of Laurie Records and the one person Dion credits as being his mentor.
[2] Dion's former producer.

input and have encouraged me. They waited for me to get all the acoustic stuff over with, and they built around me. But they waited. They care about building artists. Laurie Records was into singles, good songs, and they didn't care too much about the artist. They never built an artist. That's where I disagreed with them. They were good people, but we had different musical principles.

I had recorded "Abraham, Martin and John" and recorded a song on the "Abraham, Martin and John" album called "Clouds," by Joni Mitchell. Its three choruses were about clouds, love, and life. I had a contractual agreement with Laurie saying that all songs were mutually agreed upon as well as all edits. I got back to Miami, and they released that song and cut off the chorus about life; they put out the song with only two choruses. And I called them up and I was pissed. I said, "You got no right to do that. This is no way to start out our new relationship." And they said, "Well, it's a good song, but it's too long for radio." I was *really* pissed. And I thought that if we were going to start out on the wrong foot like that, then I didn't want to continue our relationship. So Warner Bros. were very interested in me, and they bought my contract from Laurie.

Warner Bros. amazes me. They picked up my option for this new album (*Streetheart*), it really shocked me. I made five albums for them[3] and they all just sat on the shelf without striking lightning. They were paying the rent for me, but I wasn't making money for them. At that point, I had a lot of producers interested in me and was thinking of moving to another record company for some new blood, but Mo Ostin[4] called me and he had kept the faith. He said, "I just brought a new producer to Warner Bros.— Steve Barri[5]—who you've got to get together with. He likes your approach to things. I think you'll work out together." Well, I'm so happy being at Warner's right now. And even with five albums, they've always let me hold my head up.

Steve Barri, in the studio, keeps such a state of calm—even

[3] They are: *Sit Down Old Friend, You're Not Alone, Sanctuary, Suite for Late Summer,* and *Reunion.*

[4] Chairman of the board of Warner Bros./Reprise Records.

[5] Steve Barri previously produced The Grassroots, Bo Donaldson & the Heywoods, and many other hits while a staff producer and executive for ABC/Dunhill Records.

though he's from Brooklyn. It's wonderful, because what I've heard while he produced the record was exactly what it sounded like after he had mixed it, and that's important to me. It wasn't like he got so excited about a tune that he added too much to it— like what happened with me and Phil Spector.[6] Steve is calm, professional, on the money, and he works fast. That inspires me because we didn't labor over anything such a long time that we were no longer able to maintain our perspective on it. And he's also great to hang out with. That matters to me. And, now, Warner Bros. has picked up my option *again*. What a nice company to work for.

I WANTED TO LIVE

When I was young, I lived out on the streets and I took drugs. I'm not selling it and I'm not hiding it, but I'm sure as hell not proud of it. I was thirteen or fourteen and had gotten involved with drugs before I ever thought of recording. I was taking drugs on the street corner all the time. It wasn't anything that had to do with the family. That's just the way the neighborhood was. It was a lot of things I couldn't cope with. But I never resolved that *thing,* the reason why I took drugs. I never understood it. I thought I was doing it to feel good, for peace of mind. A temporary peace of mind.

When I got into recording, there were long periods of time I was on the shelf. I was in the hospital when "Where or When" came out. I went into the hospital when I was recording for Columbia because of drugs. But there were long periods of time where I would desire to create and to work and to achieve, and it was much stronger than my desire to cop out. There were periods, though, when that kind of distraction work gave me stopped—being in the studio and being on the road—and I was still left with my problem. I never resolved it.

Until late 1967.

[6] Dion recorded an album for Warner Bros. Records in between *Suite for Late Summer* and *Streetheart* which was produced by Phil Spector and took over two years to schedule for release. Dion is reluctant to talk about it; however he finally had the entire project shelved. It was released in England, however.

I didn't make the decision of whether I wanted to take drugs or not take drugs; it was the decision of whether I wanted to live or whether I wanted to die. I was very lucky. I met somebody—who became my father-in-law—who is an extraordinary man. I've known him many years, and he's never once said "you should" or "don't." He's just brutally honest with himself and very tolerant of other people. His way of life was very attractive to me; he didn't have to sell me on anything. He was living right, and I observed him day in and day out. I said to myself, What makes this man tick? What does he have? I want it. And he led me to it. He brought me in the back door.

Today, when I look at anybody whose life is running right, I see that they have faith in themselves. Now, I have it. I was looking into bags and into bottles—it was coming out fun. Maybe the new car would do it for me. But coming off drugs has been the most important thing in my life. I feel really good about it. I feel anchored. There's rhyme and reason now. Before I didn't know how to make decisions, I didn't know how to say no. I put people down just to feel good, and today I don't have to do any of that bullshit.

People used to say to me, "Be strong, Dion, and you can kick it. Be determined." Hell, I was determined as a fucking bull. It takes a lot of determination to be a junkie. Goddamn! If people only knew.

Frank Barsalona

"Just like Cinderella when she couldn't
go to the ball,
A voice said, 'I'm your fairy-agent.
You shall play Carnegie Hall.' "

JOHN ENTWHISTLE, *Success Story*

Few people outside the rock music industry recognize the name or know the accomplishments of Frank Barsalona. Unlike Arista Records' Clive Davis, Atlantic's Ahmet Ertegun, or Elektra/ Asylum's Joe Smith—all of whom have become familiar and celebrated individuals—Barsalona maintains a low public profile, preferring to surface only on matters of intraindustry importance. Nevertheless, Frank Barsalona, as president and co-founder of Premier Talent Associates, is considered one of the most powerful men in all of rock and roll. In less than fifteen years, he has built Premier Talent into the most important rock booking agency, boasting client lists which have included Jethro Tull, the Who, Emerson Lake and Palmer, Joe Cocker, Yes, Led Zeppelin, Grand Funk Railroad, Peter Frampton, Procol Harum and Edgar and Johnny Winter—to name only a few. A majority of the acts he represents sell out the largest arenas and stadiums in the world, earning themselves between $50,000 and $100,000 a night and, in turn, have made Barsalona an extremely successful and wealthy man.

Unlike the staid reputations of many of the larger, more diverse entertainment booking agencies, Premier Talent Associates—and Frank Barsalona in particular—is well known for their creative role in the building of major careers. Their acts have not come from prior success, are not capable of selling themselves, nor are most of them afforded (or suited for) the enhanced publicity medium of prime-time television. Additionally, most of Premier's acts have not sold immediately on the strength of their recorded talent; their careers, and album sales, have been bolstered by their constant appearance in front of paying, satisfied audiences. Acts like Humble Pie, Black Sabbath, Robin Trower, and Peter Frampton have developed into big-money acts only after months, and sometimes years, spent on the road opening to more established attractions. That formula for success requires solid, strategic planning and allegiance, hours spent on the phone creating an image for an unknown quantity. But, most of all, it requires confidence in one's own instincts—the assurance that each time a phone call is made concerning a particular group you are putting your credibility on the line. That has been Frank Barsalona's underlying strength—credibility—although its foundation lies heavily in the assiduous technique he employs to ensure his position within the industry.

Barsalona's approach to creative rock booking is threefold: (1) he exercises extreme selectivity in adding artists to his client list, taking into consideration outside influences such as management and record company affiliation in addition to talent and temperament; (2) he becomes personally involved in molding the over-all appearance of the artist, sometimes even suggesting the sequencing of songs in the live act to pace the performance more evenly; and (3) he maintains an active relationship with the network of national promoters who book his acts—many of whom he started in the business and supported with top acts and seasoned advice. He deftly interweaves these qualities throughout all his dealings which serve to benefit the sundry parties with which he must contend.

Frank Barsalona is a tough, deliberate individual who speaks in definite statements which allow no leeway for interpretation. He deals in lives—artists' careers—and recognizes the pressure of re-

sponsibility he has to each person who bases his or her future on his decision making. There is little room for compromise in his negotiations; they are stringent and require precision. But, one step removed from his business activities, Barsalona is a warm individual who cares deeply about friends (which include many performers) and family. He is also exceedingly educated on the subject of fine art and is considered an authority on pre-Columbian artifacts, of which his personal collection is highly respected.

If there is any one inadequacy in Barsalona's grand design, it is the uniform homogeneity of acts he represents: loud, hard-driving rock and roll bands which appeal to younger, less musically structured audiences. But if there is sameness in his roster of acts, Frank Barsalona manages to transform the collective sameness into individual events, and, after all, the event is the essence of rock and roll.

AGENTS WERE DESPICABLE PEOPLE

My interest in music began when I was really quite young. I was singing professionally when I was eight or nine years old and continued doing that until I was sixteen and I got into college. Basically I sang country and western music working around the country. I worked on tour, on the road, so I didn't do it continuously all year round because I was in school. I worked with Hank Snow and Elton Britt and, because I came from New York and was quite young, that country-oriented way of life was really alien to me as a kid.

After I got out of college, I went to drama school for a couple of years. I went to Herbert Berghof's, which is a sister school to the Actors' Studio. I got involved in Broadway, legitimate theater, and I began to sing the normal, straight stuff. I decided that I didn't know anyone in that end of the business, and rather than going the slow route of meeting people and going through auditions, I would expedite matters and get a job at an agency. I felt that was the central point of the business. In that way, I could meet not only the performers but, more importantly, the buyers on a different level than just going to auditions. I never really wanted to become an agent. Agents, to performers, were despicable human beings.

I began in the agent-trainee program at GAC[1] and some of the agents who were the big names—those men who would floor a performer if they were sitting in the audience—well, some of them were nice, but I thought the majority of them were dummies. I thought I was ten thousand times brighter. So I decided that I would stick it out to become an agent, not wanting to stay there—just to see how well I could do it for my own peace of mind. And then I could always say, "Asshole, *I* did it, and I did it *well!*" So that was the only reason I stayed on and became an agent. Only to prove to myself that I could do it.

When I finally did get the opportunity, I really decided that I liked it. And one didn't have to be an awful human being to be an agent. You could be a normal, nice person and still do quite well.

THE DAYS AT GAC

At the time, GAC was the number-two agency in the world. William Morris was number-one. GAC had a lot of very important agents who had left MCA. MCA had been the powerhouse agency, but they were busted up by the Justice Department. So once we got the top agents from MCA, GAC and William Morris were on an equal basis in terms of importance. A lot of the guys who I was in the training program with had mentors there. I didn't. I didn't know anybody. I just went up blindly and applied for the job. While there, I became friendly with Sid Bernstein, who was an agent there. If anyone could be considered my mentor, it was Sid. But Sid didn't have the type of power that the other kids' mentors had.

We worked on acts like Nina Simone, Gloria Lynn, Little Esther Phillips, Frankie Avalon, Paul Anka, and Fabian during that Philly rock era. I didn't really like that form of music. My favorite type was show music, then country and classical. Rock was not on the top of my list. And neither were rock performers on the top of my list as far as their attitudes professionally. But I was only about twenty, so the natural position [to GAC] was to put me into

[1] General Artists Corporation.

the contemporary music department so I could relate to the performers. That was the low rung of the agency business. At the time, if I had my choice, I would have been in *any* other department. But that's where I ended up.

But I really got to enjoy it. It was in its infancy and no one could really tell you what to do because no one *knew* what to do. The executives of the company didn't like rock music, didn't like rock performers, knew nothing about the music, couldn't relate to it, couldn't relate to the audiences and, quite honestly, it was too unimportant for them to be bothered with. So subsequently, a lot of what I did I did by myself.

But the way the agency treated rock performers was a crime. If you were young and had a hit record, to them you had no talent, you were just lucky and manufactured, and they would treat you like that. There was no chance of growth for a new performer. The growth that came with [Bobby] Darin and [Paul] Anka did not come with the agency. It came with their management companies, who overcame the obstacles thrown in by the agencies. And by the whole business. Rock was really the asshole, it really was. I started getting involved and saying that we shouldn't generalize. Get as much as you can for as long as you can. If they have a hit record, they'll probably have a follow-up, perhaps a third. This consumes a year and a half and then they're out of the business, so get as much as you can while the getting's good. Consequently, we wound up killing the acts because we would overprice them. And the other disgusting thing was that there wasn't a network of promoters.

If you had $750 or $800, and you decided you wanted to be in show business, you could become a promoter. You'd call the agency, we wouldn't know anything about you, we'd try to sell you an act for as much as we could possibly con out of you, you'd try to put on a dance or a hop at the local high school, and that was it. They never had sound systems. Instead, they used a public address system. They got a local band which they paid fifty bucks, and the act went there and performed. And, generally, we put those people out of business. So we were always dealing with new people, and there was no continuity.

If an act overcame that group of promoters, they went to the second line promoters, who were only a bit better. They did maybe three or four hops. So they were seasoned veterans. Past that, if the act became like the Four Seasons or a group like them with five number-one records, then they would only go to those top promoters who got the top of everything, whether it was Tony Bennett or the Bolshoi Ballet or whatever—they got the sure shots. When I tried to sell [the top promoters] one of my acts, they wouldn't know who I was talking about. I'd say to them, "But, *my God,* they had five number-one records." And I'd wind up singing the song to them over the phone. "You must have heard it—you *must!*" It was really frustrating and totally against the act ever making it. Everything we did was for the act's oblivion.

CARAVAN OF STARS

We used to get the big acts together and package them for people like Irving Feld and Dick Clark (who promoted the packages). We did a lot of the Dick Clark Caravan of Stars. They were the creams, though. They only happened during the summer where the packages could work every night because the kids were out of school.

Clark paid as little as he possibly could, but the exposure was sensational; Clark was an important factor in the record business. He had a lot of power. You could try to get what you wanted from him for the act, and if he didn't like it, all he had to do was call the record company, and they would have given him the act for nothing. It was really hard negotiating with Clark, but we did a lot of business with him.

He treated his acts like a meat market generally, unless he was friendly with them or they were important—like Fabian or Frankie Avalon or Freddie Cannon. Someone who could headline the package he treated fine. They were friendly with Clark. *All* the acts went on the bus. But it was a joke. No one made money. But the thing is, Clark worked with the number-one radio station in every town so that it was almost a guarantee that if you were on the show, you were going to get your record played for at least the duration of the tour. It was quite important to the performers, and also to the record companies.

FORMING PREMIER TALENT

At GAC I used to say, "Hold it! Why don't we develop our own little circuit of promoters around the country, people who are committed to the business? People who, when I call them, they'll know who I'm talking about and will know about the other acts that are coming up and will concentrate on exposing that act properly." And they'd laugh at me. I was a kid, and here were all these powerhouses at the meetings. And they'd say, "Look, kid, it sounds great, it looks good on paper, but believe me—it doesn't work. You're in the business forty-three minutes, we're in the business twenty-five years. Believe us."

It seemed so simple. What I was saying wasn't enlightening, it was sort of obvious. I thought, They've got to be right or else they'd be doing that. But as I went on, I saw they were just so hung up about doing it their way and they really didn't care, that nobody ever tried to do it the other way. If you were in that business, you were only in it for as long as you had to be. And while you were there, you were trying to get into something else.

Statistically, during that period, we were coming to the age where the postwar babies were coming into their teenage years. And within five years, 50-something per cent of the people in the United States were going to be under the age of twenty-five. Those statistics, to me, seemed to tell me that this was their music and this was the music that was going to be prevalent when it happened. So I thought that they should be giving it a lot more attention than they were. Well, I was there for about three years, and I just couldn't take it after a while. I wasn't married at the time, quite young, and I decided that every agent, at one time in his life, feels that he could be doing it for himself. So, I thought, it's probably a dumb idea, but let me do it now, get it out of my system and forever more I'll never think about it. And that's how I started Premier Talent.

I fully intended to be in the business for about four months, fall on my face and get a job somewhere, and that would be it. That was in 1962.

I didn't take any artists from GAC with me. They had given me my first shot, and we didn't leave on the friendliest of terms. I had asked to be fired only because I was starting my own company. I had no money and I wanted to collect unemployment. I couldn't afford to pay myself. So I negotiated my getting fired with them. I had to give up my profit sharing. They owed me four weeks vacation, and I had to give up two of them. It was a joke. So for three weeks, I had my own little office slowdown, and finally they negotiated my getting fired, and I collected unemployment.

I started off with the acts nobody wanted. Like Freddie Cannon, who, at the time, was on the descent of his career, and tons and tons of "doo-wop" acts. Ernie Martinelli and I put Little Anthony and the Imperials back together again. They had split for a number of years, and Little Anthony had been working by himself. So they became another act for us. We had the Chiffons, but they were brand new. They became one of our important acts with a couple of number-one records. So did Randy and the Rainbows. Jay and the Americans was another act that had had a big hit and now weren't doing too much. They were another act we started with. We also had Del Shannon, Timi Yuro, Jimmy Clanton, a whole bunch of people that [no other agency] wanted.

We put into practice what I tried to do at GAC—develop young promoters who are involved in just contemporary music and are interested in staying involved so that they have to do a good job when the act comes in. And also by our guaranteeing those promoters that if they do a good job in the beginning, a fat cat promoter who's been around for a million years will not get the acts when they become big. The acts would continue to stay with the promoters who did them first. In other words, we gave them continuity with the acts, and it was in the promoters' best interests as it was in our best interests for them to do the very best job. And to do what they could to break the act.

We also took the acts and tried to break them, as opposed to waiting for the groups to get a hit record. Then they're on the charts and *everybody* makes the calls. And if you lie better than the next guy, you end up with the act. Everybody had their own pitch. Well, we couldn't compete with the other agencies because we were so tiny. So we had to get the acts before they happened. That meant developing acts, which is the other thing we did.

INTRODUCING HERMAN'S HERMITS

I booked the majority of the first Beatles' tour in America. And, as a result of that, I really didn't want to deal with English acts. Brian Epstein was really awful the first time I met him. I just found his attitude terrible, and I sort of generalized that all Englishmen were like that. The other person whom I had met was Andrew Oldham, because we booked the Stones. And he had a similar attitude. So, to me, all English people were like that, and I didn't want to deal with them.

But then I met a guy named Danny Bitash, who owned an agency in Manchester and had been here for three weeks and had made calls to everybody in the business and did not get one return phone call. I was going out to dinner that night with Connie de Nave,[2] and when I got up to her office, Danny was sitting there telling her all about this. He had to go back to England the next day, and he was asking her what she could do to get some of the acts he represented a little more exposure in America so that maybe when he came back again the big agencies would know who he was talking about.

I listened to his tale of woe and felt so sorry for the guy that I said, "Look, Danny, I've got a meeting tomorrow with Roz Ross and Dick Clark about one of his packages." Roz was Dick's buyer and co-ordinator of the tours, and she and Dick were going to be in New York and all the agents had meetings with them, as did I. "Danny, I'm sure you can come up with me. I'll call Roz in the morning and I'll get ten minutes for you, and you can give him your sales pitch."

So he came up with me, and after I had met with Dick, they agreed to give Danny ten minutes. I was about to leave, but something in the back of my head said, DON'T LEAVE. This guy was so desperate to go back to England with something, I think he would have given Clark and Roz the whole agency. So I just sat there. I didn't want to represent the acts that he had. And, sure enough, Roz was taking him over the coals. She was a hard lady,

[2] Connie de Nave is a well-known entertainment publicist and currently manager of Robert Palmer.

the great negotiator. The act that Danny was most anxious to get something done on was Herman's Hermits. They had had a few records here that really didn't do anything, and they had a new record coming out and he wanted to get a tour for them. It happened that Roz liked Peter Noone's face and said, "Aw—I'll throw him on the show. They can open." This was like opening for seven or eight acts which were billed on the show. They only did one or two numbers, not a set. Only the headliners got to do four or five numbers.

Anyway, Roz wanted to buy Herman's Hermits for four weeks for $250 a week, which is terrible. It was even low for Dick Clark. He didn't pay that much higher, though. I decided to step in, because Danny was about to do it. I worked out a $750-a-week deal with graduating increases depending on whether or not the record got on the charts and how high it went. If it went up fifty points, he got $1,000, if it went up to forty, he got $1,250, etc. I did a really unique thing. Because Roz really liked Peter's face, I got Clark to do something he never did. I got him to box off Herman's Hermits. Because he would have so many acts appearing in the bill, he would have DICK CLARK'S CARAVAN OF STARS in gigantic lettering. Underneath, the acts' names would be scattered all over the place. So your eye never caught any one particular act. So I got Dick to give them a box at the bottom: Introducing Herman's Hermits.

The significance of all this is that Dick did the tour with the number-one radio stations in every city that he played. They co-promoted the shows. Once that station bought the package, they would look and see what acts were on the bill and would pull those records, and those were the acts they really laid on . . . because they were getting half of the bread [as co-promoters]. So by the time that show came in, as far as that city was concerned, these were the top selling acts in the world. "And we've got 'em all on one show!"

And exactly what was supposed to happen on the tour happened. The stations hopped on Peter's record "I'm into Something Good," and it started to happen. There were such a vast amount of important stations going with the record, that the rest of the country picked up on it. It went to number-one four or five weeks before the tour was supposed to start.

Clark was really excited. Even though he now had to pay them their top price of $3,500 a week, it was for two shows a day. So now he started adding on afternoon shows not only in one city, but an afternoon in the city he was in and an evening in another city. In those days, there was no sound. You used whatever the local hall had to announce the fight's on. So all it meant was getting into the bus and going.

ON DEE ANTHONY

After I had been with Premier Talent about five and a half years, I got a call from Sid Bernstein one day, and he said, "Kid, do you remember Dee Anthony?" Now, when I was at GAC, Dee Anthony was one of the top three managers in the business. He had Tony Bennett, Jerry Vale, Buddy Greco, Martin and Rossi. And after I left GAC, I didn't keep track of Dee Anthony's career because I really didn't know him well. So Sid said, "He's had a couple of rough years. He lost all of the acts, he went through a bad divorce, and the guy is really in a rut. He's thinking about getting into contemporary music, and he called to ask me if I'd arrange your seeing him." So I said, "Sure I'll see him."

Anyway, he came up, and I could see by looking at him that he really had a hard time. He had this act called the Mississippi River Boat Soul Band, and I took the act. At this point, we were quite important because we had developed from the Hermits and Freddie and the Dreamers. We were also handling acts like the Animals and Mitch Ryder. I never saw [Dee's] act, but because I felt sorry for him, I took it. As a result of that, we became friendly.

We then went through a whole fracas together where Dee was the New York representative for a rock management company that was screwing their acts. I finally had to tell Dee what was going on, but he already knew and was preparing to leave. At this point, I was going to London to tell the acts and suggest that Dee manage them in the States from now on. But Dee didn't want it that way. He felt as though he had a lot more to learn about contemporary music and needed to get his feet wet before he actually assumed American management. And I told him, "Dee, it's the same thing you used to do with Bennett, Vale, and Greco but with a different cast of characters. Trust me. I know, at least, as much as anybody in this business about the contemporary music business, and I'll help you. You'll get the hang of it. It's not hard."

So he gave it a shot. I went over to England and revealed what was happening to the acts and got this guy out and Dee in. And that's how Dee got into the American management [of rock groups]. Together, we've been associated with Joe Cocker, Traffic, Ten Years After, and Jethro Tull. As his own management company, we've had Humble Pie, Peter Frampton, Gary Wright, J. Geils, and a few others I won't mention.

The main reason that Dee is so good is that he does what a lot of the young managers don't do. In the old days, when an act played clubs, you helped them put together an act with a strong opening and hills and valleys. You constructed an act for visual effectiveness, for emotion appeal and all of those things. The young managers today have never been involved in those things. They don't know about putting together an act. So, it's by trial and error. And it's during that trial and error period that a lot of acts get lost. Dee works with his acts and molds their show. Humble Pie, for instance. The first night they played in America, we went out to see them in Detroit; the show was all wrong. We had a meeting the next morning with Humble Pie and we changed the whole show around. That night, they barely got any applause. The next night, they got two encores. Dee can instill incredible confidence in his acts. He will huddle with the group before the show like Knute Rockne. It seems funny, but it works. His acts really believe they're stars before they really are. And Dee believes it too.

CRITERIA

We have a number of criteria on which we base taking on a new act. Logically, one of the criteria is that the act is good onstage. I don't really care about records. I listen to them, but we've had a lot of acts who have sold records as a result of what they did onstage. Peter Frampton is a good example of that.

I also care about who manages them, whether we can have a good relationship with the manager and the group. Whether they're going to be easy to work with. If the act or the manager is going to be a nut, there's no use doing it. A lot of times we get involved with nuts, but they weren't that to begin with, and we had no way of telling they were going to develop into that. But we remind the manager that you don't live and die with one act. You've got to come around again. There have been a number of managers who have been horrendous people to work with, and we just never dealt with them again, and we never will. They call and say, "I've learned my lesson and I've grown up." No! Pass! And we have to let people know we do that if they are thinking of becoming tyrannical when the act is on top. We let them know that they might be closing the door to Premier Talent.

The record company the artist is with is important to us, too. Certain record companies you can deal with easier than others. They're more involved and realize the importance of what the act does on the road, and that it's eventually going to sell records for them. We like the record companies to support the dates in terms of advertising, but that's not our job to get it—that's the manager's job.

Most people outside the business aren't sure what an agent does. A manager is personally involved in the act's life, his career. He's the liaison with record companies, agents, publishers, and whomever else. The agent works primarily with the managers. We assist the manager, the record company, and everyone else in breaking the act. And, thereafter, in getting the act work. Our commissions are determined by the guilds who franchise us, so it's not a negotiable thing—we can only take a certain amount. Past that, what's made Premier successful is how we work so closely with the managers. Also, what we did in Detroit with Humble Pie —which we have done many times—is above and beyond our bottom line responsibility as agents.

THE WHO: IT'S MY ACT!

I had passed on the Who about two or three times. At that time, they had left Decca and were on Atlantic, and I got calls from everybody at Atlantic, then I got calls from Chris Stamp and everybody really wanted me to sign them. But I had seen Chris and Kit Lambert with Allen Klein at a Herman's Hermits party—because at the time he was representing Mickey Most—and I just felt that they were climbing into bed with Allen Klein. Allen and I didn't get along very well, and I just didn't want to get involved in another act that Allen Klein might be involved in. Consequently, I passed on the Who again.

I went out to California, and Chris came up again while I was away to see my partner. While I was away, he signed them with the agency. I didn't know about it, and somebody in my office came up to me and said, "By the way, what are we going to do about this act, the Who, that Freedberg [one of the agents working for Barsalona] signed?" And I said, "You're *joking!*" And I went into his office raging mad. He told me that he didn't know that I had passed on them before. So we were now committed to the Who. I had no idea about what we were going to do with them. They hadn't had any record success here; they had a ton of records out and nothing ever happened with them.

The next day, I was having a meeting with Murray Kaufman[3] about his Easter show at the 58th Street Theatre, and he wanted Mitch Ryder to headline. We represented Mitch, who, at the time, was about the biggest male vocalist in contemporary music. Murray wanted him really bad, and Mitch owed Murray the appearance because of something Murray had done for him in the past. It was one of those: "If there's ever anything I can do to repay you, Murray . . ." And now Murray wanted the favor returned. Mitch said that he just couldn't face ten days, five shows a day. But he said, "Look, I'll do it, but can't you make it so difficult that he'll pass on me?" I told him that I would give it a shot, but got him to promise me that if I couldn't get Murray to pass that he would do the show.

So Murray came up to my office, and he freaked out when I mentioned the price I wanted for Mitch to do the show. But after a while he said, "All right. If that's what I have to do, I'll pay it." I thought, *My God, what do I do now?* But I remembered that, when I was at GAC, I saw a Zsa Zsa Gabor rider attached to her contract that had to do with something like her liking the color lavender, and whoever bought her had to do her whole dressing room in that color. So I told Murray, "Look, Mitch has this thing about the color blue, and as long as he's going to be at the theater for ten days, all day long, he wants to have his dressing room

[3] New York disc jockey Murray The K.

done in blue." Murray had never heard of this, and he almost died, he really carried on. He argued and threatened that he was going to destroy Mitch, he would destroy me, he would destroy anyone involved with us—but he finally accepted it. I was shocked. I didn't know what to do then. But I thought I'd give it one more shot.

We had just signed the Who, and they were fresh on my mind. I said, "Murray, Mitch has this thing for an act in England called the Who, and he wants them on the show." And Murray said, "But they don't mean *anything*. I've gotta sell tickets." But I was adamant, and I really thought I had him then—he was almost to a point of banging his head against the wall. And he said, "I've just seen something on them." And I answered, "Yes, they just went with your friend, Brian Epstein." Then I told him how much we wanted, a whole lot of money for those days. He told me that he was going to call Brian in England and see if he could get the price down.

Well, right after he left, I called Brian Epstein and said, "Murray is going to be calling you. It's on the Who and it's for the Easter show. Just remember that the price is $7,500 plus $1,500 for his TV show." Brian said, "Well, Frank, you should be talking to my associate, Robert Stigwood. He's the one handling the Who for me," so he put him on. I told Stiggie the same thing. And he said, "Quite honestly, Frank, we'll do it for nothing. It seems like a high price." I said, "No, no, no, no, no—*that's the price!*" And he agreed. I called Murray two days later, and he told me to put out a contract to include the Who—and it was for a *much lower* price. They were going to do the five days *and* the TV show for something ridiculous like $5,000. I couldn't tell Murray that I had called Stiggie, and that I knew the price was too low, so I said, "Okay." And Mitch had to do the show.

So now it's the day before the show—dress rehearsal—and I was going out of my mind. I said to my wife, June, "They're [the Who are] probably awful. How did I ever do it without seeing them? I'm going to be the laughingstock of the business." I just didn't want to go to dress rehearsal. Finally she said, "Look, you've got to go. You've got Little Anthony, Mitch Ryder, and a few other acts on the bill and you should be there." I said, "But if the Who are terrible, the abuse I'm going to have to take from

Murray will be too much." But, in the end, she convinced me I had to go.

I got there after dress rehearsal started, so I sat in the back [of the theater] in the dark. There were workmen there getting it ready and several people in the business. Well, I saw Little Anthony, and then the Who came on. I was hoping that I would have gotten there late enough so that they already would have rehearsed. But no. And there was Townshend, who was wearing this suit that lit up with Christmas lights in it; they weren't the greatest-looking act in the world. And these were the days when physical appearance was quite important. I said to myself: "Oh Jesus, they're going to be horrible. I know it." I'm now sitting way down in my seat as they're ready to start. They did the first number—I had gotten Murray to allow them to do two numbers on the show—and I said, "June, you know, they're really not all that bad." Well, they finished that one, and I didn't think Murray had much of a complaint. Then, they went into "My Generation," their last number, and it was really a good song. And they were really moving around on the stage. So I began to sit up a little higher in my seat. Well, they came to the end of the song, Townshend throws up his guitar, goes to catch it, and misses it. I said, "Thank God he didn't do that in the show. What a klutz!" He picks up his guitar, throws it up and misses it again. Then he picked it up and smashed it on the ground. I looked. My wife looked. Then I said, "I don't believe it! This guy just smashed his guitar. It's only a fucking rehearsal. What is he getting so angry about?" At his point, Roger Daltry picks up his mike stand and smashes it into the amplifier. I said, "I don't believe it. They're going crazy." The guitar is smashed on the floor, and now Townshend takes a flying leap into his bank of amplifiers and kicks them over.

Now there's bombs going off, and I'm looking for Chris Stamp to get them off because I'm wondering what kind of equipment they're going to use for the show. I look all over for Chris, and finally I see him and Nancy Lewis, who worked for him, sitting in the audience as calm as can be. I said to my wife, "What—are they crazy? This act is obviously going through a breakdown here in the theater." And then it hit me. I thought, Why aren't they concerned? They're just sitting here. I said to June, "You know what?

This is part of the show. It's got to be. Look at Chris and Nancy. It *is* part of the show, it *really is*." Now Moon had kicked over his drums, and everybody in the theater had stopped what they were doing and were staring at the stage while the bombs went off. Everyone was extremely frightened. I couldn't even see Murray through all the smoke. I'm now standing up screaming, *"They're fucking great! They're brilliant!"*

They bowed after they were finished destroying everything, and everyone else in the theater realized it was part of their act. It was the first time I ever saw a standing ovation from people in the business. Now, I'm running up to the stage screaming, *"It's my act!"*

I found Murray backstage and slapped him on the back and said, "Now what do you think of that?" And he said, "They still don't mean anything in New York." I told him that after opening night, word of mouth would fill his shows with people all wanting to see the Who. So he said, "I'm willing to concede that. But what about that other piece of shit you made me take?" I said, "Mitch?" He said, "No, not Mitch." I asked, "Anthony?" He said, "No, not Anthony. That other piece of shit—the Cream." I couldn't believe it; I didn't book them. I said, "I saw them on the placard outside. I don't know who they are." He said, "Frank, don't be cute to me. We've never lied to each other." I said, "Murray, I swear to you on anything holy that I don't know anything about the Cream." He said, "You don't know that when I called England to get the Who, I had to take the Cream?" Now I realized where the additional money had gone. Stiggie was the Who's agent, and the Cream's agent and manager. And as a result of that, I had a fight with Robert Stigwood and told him that I thought it was terribly unethical that he had done that. And I never did anything with Stigwood after that. Although he seemed to do all right without me.

GRAND FUNK

I didn't pass on Grand Funk, but somebody else at the agency had. In fact, they passed on them rudely—they had been rude to Terry Knight,[4] who had been a friend of the agency. We had

---

[4] Terry Knight managed Grand Funk through their initial success.

booked Terry Knight and whatever-his-group was years before. And we should have been a lot more courteous to him. I found out about it and felt badly. As a result, I took the act because I'd felt badly about how he'd been treated.

Thank God!

A lot of the biggest people in the business said to me, "How could you mess up your list [of acts we represented] with crap like that?" Actually, I was *looking* for an act like Grand Funk Railroad because, in trends, you get the purists in the very beginning. If they, in fact, capture the fancy of the regular population, you then have weekend purists—those people who during the week lead a normal life and on the weekends they become something else. You also have the younger kids emulating the older kids. I started seeing that down at the Fillmore [East], where the audiences were getting younger and younger. Now, whenever the audiences become younger and not as committed, then elements such as hype and sex appeal come into play. So I was looking for an act that played the type of music these younger kids were going for but also incorporated sex appeal, showmanship, and hype. A Grand Funk Railroad, who was younger than the regular groups and played harder, filled the gap. And they worked at their sex appeal.

We couldn't break the act in the major cities because they were too sophisticated—they thought. So we broke them down south, an area that was just emerging into the FM thing. They weren't as jaded as the kids who had been seeing it for a couple years in the larger cities like New York, Boston, and L.A. So, to them, Grand Funk Railroad was FM [music]. Then they broke in the Midwest and, finally, the East and West Coasts. We didn't create the trend, but we recognized that there was indeed a trend, and we took advantage of it.

RIDERS

Riders are one of my pet peeves. I hate riders in artists' contracts. I think they're a joke—they're indulgent. I'm truly embarrassed by the riders. And act gets $30,000, $40,000, or $60,000 or whatever, and they have the fucking gall to demand the type of food they want in the dressing room. And three quarters of the time, they don't eat it. And wines, and feeding the road crews. All these people make money! If these road crew people are setting up sound in the afternoon, they are getting paid to do that and they should be able to feed themselves. It's a horror.

I'm against limousines, and this has been going on for years. But if I were a promoter and I was paying a group $50,000, that's their problem of how they get to the hall to get the $50,000. They could come by scooter for all I care. I wouldn't do any of that. But, unfortunately, a lot of what we do is governed by what everybody else does.

If a promoter gives Elton John or So-and-So limousines and food and everything else, then I am not doing my job if I don't get the same for my act. I can't tell my act it's wrong if everybody else is doing it. The promoters, as soon as this started, should have put their foot down. And that would have been the end of it. But the moment you give in once and say, "All right, the Rolling Stones are unique," that's enough to justify giving it to all the other acts. Because all the Rolling Stones do is sell out, and so do all the other big acts. You can't give me the bullshit about them being legendary.

We don't have the promoters by the balls. Unfortunately, all everyone in this business thinks about is *big* acts. Sure we have them by the balls for acts like the Who and Jethro Tull and Yes. But we need all the promoters, as well, for the small acts, and the moment they realize that's where their strength is, then nobody's got them by the balls. They don't realize that. They're so afraid that someone else is going to get Bob Dylan. So fuck it! *Let* somebody else get Dylan. But you can't tell [the promoters] that. They say, "But I can't let somebody else bring Bob Dylan into my town." Like the kids really give a fuck who's doing Bob Dylan. Do you think they even look to see who is presenting him? No chance! One of these days all the promoters are going to stop their crying, wake up, and discover they've got us booking agents licked. And, when that time comes, everyone—*everyone*—is going to peacefully coexist in this crazy music business.

Neil Sedaka

"Change—I guess you're bound to have
   your way with me
Time—no time to think about what used
   to be
Just the never-ending motion of a clock
   upon the wall
A deep, uneasy feeling of the axe about
   to fall
Say, my God, I'm getting older
Waiting at the crossroads of my life."

N. SEDAKA AND P. CODY, *Crossroads*

Like a professional athlete, a rock star lives in constant trepidation of an end to the hits. The pressures of longevity are most severe for a creative artist, seldom fulfilled, never obliterated. Each performance must be better than the last; every new record must challenge the listener and win; all interviews become critical; every choice of association becomes a key career factor. The end, never being in sight, comes totally unexpected, and with it come bitterness and a lack of self-confidence. In rock music, as in any other entertainment form, a fan's impatience leads to a short memory and loyalty becomes a trying test of time.

Comebacks are even rarer than durability. They ask the audience to forgive and forget and generally frustrate the performer who attempts not only to entertain but also to overcome. And the few who do manage to rekindle their careers find that they are

never able to attain the degree of success which they formerly en-
joyed.

*Neil Sedaka is the unique exception to almost each example
given concerning an artist's career. A teenage star of the late Fifties and early Sixties, he recorded a string of international hits
which have become rock and roll standards: "Calendar Girl,"
"Happy Birthday Sweet Sixteen," "Stairway to Heaven," and
"Breaking Up Is Hard to Do" evoke instant memories of innocent
young love.*

*Sedaka was well aware that his success was dwindling with the
advent of the Beatles, and he tried to revive it. But when it became
apparent to him that the tra-la days were, indeed, over, he rechan-
neled his talents and became a more prolific songwriter. No bitterness, no loss of self-confidence, no beating his head against the
wall for want of a cheering audience. Instead, he listened, an-
alyzed, and contemplated the new trends, and he adapted his lifestyle and his talents to the 1970s teenager so that he might enjoy
another string of hits.*

*The next logical step had to be the re-emergence of one of the
all-time great musical talents as an entertainer, and with the help
of Elton John, Neil was again in the spotlight as a major recording
artist and concert performer. Now Sedaka's audience is much
larger and stronger than before. He has found an entire new generation fifteen years later, and brought the old fans back for a
renewed good time.*

*Sedaka in the 1970s is an extension of Sedaka in the 1950s and
1960s. His songs still exalt young love. They are hopeful, eu-
phoric, spirited, and express a certain optimism. His characters
are plain—you and I—and tackle everyday problems of contemporary love to which any listener can relate. Songs like "Laughter
in the Rain," "Love Will Keep Us Together," "Lonely Nights
(Angel Face)" and "Bad Blood" are straightforward and well
constructed. And if there is any one secret to Sedaka's endurance
as a writer, it is that his compositions lack self-indulgence both
lyrically and musically. There are no obscure references, no sym-
bolism, no complicated melodies. His songs are written for people
to enjoy and hum along with. And yet, both the lyrics and the
melodies have matured significantly, have become more intelligent. The early Sedaka-Greenfield songs were constructed on*

verse-chorus-verse-chorus-verse-chorus-chorus-end of song. They were formulas, and they worked. Today, his material is still referred to as a formula construction; however, an intense listen to "Love Will Keep Us Together"—probably one of the most commercial standards of all time—reveals three constructions, any of which could be dubbed verse or chorus, equally important to the over-all effect of the song. His new association with lyricist Phil Cody has afforded him new room in which to move. Cody's lyrics are less structured, slightly more intense, and more imaginative than Greenfield's. It has allowed Sedaka to be more introverted in what he reveals of himself to his listener. And yet, Howard Greenfield has fashioned contemplative lyrics such as "The Hungry Years" and "Stephen" for Sedaka to interpret, which purveys a diverseness to the over-all quality of Sedaka's recent albums.

Yet, Neil Sedaka hasn't lost sight of the fact that his purpose is to entertain on the most universal level. He is that type of total performer who is capable of maintaining both a creative and commercial perspective on what he introduces to his public. He has maintained his prominence in contemporary music for almost two decades—two decades which have witnessed a complete metamorphosis of the teenager with new mores and new desires.

I CAN'T KEEP UP WITH HIM ANYMORE!

I came from somewhat of a musical family: Aunt Freida sang, Uncle Joey sang, and my grandmother, who died very young, played the piano and had studied with Walter Damrosch.

As far back as I can remember, I have always been in love with music and records. I must have been about three years old when my mother bought my first record by the Moylan Sisters. I have not heard hide nor hair of the Moylan Sisters since then—I don't even know who they are—but I was so excited that I ran to my grandparents' Victrola with this record, and I fell and it broke into a million pieces. My mother had to buy another record.

When I was young, I used to sneak across the hall of our apartment building in Coney Island and play the piano in a neighbor's apartment. I started picking out tunes when I was seven and a half. I loved being able to play by ear.

When I was eight, my third-grade teacher, Mrs. Glantz, noticed that I had some ability and put me in front of a choir of my fellow students, and I wound up conducting for them. Afterward, she asked my mother to buy a piano, which she did, so that my sister, Ronnie, and I could learn how to play. At that point, my parents encouraged me so much that they had to bring the food to the piano. I worked at it day and night.

I studied with a private teacher from about the age of eight until I was nine—a guy named Murray Newman—and he finally had to say to my mother, "He's gone through all the books. I can't keep up with him anymore! Let him try out for the Juilliard Prep School." I did and I was accepted. I was a very good student because I had a very good teacher, Edward Roberts. I was conscientious and practiced six or seven hours a day. But we were expected to give many recitals, and I would vomit a lot before I had to give a recital, because all the mothers and fathers and teachers were there and it was a very traumatic experience.

WELL, LET'S GIVE IT A TRY

I knew Howie Greenfield from my apartment building. He lived on the fifth floor on the other side of the building. We were not that close socially.

While I was on vacation with my parents in the Catskills, we met his mother, Ella, and she heard me play the piano and arranged a meeting between her son, Howard, and myself. I was thirteen and Howie was sixteen when he rang my bell in 1951. He was, like me, kind of an introverted kid. When he came to see me that first time, he asked me if I had ever written songs and I said, "No, I don't know how to write." He said, "Well, let's give it a try. It can't be too difficult." We had to wait for my mother to leave the apartment—I think she was on her way out to go shopping or something—because here she had encouraged me to study the classics and I was considering writing pop music with this heavy kid who had just rung my doorbell. She would have had a fit.

Well, we sat down, and in about an hour we wrote "My Love's Devotion." We had a Webcor wire recorder, and we made a demo in my high soprano voice, and I was totally enthralled with the idea of creating something. I'll never forget the words to it:[1] "My life's devotion is loving you only/My heart says to you I'll always be true/You'll never be lonely." Thank God Howie got better! "I just adore you/I only live for you/I'd give all the gold/A treasure can hold." He was obsessed with rhymes.

We wrote the kind of music we were listening to, which was being recorded by Johnny Ray, Rosemary Clooney, Patti Page, and Guy Mitchell. This is what we now call "pop." It wasn't until I was about fifteen or sixteen that I heard my first rock and roll song. I was carried away by it. Howie wasn't so sure. He thought we ought to stick with what we were doing, but I knew rock and roll was where I had to be. It was so exciting.

THAT GAVE ME A PURPOSE

We wrote a song a day—it's true—for a couple years, and it got easier and the songs got better. We said, "It's finally about time that we do something with our songs," and we started hanging around 1619 Broadway—the Brill Building[2]—showing our material.

The first song that was recorded was "Passing Time" on Atlantic Records by the Cookies. It was such a thrill. I can't even describe the feeling I had of riding the BMT [subway] from Atlantic Records back home to Brooklyn with Howie holding that label—that red and black Atlantic label, seeing our names on that label. I had knocked on Jerry Wexler's and Ahmet Ertegun's door and sang the song live for them. It took several weeks to get an answer, and they finally told us that they were recording it. But the realization of seeing the record, of playing it on my record player in Brooklyn, was just overwhelming. I brought it to high school and played it during one of the free periods in front of the class, and they screamed, "Let's hear the other side! Let's hear the

[1] Neil asserts that he remembers all the words to every one of his songs, which now number well over eight hundred.

[2] The Brill Building was the focal point of the New York pop music business during the 1950s and the early 1960s. It was headquarters for all the major publishers, independent producers, and some of the independent record companies. Writers walked from door to door trying to have their songs heard.

other side!" So I flipped it over, and it was called "In Paradise," and the kids said, "We like that better." The funny thing is, it wound up being an R&B hit. Jerry and Ahmet called me as the record was taking off and said, "Would you mind terribly if you were the B side? It seems that 'In Paradise' is the hit." I felt terrible. But the thing sold about 100,000 copies, and that was the first money I received as a songwriter. We always got paid our royalties, even though so many of the other artists got screwed.

It was wonderful breaking into the business in those days. Absolutely wonderful. My whole existence was waking up, writing songs and making demos. That gave me a purpose, it made me a big shot—I stood out from the rest of the people—it ensured me invitations to parties where I could play and sing my songs. The music executives seemed fascinated when Howie and I walked into their offices. We were so young. It took us a couple years at the start to be recorded, but it became easier and easier as we went along.

The first hit we had was "Wishing Well," by Jerry Dorn. It was a New York hit only, but it was a hit! "Stupid Cupid" was our first big national hit, but "Wishing Well" came years before "Stupid Cupid." There were a few national hits, not as big, before "Stupid Cupid": "I Waited Too Long," by Laverne Baker, "Since You've Been Gone" by Clyde McPhatter, "Time Marches On" by Roy Hamilton, and "Another Sleepless Night" by Jimmy Clanton. I was about sixteen when we had those.

THE BROOKLYN CROWD

I started the Tokens when I was at Abraham Lincoln High School in Brooklyn. Jay Siegal sat on my right in math class, and Hank Medress[3] and I had been friends for several years. Cynthia Zolotin was in the group because her parents knew Happy Goday[4] and we thought that would be a good "in." Eddie Rapkin was the fourth member.

Hank and I had sang on Brighton's Twelfth Street for a long time, and we always had the thought of getting a group together,

[3] Hank Medress produces Tony Orlando.
[4] Happy Goday was an influential New York publisher.

so we became the Tokens. We started out by singing at local hops and bar mitzvahs and weddings—it was wonderful. I left when the original group started to break up. This was many years before they had "The Lion Sleeps Tonight."

A young friend named Carole Klein used to sit in on those sessions with the Tokens. Of course, she's the same girl who later changed her name to Carole King, and she had a group called the Cosines. All the musical people used to congregate together, and when the Tokens rehearsed, she would harmonize and then play for us. Carole was into rock from the beginning.

Carole was very confident both of herself and her music. She was very energetic, and a chain smoker whom my mother didn't like. We were only fifteen, sixteen, and my mother thought that her bad smoking habit would rub off on her son. Carole became my girl friend. Later I took her to Lakewood, New Jersey—chaperoned, of course—for a weekend. I was infatuated with her. It was a couple of years of singing and hanging out together in Brighton in Brooklyn. I finally convinced her mother that she was very talented, because her mother was not enchanted with her popular writing. Her mother was a drama coach and didn't think her daughter should pursue rock and roll.

WE LIKE THE WAY YOU DO IT BETTER

One day, Howie and I had gone to Hill & Range[5] to play our material for Doc Pomus and Morty Schuman.[6] They told us that there was a new publishing firm opening downstairs on the third floor—actually it was a polite way of passing on us—and they suggested we go down there. I knocked on the door and Al Nevins answered it[7] and said, "I'm sorry, we're in conference. Come back later." He had been in business for only two days [with Don Kirshner], and he became our publisher.

Nobody ever made the overture to record me during those early

[5] One of the larger publishing houses on the East Coast representing the Elvis Presley catalogue.

[6] Writers of many of the early rock and roll hits, they were employed at Hill & Range at the time.

[7] Elsewhere in this book, Don Kirshner recalls the same story in a different way.

days. I don't know why I didn't try to get a recording contract, but I suppose being an introverted person—not the exhibitionist type—I was satisfied with the songs, being a writer and hiding behind a piano and having other people record them. Until it became a frustrating thing.

In many instances, the record producers would produce the song as they felt it should be done. And in more cases than not, they ruined the song. Killed it! Then I began to feel that they couldn't feel it the way I could. I used to play my songs for people and then play the record, and they would say, "We like the way you do it better." I always loved my own voice, but I was a bit embarrassed because it was so damn high. And it got to the point where I thought, "Gee—why don't they take *me* along with the song?" But no one ever did. Until RCA Victor Records.

I had been writing for Aldon Music. We had "Stupid Cupid" for Connie Francis, then "Frankie" and "Fallen." Then Al Nevins, who was part of the Three Suns on RCA, approached Steve Schoals at RCA about me. Al always wanted to "wait for the right time." He took [them] my demo of "The Diary." It had been written for Little Anthony and the Imperials as the follow-up to "Tears on My Pillow," and George Goldner [their manager] chose something else. It was a blessing in disguise, because the song turned out to be mine and became my very first recording.

I had played the song live on the piano for Steve at RCA—I had been taken there by Al and Don Kirshner—and he said, "Yes, we are looking for more teenage attractions because of our immense success with Elvis. Being that you write songs, you are very interesting."

It's no secret that RCA spent $100,000 to make "The Diary" a hit.

Sessions, in those days, were panicked, fearful. We watched the clock at all times because we had to do three songs in four hours. And we did it with forty musicians, all together at once. I would get together with the arranger several days before. I'd write out a bass line—the bass line that I would play with my left hand on the piano—so it matched exactly. But the sessions themselves were very hectic and very tense. I would sit at the piano and do live vocals with all of the pieces—strings and everything—playing at one time. Al Nevins produced the sessions.

"The Diary" became a national hit, and then "I Go Ape" came out and did less and "Crying My Heart Out for You" did even less than that. And then the famous "Oh Carole" came out. Thank goodness it was a hit, because RCA was getting ready to drop my contract as a recording artist. It took off right away and was my tribute to my friendship with Carole King. She, of course, did an answer record on Decca called "Oh Neil."

THEY HARDLY BOOKED ME

I didn't perform right away. Don Kirshner and Al Nevins had sent Little Eva out on the road—and even people before her—and they found that if the record artist was a disappointment in person, the record sales would stop. So rather than [have] me perform in America, they waited a while. Later on, the offers were rolling in and they didn't want to turn them down, so they booked me in Brazil in 1959. They had no faith in me as a performer; they thought it would ruin their record sales and publishing rights. So I hardly worked in the United States. They put me on a tour which started in South America and took me to Italy, the Philippines, and Japan with great success. Then they got brave and booked me in Pittsburgh. But they were afraid of any negative situation happening, so they hardly booked me.

Once I got back to playing the United States, I never played tours. I would do two-week engagements in places like the Copacabana, the stand-up supper club act places with bow ties and tuxedoes. There were no fees involved with the hops, so I did them rarely and for record promotion only.

I didn't do the Dick Clark tours—never—but he was one of the most important people in my career because he put me on his Beech-Nut Saturday Night show with an unknown song called "Ring-a-Rockin' Music," which was the record before "The Diary"—before RCA signed me—on the Jaimie/Guyden label out of Philadelphia. And I always did Bandstand in Philadelphia. Dick was a terrific guy and treated me very nicely. I suppose that he was the guy who really started me.

One day I was sitting at home in Brooklyn with Carole King—we used to run home from school to watch "Who Do You Trust?"

with Johnny Carson and then Bandstand—and he was playing
"Ring-a-Rockin' Music," and I got so excited that I was being
played on the air that I fell off my chair.

THIS DOESN'T LAST FOREVER

I realized that my star was fading when my brother-in-law,
Eddie, said, "Neil, you know this doesn't last forever." And I
said, "It doesn't?"

I had had four solid years as a hitmaker—1959 to 1962—and
after "Alice in Wonderland," my last substantial hit, I realized
that it was going to be hard to make it last much longer. I tried to
change my style. I tried to change that kind of formula song, but
they didn't want to hear me that way—RCA nor any of the executives nor the stations. They knew that even if I did pull it off, it
would be such a difficult thing to sell: Neil Sedaka doing something other than that type of song. It would be too monumental
for them to handle.

But I loved the Beatles and I loved the new songs and I continued to listen—always listening, always keeping aware of what was
happening, what people went for, what type of tune, what kind of
chord changes, what tempos. Tempos are very important. Those
old records were repetitious, but the tempos were all different.
"Stairway to Heaven" was one, "Little Devil" was different,
"Breaking Up Is Hard to Do" was completely different from the
others tempowise. And, most important, I continued to write after
I stopped recording. I went to the office every day. I stopped performing except for going to Australia once a year beginning in
1965. They paid well, and I liked it there.

GEE—I COULD DO THAT AGAIN

Around 1970, after writing a string of hits (including a song
called "Amarillo," which sold three million copies and never
made it into the United States), Carole King's new success took
its toll on me. I bought her first two albums—when she was with
The City and her first Ode [Records] album. She had made the
big move to California to try to become a singer. And here I had

gone through it. I had sort of settled into a family life, I was happy writing. But in 1970, when she started to hit, I said, "Gee, —I could do that again." I felt as though I had been neglected.

I was still with the William Morris Agency—hardly working, though—and Dick Fox, my agent there, mentioned a tour that was coming up in England, a tour of their cabarets. Real holes! They were just terrible places with drunk people, loud, noisy. And I knew that I *had* to do my oldies. I thought that if I could incorporate some of the newer material I had just written into my act someway—if I could break in England—perhaps it would be the back door I was looking for. The back door to America. So I took the job. It was for something ridiculous like $1,500 a week. I did my oldies in these clubs, but I used to stick in one new one here and there. And they went over good. I loved performing again.

Then I was offered a concert at Albert Hall, and that was in London, a big deal. I said, "Yes, I'll do that one, but only if they allow me to include stuff other than the songs from the late Fifties and early Sixties. That was a semitriumph for me. Now, the Albert Hall seats about six or seven thousand people and only about two thousand people showed up—empty! It took a lot of guts. It also took a lot of guts to go into the radio stations and say, "Yes, 'Oh Carole' is nice, but I have this new record called 'Beautiful You.'" Soon after, I was asked to do Top of the Pops. I had two songs on the English charts: "Beautiful You" and "Oh Carole," the original recording which had been rereleased. It was, at that time, fifteen years old or near that, and all of a sudden it was back in the top twenty.

Well, I was under the impression that I was going over to London to sing "Beautiful You" on the TV show, but when I got there they said, "You have to do 'Oh Carole.'" I said, "Oh *shit!* Back to the same old shit again." My wife, Leba, and I looked at each other and we said, "Well, maybe if the kids of 1971 don't know 'Oh Carole' it will be a good steppingstone." And it was. Soon after, I recorded with 10cc an album called *Solitaire,* and another called *The Tra-La Days Are Over.* I spent three or four months each year going to England and working on my new career. By that time, in 1973, I had garnered a reputation for being something other than a ghost from the past—which pleased me.

WHAT A BRAINSTORM!

I had met Elton John at a Bee Gees concert backstage, and then at a lot of parties. My lawyer thought that I should approach Elton to put out my records in America (on his Rocket Records) since I was available.

I sure was available. Nobody wanted to record me in America. All the companies passed on me. I couldn't understand it. They were so stupid. I had at least four or five top twenty singles in England, and I had two albums that had sold 100,000 copies each. Now, you'd think that any American record company would take a chance on it. Or that they'd say, "There must be *something* there." But they did not. If the company is not prepared to spend dollars or go out and co-ordinate a tremendous campaign—especially at the time a wave of nostalgia was sweeping the country—it would take an awful lot of work to get me out of that box, out of the oldies category. Unfortunately, American record companies don't want to really make an effort. Even my old record company, RCA, passed on me. Elton was immensely successful, and he had been a fan of my old records. It would be a challenge for him, kind of a labor of love.

I was in England and was giving a party after one of my concerts. Elton and John Reid[8] came. We had a little to drink, and we began singing and playing. I took both of them to one side, and I asked them if they might be interested in putting my records out in America. They looked at each other and said, "Oh my God, what a brainstorm! It's a marvelous idea. We'll do it." I said, "All I ask for is Elton's endorsement on the back of the first album. I don't need the money, and I don't want the royalties from the first album and single. Put it into promotion. You know how difficult this will be."

I'll never forget—Elton said to me, "Will we remain friends if it shouldn't happen?" I said, "Yes."

He invited me to Caribou Ranch, where we discussed it during his recording sessions, and out of the successful English albums we constructed my first American release in fifteen years. He asked

8 John Reid manages Elton John's career.

me what I'd like as the first single, and I said, "Laughter in the Rain" because it had been a hit in England. I felt it was right. It was released [on Rocket Records in America] the end of 1974 and took sixteen weeks to hit number-one. The record just crept and crept up the charts, and I went out of my mind. I couldn't believe it. I was back on the charts again. It was a miracle!

SO I FOUND PHIL CODY

Phil Cody is a great writer. I met him in Don Kirshner's office when Howie and I were on the outs. We felt that the writing was getting stagnant. I had an album (co-written with Howie) called *Emergence,* which was the last album on RCA. My contract with them had run out. And I felt that it would have been healthier for Howie and me to write with other people and not keep an exclusive collaboration. He did not agree. He wanted it to be exclusive, but I wasn't getting anywhere. *Emergence* was brilliant, but I felt that the songs were going in the wrong direction, and it wasn't right for the time.

So I found Phil Cody, who had made an album called *Laughing Sandwich,* and I took the album home to listen to it. He was writing with someone who he had just split up with. I read the lyrics on the back of his album very carefully, and they were "young." They were poetic and elusive, they had moods, they changed. You know, when you hear a song lyric and you know what the song is going to say after the first eight bars, that's one kind of song—the establishment song, of which Howie Greenfield is a master. Then there is the singer/songwriter song—the Joni Mitchells and the Gordon Lightfoots—which I have never written before. And Phil Cody fit that bill perfectly.

We wrote seven songs in one week, and I found him a delight to work with. He is a quiet, sensitive person, very considerate, multitalented. He sings, plays the guitar and piano, and writes his ass off. He can sit at the piano for hours with great concentration. It was a completely different type of writing than the Sedaka/ Greenfield collaboration.

Working with Howie Greenfield is an institution, it goes on forever. It started when I was thirteen, now I'm thirty-seven and we're still writing and growing.

ON WRITING AND HIT SONGS

I suppose that writing is an ego satisfaction for me—the need to be recognized. I always sat at the piano and played for my friends. It's no satisfaction playing somebody else's songs, but playing my own songs and watching my friends' reactions is a very satisfying feeling. The ability to turn somebody else's emotions "on" with my creations is a drive that's always been in me.

Today, writing is something that I know I *have* to do, and I set aside a couple months for it. It takes discipline and self-confidence. It's scary. But I've found I can write anywhere there is a piano.

When I write, the first two weeks all I get are Stephen Foster melodies, and that's frightening. That's why I wrote "Stephen." I vicariously think I may be him reincarnated. I don't know. Anyway, the first two weeks are like climbing mountains. I try to satisfy myself. I try to take the first piece of melody or lyric and say, "Yes," and go from there.

A hit song is a combination of chord progressions, of wonderful chord changes, where those chord changes come from, what the lyrics say at a certain time in the song, how many hooks there are, the mood that the song paints, the picture that it paints. I strive for something that doesn't hit you over the head, that can be heard more than a few times without getting boring, and something that is predictable and not predictable at the same time.

"LOVE WILL KEEP US TOGETHER"

Howie decided he was moving to California. The last two songs he wrote were "Our Last Song Together" and "Love Will Keep Us Together."

In "Love Will Keep Us Together" I wanted to put together a bit of Diana Ross and the Supremes with the Beach Boys and Al Green—three of my favorites. I wanted to incorporate those three sounds together with lots of hooks and tunes. I had written the first verse, and I was stuck and didn't know what to do. Howie came in and said, "I love that so far." And I sang it again, and he went, "Stop!" I said, "That's it!" And then he said, "Why don't

we put in a catchy phrase like 'I will, I will, I will'?" And all of
the secretaries starting singing, "I will, I will, I will." And that's
how the rest of it came about.

Now, I always knew that song had what it takes to become a
hit, but it lay around for three years. I recorded it on my album
The Tra-La Days Are Over, yet people just couldn't hear it. They
just couldn't hear *that* song. Except for me, the only other recording of it until the Captain and Tenille did it was by Mac and Katie
Kassoon out of England. The record was no good, though. I made
a piano and voice demo of it in England before I went into the
studio to record it, and I listened to this song and said, "Jesus
Christ, this is good!" The reason I didn't put it out was because it
was between "Love Will Keep Us Together" and "Standing on the
Inside," and we went with "Standing on the Inside" because I had
actually managed to write my own lyric to it and I was taken by it.
And the mastering of "Love Will Keep Us Together" was bad—it
was overcut. So I said, "To hell with this, I'm not going back into
the studio. Let's put out 'Standing on the Inside.' "

Kip Cohen, of A&M Records,[9] heard the *Sedaka's Back* album
and liked the song. The Captain and Tenille had come with him to
the Troubadour in Los Angeles, where I was singing, and said,
"My God, that's a fantastic song. If we could only get Neil's enthusiasm." Which they did. And I think they improved on my record with Darryl's keyboards and Toni's marvelous voice. It was a
marvelous pop record. Almost perfect.

THE ROCKET ALBUMS

The *Sedaka's Back* album, the first one for Rocket, was a com-
pilation of the albums *Solitaire, The Tra-La Days Are Over* and
Laughter in the Rain, which I had done in England.

The Hungry Years was recorded in Los Angeles with Robert
Appère as co-producer and some marvelous musicians. I was
very confident with the songs. I had "Hungry Years" and "New
York City Blues" and "Stephen" and "Bad Blood" and the new
version of "Breaking Up Is Hard to Do." The writing went very
well for that album, and that's usually a good indication of the

---

[9] That record label's West Coast director of Artists & Repertoire.

outcome. So I was confident. Oh yes, and "Lonely Nights (Angel Face)" was in that album as well. That song was one of my lyrics, and I was exceptionally happy with it. That song took me two martinis to write. I had been writing with two of the most fantastic lyricists of all time, and I was unsure of myself lyrically. But I wrote "Lonely Nights (Angel Face)," the music first, and came up with the line ". . . tell me, what am I gonna do?" and I really liked it. So I said, "Hell, I'm not going to give this one to Howie or Phil!"

I loved making *The Hungry Years* album. It seemed like an eternity before it came out in this country, because it was released in England months and months before. A lousy front cover in England, a beautiful cover here. The cover was not my choice. The clown face was supposed to be the cover, which I felt would have been more identifiable and a better eye-catcher for the window displays.

"Steppin' Out" was a fearful, frightening recording experience. I knew I had a following, and there were people out there waiting to see what I was going to do next. Therefore, I became more critical of myself, much more demanding. I felt as though I had to top the last album—which I think I did. I had more of an obligation to my public and myself.

Ron Delsener:
Concert Promotion

Since the beginning of the rock era live concerts have paralleled the growth of the record industry and assumed a dominant role in our music culture. They are no longer only venues for musical recitals, but have become events, a musical environment where the price of the ticket can include anything from exceptional people-watching to Frisbee exhibitions to conceptual theater to simple congregation and, oh yes, to music. Coincidentally, the music has become bigger and more technically sophisticated, and the audiences have grown in size from seventy-five kids gathering in a high-school gymnasium to an audience of thirty thousand packing the local sports complex for the several shows scheduled to accommodate the demand for tickets.

The rock concert has taken on another identity affecting the artist's careers in that, it is virtually impossible for new talents to break without first proving themselves in the performance arena. Records alone are no longer a sufficient criterion for absolute acceptance. Where we were once able to go into a record store and speculate on intuition (maybe a cover caught our eye or we knew at least two of the songs in the album were good), records do not reveal enough about the artist to substantiate over-all talent. Now, more often than ever before, it is the word-of-mouth evaluation of an artist's live show which differentiates the eventual success or failure of the act. Few acts can exist without first going on the road—the Harry Nilssons and Steely Dans being rare exceptions—and most record companies will not sign an act before they are sure they are able to represent their music properly to an audience and sell records. Peter Frampton mentions in this book how his album sales automatically pick up immediately after his show in the city where he performs. Bruce Springsteen, by keeping his act in front of an audience for three years before Born to Run broke, was able to build up a devoted following who spread the word. Loggins and Messina continued to sell gold albums even after radio response diminished by doing a certain number of concerts each year and getting their new material to their public via the stage.

But even though the business demand for concerts is great, attendance has been spotty and what were once guaranteed sellouts are now work projects for the promoters. This sagging attendance has arisen out of more acts being on the road and competing against one another even on the same night in the same city, more discriminating audiences being selective with the $7.50 average ticket price and sky-high talent costs that raise the amount of work necessary to sell the show and lower the profits. Combined with ludicrous union bills and advertising costs, the promoter puts himself on the line for each show. Promoters no longer lose two or three hundred dollars a night on near-misses. The astronomical inclusive fees can put a show under by several thousand dollars while a successful show, after all costs have been accounted for, only provide the promoter with a token financial reward.

The face of the concert promotion business has changed over the past few years, bringing with it new faces and new ideas. But in New York City, probably the toughest concert market to maintain, Ron Delsener has been churning new ideas and top entertainment into rock arenas for over a decade. Above all, Delsener has been a champion of the music, fighting city administration *after city administration to prevent rock and roll audiences from being treated as "second-class citizens."*

Delsener is a perfectionist and demands that his productions reflect his ideals. Groups love working for him. Besides knowing that they will be paid fairly, they know that he caters to their utmost needs and treats them with dignity. In return, some of the biggest performers will not work in New York unless they work for Ron. Confusion is obsolete at a Delsener show. The stage is always ready on time and the crews know what they are doing so that nothing detracts from the show.

Ron Delsener would love others to think he is a tough character. His manner of speech is tersely businesslike, brusque, but is more of a guise which he comfortably assumes to keep things moving in his line of work. He is a city boy and a fighter, and he uses his urban background to get what he wants. And while he might seem aloof, he is a thoughtful, intelligent human being who cares more about his young audiences than anything else . . . although he'll probably cringe when he sees this in print.

Presenting rock music in concert is probably the most chaotic experience in the entertainment business. It is multilateral, multicomplex, and probably a bit masochistic, but when presented properly it is the ultimate musical experience.

THIS MUST BE SOME BUSINESS TO GET INTO!

When I was a young guy, I used to be a Lenny Bruce fan and would try to see him in concert as much as possible. Before I got into producing concerts, I went to see Lenny at a midnight concert at Carnegie Hall. It was in a fierce snowstorm, but I *had* to see him and I wouldn't let the snow stop me. I lived in Queens[1] at the time and I had to take a bus to the subway station and then a subway into Manhattan. It was murder traveling that night! Anyway, I was real lucky to get a seat in the orchestra. There was no Ticketron in those days and I had hoped to get a good seat at the door. I was shocked when I got inside because the place was packed.

[1] Queens is a borough adjacent to Manhattan.

I looked around the hall that night and said to myself, There's only one guy onstage—Lenny Bruce. One microphone, one spotlight. I got out a paper and pen right on the spot and figured what the gross must be. I thought, This guy, Don Friedman, who had come out on the stage and introduced Lenny, as promoter must be making a fortune. I figured he paid Lenny $500 or $1,000 for the night, maybe the same to rent Carnegie Hall—he probably went home with $10,000 for the night. I didn't know anything about what you *really* have to pay an act or anything about percentages. I said to myself, "Wow, this must be some business to get into!"

Later I worked with Don Friedman, the same man who had promoted Lenny Bruce at Carnegie Hall, and then I decided to try doing a show of my own. It was with Patrick Sky and Mississippi John Hurt and the Greenbriar Boys at Town Hall in 1965. I lost forty dollars on that show and thought, "This is no way to make a living!

ROSIN? WHAT'S THAT?

After that first show, no one would sell me any acts. So I went to an old friend, Edward Villella, for my next show. I had gone to school with Edward, and one night I stopped backstage at the ballet and said, "I'm a promoter now." I conned him into doing a ballet without an orchestra—we could use tape-recorded music. He had always wanted to dance a *pas de deux* with Melissa Hayden, so I arranged it, and he said, "Okay, let's do it."

At that time, I had to do everything *by myself*. I used to give out handbills in the street every night with my wife-to-be. We'd hang around the ballet handing them out, really promoting the show, in all kinds of weather.

Come the night of the show, Edward arrived and said, "Where's the rosin for the floor? I can't dance on this floor." I looked around and said, "Rosin? What's that?" So he told me, and I ran up Third Avenue looking for any place that had one of those skiball machines like they have in the bar and grills because they always used rosin on the lanes. But nobody had any. So I figured, "I need something abrasive like that," and I got a bright idea. "I'll use Bab-O." So I bought a lot of cans of Bab-O, and I ran back to the hall and we started throwing this stuff all over the floor. Edward thought I was crazy—Comet and Bab-O all over the floor. But we finally got through the night, and I don't think Edward spoke to me for two years. But it was my start.

THE ONLY BALL GAME IN TOWN

In those days, the late Fifties and Sixties, you could make a lot of money as a promoter because you paid [the artists] flat. In other words, if you were a recording artist, you worked for a flat fee . . . a thousand dollars, for example. Today, there's a percentage of the gate that has to be paid to the performer as well as the flat fee. They get the flat fee plus a percentage of the gross. Sometimes it's a straight 60 per cent of the gross, sometime it's a 90–10 split. Performers like the Who or some other big stars will say to you, "We know we're going to sell out, so we're going to let you make 10 per cent—not of the gross, but of the net, what's left." I take all the expenses at the end of the night, show them the bills, and say, "Well, my expenses are $50,000. Here's the gross— $100,000." Then they'll say, "Your share is 10 per cent of that remaining $50,000, which is $5,000, and we get $45,000." Now, things are even getting worse. A David Bowie or an Elton John or Who will say, "We want a minimum of $70,000 guaranteed against a 90–10 per cent." So they'll get at least $70,000, and then, after you pay them, you split what's left with them 90–10 per cent.

There are several "sure" acts that *will* sell out a place like Madison Square Garden, but a lot of other things could occur to screw things up. I might be sold out and one of the acts will get tonsillitis. That happened to me with Dan Fogelberg. Or Neil Young: vocal chords sore, couldn't talk, has to whisper and whistle. These things happen. But when they *do* work and they're healthy and aren't crazy and haven't had a fight with each other, there are a lot of artists who are money in the bank. And those are the acts that say to you, "We know what the gross is, we know what your expenses are, we know *everything*. We really don't need you to promote the show, but you play all our other acts or have a history with us, so here's a fee. You do all the work, guarantee all the expenses, and here's $5,000." Of course, out of that,

you have to pay your office overhead—mine is about $3,000 a
week. It sounds like a lot of money when you make three or four
thousand dollars a night, but the overhead is great and so are the
losses. You lose big money, and today you don't make big money.
That's why I have to do one or two hundred concerts a year, because the profit margin is small. And you have to have the city
wrapped up—be the only ball game in town. That way, the managers need you for their other acts. Then you can say, "I played
this act of yours and I lost $6,000. How can you only let me make
$4,000 with your big act. So you have to come on pretty heavy—
you have to be forceful and scream a lot. I'm starting to do that
more and more now.

Lots of acts know what they make, and they'll come off the
stage and flip for the money. And that's what it's all about. They
don't get involved in negotiations, though. It's a taboo thing to
talk to an act about money directly. But they'll talk about how
much money they've got off the stage—what they're doing and
what they're buying with it. Then some acts will dress down,
look like they haven't had a meal in six months, go on the stage
and the kids think, This is great! They're one of us. Then, after
the concert, right into the limousine for steaks and champagne.

BOOKING THE SHOW

The first thing that happens when I book an act is that the agent
calls me and says, "So-and-So is going out on the road in Octo-
ber." And I'll say, "These are the theaters that I think they should
play in New York." We'll then decide on where I'm going to play
the act. Then we'll haggle about the money. Based on the price on
which we decide, I'll tell the agent what I'm going to have to
charge for tickets, because that has to be approved ahead of time.

Then the agent asks me what the cost is going to be for provid-
ing the entire concert. This I can't fudge. I have to know the actual cost or I'm going to misrepresent myself and be embarrassed
later on. They always find out. We discuss the cost of the theater:
the rental, the stagehands, the food. Then we discuss the rider.
When you make a deal, you have to ask yourself, How much will
the rider cost me in addition to the act? If they bring an orchestra,
do I have to pay for that? Do I have to pay for an organ? A

piano? Do they need a limousine? It all gets spelled out in the rider. I estimate the cost of everything and include that in my expenses. This happens before I make the deal. Then we agree on the final price for the act and the percentage the act will receive after my expenses and his base costs are paid, and only then I am allowed to make *my* small profit.

Once I get a contract, the first thing I do is give it to my production associate, who checks it out for any crazy things. He'll call up the group's production man and—in a nice way—say, "You can do this, this you can't do, and this is what we can give you." And the group's production man will say, "But the rider says we want fourteen spotlights [in a hall where we are only able to use two] and limousines with beds and blah blah blah!" My man works that down and smoothes over any rough edges. Years ago, many promoters didn't even bother to call the act. The group would come to the hall on the night of the show expecting everything in the rider, and nothing would be there. There were always arguments in those days, and that's why the rider came into practice.

The riders are getting crazier all the time. They include things like: we want Chinese food at two o'clock for the crew—all sixteen of them—and then, at six o'clock the act wants a specified menu for guests including various wines and hors d'oeuvres. And there are always two vegetarians. I remember for Cat Stevens we had to supply curry and Chinese bamboo shoots and Orange Julius. So I had to go out and buy an Osterizer, because I also played Cat in New Haven at the time, and they didn't have Orange Julius. So we brought up the Osterizer and mixed it ourselves. If I play a big show at the Garden, I get a bill for $1,300 for dressing-room food, and this has to be figured into my deal. But there may be hope yet. I just saw the Johnny and Edgar Winter rider and it's very simple: no food—just cheese and some fruit. But the crews' riders are bigger than ever: Monday it's a steak, Tuesday it's Chinese food, Wednesday it's turkey. Then they want things like organic vegetables. But there's enough money in the gross where I just figure those things in. Now, I'm basically in the catering business as a promoter.

After that's all squared away, the ticket lady looks at the contract, the rider and works out how many seats to hold per show for the act, the record company, and our guests, and pulls the seats. Then we have an ad team, and I tell them when to break the ads. The act usually sends you the copy they want to appear in the ad. Then we co-ordinate the tickets and everything else for the day that ad breaks. Tickets have to be in, Ticketron has to be notified in advance, the box office has to be notified. After that, I watch the sales every day. We have a machine in the office which we punch into to see how the outlets are doing with the tickets. We check the box office, and I know whether or not to book radio or to kill print or whatever.

It all sounds like an unreal process, but it comes together for each show, and I have a great staff helping me.

THE NEW YORK SITUATION

The concert scene has really changed in New York over the past few years. Carnegie Hall used to be the prestige place to play, but they don't want rock and roll, amplified music, and they're outspoken about it. They have a blacklist of acts which they don't permit to play there, like Poco, and there are also certain penalties they impose on you. The stagehands' union charges more for putting a show in Carnegie Hall because they call it a special event. The hall charges you a rehearsal fee, a taping fee, all sorts of surcharges. And that's only *if* they want you in there. Avery Fisher Hall[2] is a little bit looser, but they've built an entire new inside to the hall and they may be a little stricter now that they're finished. They have new rugs and don't want cigarette burns on them. Then they keep the house lights on at half intensity so they can watch the crowd. You can't bring drinks backstage. But I've slipped a few goodies into there in my day—like Jimi Hendrix on Thanksgiving evening a few years back. That was a *real* chore getting him in there.

The Felt Forum costs me four dollars for every seat. There are 4,200 seats, and it costs me $16,000 for the Felt Forum. That's four dollars out of every five-dollar ticket you charge goes to the management. And that breaks down even more. Six thousand dol-

2 Formerly Philharmonic Hall at Lincoln Center for the Performing Arts.

lars goes to the Garden for rental of the Forum. There is another five to six thousand for staffing—electricians, not stagehands. And the other four or five thousand is for the stagehands, whom you pay directly. By the time you get done: $16,000. The gross is usually—with a $6.50–7.50 top price—$30,000. So you have $15,000 left to pay the two acts, the lights, the sound, the advertising and still figure in your profit. Because of that, I have to do two shows to make any money there.

Madison Square Garden is the biggest and most expensive indoor place to put on a show in the country. They have an awful big operating nut to crack there. They have an office building to maintain as well as the rest of the complex, so they charge a lot of money. It costs me $30,000 to rent the arena for one night on a potential gross of $130,000. Anything over $130,000 they get 22½ per cent of, besides the basic $30,000. Then you have their staffing charges, which can run anywhere from $25,000 to $27,000. Stagehands are paid separately, and that runs anywhere from $5,000 to $10,000. So by the time you get done with a decent show at the Garden, it costs between $65,000 to $75,000. The gross is $130,000, so, in essence, 50 per cent of the evening's income is for basics. Which means for every $7.50 ticket the Garden gets almost $4.00. Most other halls average out at $2.00 a ticket, but if you want to play the Big Apple, the Garden's *the* place to play. It's prestigious, and many acts want to play it for that reason. They don't care about the money and they know up front that they're not going to make a lot there. I do about fifteen or twenty big concerts there a year.

To book the Garden, I have to go around their basketball and hockey schedule. I clear dates anywhere from four to six months in advance. I tell them that I want every date available over a five-month period. Now, I can't hold the dates forever, so when they get uptight about it, they call me and say, "Hey, Ron, somebody just called about that date you're holding." Either I'll release it, or I'll tell them that I have a shot with Chicago or the Beach Boys or whomever. Then I go back to the group and tell them that the Garden needs a definite answer on the dates. And the larger acts will usually give me an answer long in advance to help me book them into the Garden.

I'M WORKING FOR THEM

The unions are exceptionally strong in New York City. The big problem with the unions is that they have a large cost-of-living increase built into their contract which increases every three years. I work pretty well with the stagehands' union; however, it's not the best deal in the world. They tell me how many men I'm going to use and that's God's word! I'm working for them. What am I going to say—I don't want them? No chance. So I'll cry a little and do the best I can.

For an Elton John concert at Madison Square Garden, I have to have twenty-four stagehands, and I'll probably only have sixteen actual men work on the show. But I'll pay for twenty-four. Then the electrician's union puts a minimum number of men on me. With the spotlight operators, I could have as many as twenty-five additional men where, if I did the show in another city, I'd only have to use ten men.

And if the group comes in with ten roadies,[3] I have to take an extra ten union men. Many times the roadies are not even allowed to unload the equipment from their own trucks—they're only allowed to tell the union men what they want unloaded and where they want it. Because of that, the setting up of the show is slow. The union people aren't familiar with the act and where they want the equipment. And many times the union man won't even let the kid work alongside of him.

Some good stagehands can make $50,000 or $60,000 a year. But, on the other hand, most of them are unemployed. Yet at a single concert at the Garden, a stagehand bill can be as high as $10,000. The average man can make six or seven hundred dollars a night. That includes working a show and taking it out afterward—anywhere from twelve to fourteen hours' work.

CHOOSING THE ACT

I always look for acts that sell out. Some people forget that this is a business first; you've got to be able to sell tickets. But I listen to a lot of word-of-mouth before deciding the acts I'm going to

[3] Members of the group's equipment crew.

play. I check to see how they did in places like Cleveland or Los Angeles. Many groups don't break out of San Francisco like they used to. Most of them are now breaking in the New York area. So I go to the clubs all the time to see if there's somebody hot playing there. I keep in touch with the club owners who usually have an inside track on the new talent. If a manager who I know and trust says, "I've got a new act I want you to see," I'll go and see them. I stay closely in touch with the record companies. They're interested in hyping their artists to me because they want me to play them, but I'll listen to the record first. Or I'll go to the Columbia and Warner Bros. conventions and see the new artists. I use all those combinations, plus I hit on a few people in New York whose opinions I respect and speak to them about what's happening. I put all these things together.

But many acts are record acts. You go see them in person and they put you right to sleep. There's a difference. If artists have both qualities—if they're exciting in person and great on records —that will sustain them. There are a lot of acts who will never have a hit, but they're exciting as hell in person. Springsteen delivers in person, and for a long time he couldn't get over with his records. But now he's got it both ways. Elton John—there's an act that delivers in person and on record. There are also a lot of regional acts. Acts like Z Z Top, who I don't particularly care for musically, will play a place like the Houston Summit, do two shows a day, and sell out in front of 30,000 people. Arrowsmith is another group like that.

Today, everybody wants to headline. It's an unfortunate problem because everybody should have the chance to open a show. It gives them experience, poise. Hell, it's scary playing in front of ten or fifteen thousand people. You take an act like Minnie Riperton, whom I adore and whom I took a chance with twice because I liked her. Right away, they wanted $5,000 for one performance when everybody knew she should have been getting $750 to $1,000 as an opening act. But she went out at five grand and nearly everybody lost money. It's going to take two years now to convince us to buy her back and to convince people to come out to see her again. By people saying to her, "Minnie, look what I got you the first time out: $5,000 a night," well, they could have ruined her. Anybody can hype. Luckily, Minnie Riperton is a great artist and will bounce back, but it definitely put a snag in her career. Sometimes, people should say, "We'll take less money and a percentage. We don't want to be greedy." You have to be honest with people and with the acts you represent when it comes to their drawing power in a market.

I definitely need an opening act. Many times, a headliner won't fill two hours, so I need that opening act to fill the time. Also, the headliners don't want people walking in while they're starting their set.

Opening acts used to be my decision, but those days are practically gone. The only way I get a choice is if there are three acts on the show. A talent agency who has the headliner also has a million acts for whom they are looking to get work. So they'll tell me who the opening act is going to be. Today, a lot of opening acts are on the show because the manager of the headliner also manages other acts and he wants exposure for them. So you may not get his headliner unless you also agree to take his opening act. And often the agency wants their own opening act on the bill.

But today's opening acts are tomorrow's headliners. I always hope that one of my opening acts breaks. And hopefully I'll be afforded the courtesy of being the first to present the act again when they're big. On that, I have to keep my fingers crossed.

ON TICKETRON

Ticketron has built a real monster. It's not their fault, but for every rule there's an angle, and people have certainly found a way around Ticketron. When they first came to New York, there were two agencies vying for the promoters. Ticketron won out because they were backed by Control Data, a big computer firm.

They went to the stores and said, "You're going to charge the patron fifty cents over the cost of the ticket, and we'll give you twenty-five cents of that." Then they taught the clerks—who were probably selling jewelry or ladies' lingerie—how to punch into the machine. Now Ticketron is solicited by scalpers who come into the stores and see their favorite little clerk. These clerks get a Ticketron supplement that comes out in advance of the tickets going on the machine. The supplement says, "Programmed in your machine will be the following shows." Well, the scalpers go in the store every week and take care of this person. They say, "Here's a hundred bucks. Did you get the latest book? What's coming in?" And the clerk says, "Well, now, let me see—oh yes, we have a Bob Dialin concert coming in. It goes on sale in the machine on Monday, and the price per ticket is ten dollars." And the scalper says, "You just pull a hundred tickets off for me. I don't have to wait in line. Here's fifty dollars." Come Monday, he rolls up to the store while all the kids are waiting in line, she hands him his box of tickets, and he sells them on the street for thirty dollars apiece. That's why you can be first in line on that Monday when the ticket counter opens and the person behind the window opens up and says, "Sorry, they're all gone!" They tell the kids that the promoter took them all.

COMPETITION IS NOT FRIENDLY

People are always trying to knock me off! Right now, I have fierce competition from three or four people. As a promoter, I have an undefined territory. Mine is New York, and it kills me when other people do shows in my territory, but they're always trying to do it. People want to play the best facilities, and if you have them, then there's no competition.

The only thing I can do is to try to develop a relationship with an act so they'll play for me again and again. I try to stay very close to the managers—some of whom have become my close friends as a result of our business ties. The agents, too. The agents protect me from other guys moving into my territory. They know I'm reliable, and they know I'm guaranteed to take x-amount of shows from them a year.

But competition is not friendly—it's vicious. It's a very insecure feeling. So it's had to become a day and night thing for me. I have to be on top of things all the time or I *will* get knocked off by these guys waiting in the wings. I can't remember the last time I had a good night's sleep worrying about a show or about my image in the business. I really haven't had time to read or go to the movies because of this. But, I'll tell you, it's a great business. I love putting on shows and I can't think of another thing I'd trade it for. It's worth all the trouble and worry, because I really enjoy what I do and I really enjoy the kids' appreciation of being able to see their favorite acts. And that's the name of the game.

Peter Frampton

"Music is my fruit of life
Don't take it away.
I want to wear it to see
I don't care when it will be."

P. FRAMPTON, *I Want to Go to the Sun*

People outside the rock music industry are under the erroneous impression that stardom comes to its performers quickly and ephemerally. Too often, by virtue of longevity being reflected by the quality of music, the abrupt acceptance of a particular artist reinforces this misconception. Hence, there is a tendency today for many of the new recording artists to anticipate that "instant success" and, often, to expect their record company to manufacture the impossible. That, I'm afraid, is a thing of the past. A lot of critics attribute its demise to the corporate takeover of rock and roll; however, the bottom line is clearly that the talent has become better and quantitative, and the audience has become most discriminating. Therefore, record companies are beginning to practice a greater degree of patience. They are living with the product longer and working harder on creating an image for the artist and his music. First albums are the tools; they are no longer expected to immediately break the artist. They are "work" records and, while the company puts its promotional and publicity machinery into operation, it affords the artist the time to introduce himself to his prospective audience, to develop his act, and, ultimately, to formulate a lasting career. It is difficult work, often creatively frustrating, but should the talent be strong enough to gain public acceptance, the rewards are infinite.

Peter Frampton is fully cognizant of the rigors of paying dues and being amply compensated for his work—although, in Peter's case, it took two groups and four solo albums to expand his cult following and to gain universal acclaim. He has been on the road writing and performing professionally since he was fourteen working toward the success which eventually arrived with the release of Frampton Comes Alive. *That success was not dependent solely upon the release of that exceptional album; rather it was an accumulation of that album and the twelve years of exposure which provided Frampton with the total package which just about guarantees his longevity. For today, it has indeed come alive for Peter Frampton, who is playing to sold-out arenas and stadiums across the United States and whose latest album continues to sell in extraordinary numbers.*

For a good part of his career, Frampton's music has been closely associated with that of hard rock, which subsequently alienated a portion of his potential audience. He played the cement-and-concrete circuit, opening to mostly English groups and working for progressive music promoters. In essence, his music has not changed. The only facet of his career which has been altered is the context within which he is being presented. If anything, Peter's wavery voice subdues any musical resemblance to hard rock and emotionalizes his intentions. His music is deeply personal, yet it has a way of conveying just as personal feelings to the listener. And the energy with which he delivers each of his songs, the driving arrangements and vocalizations, delineate his talents from those of similar rock acts.

Frampton is more a musician than a lyricist, and a close listen to his catalogue indicates that, while his lyrics are competent, his musicianship is exceptional. His guitar work is expressive of feelings and often serves his compositions lyrically better than his vocalizing of the words. He is an articulate musician, nimble, technically perfect. And yet in over-all appearance, his instrumentation is almost incidental. This is the mark of a clever artist—one who thinks his music through in terms of a total composition. There

*are no riffs in Frampton's work, no lengthy jams—just accentua-
tions which constantly weave throughout the other instruments
into the total musical entity. And of all Peter Frampton's crafts, it
is that weaving at which he is most skilled.*

*Frampton's music is not depressing, nor is it particularly hope-
ful. He writes of the present and the things which are just within
his reach. These metaphors ("I Want to Go to the Sun," "Show
Me the Way," "Something's Happening") are marked by uncer-
tainty, almost a naïve hopefulness which remains unresolved.
Frampton is a young man who has been protected by the
microcosmic rock group all his adult life, and his songs reflect the
questions which might have been answered or worked out for him
had he grown up in a less constricting environment. But there has
been a constant maturity in Peter Frampton's writing—a sign that
he is looking around him and learning, a sign that he has a long
and embellished future ahead of him as an artist and an entertainer.*

I PLEADED FOR A GUITAR

Until I was nine, I had my grandmother's banjulele, which is
like a ukulele, but it's shaped like a banjo—a real strange-sound-
ing instrument. It had four strings and was tuned in a my-dog's-
got-fleas tuning. But I got bored with it quickly because it only
had four strings; that was no fun. So I pleaded for a guitar, and my
parents finally broke down and got me a steel-string guitar for
Christmas in 1959. My father had shown me a couple of chords
on the banjulele, and now I had to learn how to use the other two
strings.

After I'd been chomping away at chords for a while, they said,
"Well, if you're going to learn how to play properly—if you're
going to bug us so much—then you're going to go to Spanish guitar lessons." So they sent me to this private Spanish guitar teacher,
and whenever her back was turned, I was playing something else.
I never practiced for those lessons really that much. But it taught
me how to use all the fingers on my left hand and how to pick a
little.

My parents were real pleased with my progress. Both my

mother and my father were musical, both could sing. My mother had even been given a scholarship to the Royal Academy of Dramatic Arts by Dame Sybil Thorndike, but she turned it down because she had to go out and work. So my mother has always been a frustrated actress, and she could have been fantastic. My dad played guitar in a prewar college dance band and could handle the instrument pretty well. He was into Django Reinhardt and Stephane Grappelli stuff, and that's where his interest in the guitar really came from.

One day, my father decided to buy a record player for our house, and when he came back with it, he brought along two records: one for him and one for me. His album was Django Rhinehart, and the one for me was The Shadows, which was Cliff Richard's band. It's funny, because I listened to that the first day he brought them back for us and I said, "Yecch! What's that junk?" And in the end, I went full around going through jazz. I've still got that first album; I brought it with me when I came to the United States.

While I was growing up, I listened to people like Buddy Holly, Eddie Cochran, Gene Vincent, Elvis Presley, Little Anthony and the Imperials, Cliff Richard, and Adam Faith. I never got to see many of these people perform at concerts, but we did have two TV shows that did rock. Apart from Cliff Richard and Adam Faith, American rock dominated the British charts. Then The Shadows happened and they had a string of instrumental hits for about three or four years. They were my favorite band. I could play any Shadows number backward, forward, with the echo and everything. And their guitarist, Hank Marvin, who I really admired more than any other musician, wore horn-rimmed glasses like Buddy Holly and had a red Stratocaster, so I went out to Woolworth's and bought some red horn-rimmed sunglasses, knocked the glass out, and I used to wear those whenever I played.

THIS IS THE CHOICE

My parents really never had to encourage me to get involved in music. They never really stopped me from doing anything, even when I began doing all-nighters while I was still in school. I'd go to school the next day, and the first thing that would happen to me was that the math teacher would have a mental arithmetic test and he'd always ask me the first question because he *knew* I'd be the sucker, that I'd be nodding off at nine o'clock in the morning having just gotten in from the gig.

The only time my parents ever stopped me from doing music was when it became an obsession. When I was eight and nine years old, I never did anything but play the guitar. I hated football and would never go out and play. I played guitar from the time I got home from school until bedtime. But when it got to the point where my academic future became jeopardized, then my parents took hold. They wanted me to go to music college, so they took me away from the group that was doing these all-nighters because it was affecting me in many ways. But that was a good thing because I just got a chance to practice more. I never went to music college, because after I took the General College Examinations, I got grades that were nothing to be proud of. And, also, Andrew Baum met me. He was with a rock group called The Herd, who I had sat in with, West Wickham's top group. And they asked me if I'd like to join.

I said to my father, "This is the choice. Do I go back to school and take some more examinations and try to go to music college or do I get to work professionally with a group?" And he asked me, "What do you want to do?" I said, "Join the group!" So my father negotiated this deal with Billy Gaff, who was then The Herd's manager, and I got fifteen pounds a week. That was a terrific wage for me after having just left school. And that was fifteen pounds a week, come what may. Some weeks the other members in the group only made three pounds a week each, but I always got my fifteen. My father made the best deal ever for me. That was the only proviso he gave. But one week we worked a lot and the rest of the group got twenty-five pounds—and I got my fifteen. So karma came back to me.

I LOVED BEING WITH THE HERD

We did our residency at the Marquee Club. It was a great place which was a stomping ground for any good talent scout. The Who started there, so did the Stones. It was the type of club that if your band got the residency, someone was bound to come along and offer you a recording contract. After we had played there for about a year, Steve Rollins, a manager, came down and saw us and asked us to do a few demos for a popular group called Dave Dee, Dozy, Beaky, Mich and Tich. So we did all these demos which they would then redo and turn them into big hits. Pretty soon, their producers said they'd try *us* out and would even write some songs for us. It was our big break! The first song was called "I Can Fly," which flubbed. Then they tried with another one called "From the Underworld," which went straight up the charts. It was a Top Ten hit for a long time. And soon after, I got named the Face of Sixty-Eight.[1]

I loved being with The Herd and doing commercial music. The way we started off was much more jazz-oriented, Motown-oriented, than the way we ended up. We did Martha and the Vandellas numbers and things like that. But we also did Jimmy McGriff and Jimmy Smith numbers. Andrew was into all those Motown groups and I was into people like George Benson, Kenny Burell, and Wes Montgomery. So when we played the Marquee Club we'd do a twenty-minute jazz spot in the middle of our set. All of a sudden—now that we had all these hits—we couldn't do that anymore, not with the teeny-boppers. But we had a string of big songs, and it was a real nice time in my life.

WHERE'S YOUR ROLLS-ROYCE?

While I was with The Herd, we thought we were being screwed financially—and we were! There were so many production companies involved, and we weren't actually signed to a label. So someone was taking this and someone was taking that and when it came down to the band, we couldn't afford to pay ourselves. All the excitement of being on the Top of the Pops[2] every week for about a year had died down. And the killer was that my *milkman* had predicted our demise. He was always delivering the milk when I was arriving home from all-night gigs, and he kept asking

[1] A name given him by the press which characterized his handsome appearance.

[2] One of the few English rock and roll television shows that demand that guests are on the very top of the English pop charts.

me, "Where's your Rolls-Royce?" And then it sort of struck me that there were all these other people riding around in limousines, and I still had a Morris Minor. I couldn't afford to buy anything fantastic for myself. I was earning peanuts—my same fifteen pounds a week. When we finally got rid of the whole organization which had been running our careers we were able to pay ourselves almost fifty pounds a week, but our deal was so bad that we never received any record royalties. We got one English penny per record, which was split between the four of us. And we had to pay ourselves out of that as well. That's how we were being screwed.

Our managers had been fair to us—more fair than our production company—but they never managed us for longevity purposes, they never looked ahead. They never said, "We'll put this away for the group so that when they stop having hits they'll be all right."

So we got this offer from Andrew Oldham to be signed to his Immediate Records,[3] and we were given his Phantom Five Rolls-Royce to drive around Scotland. Steve Marriott and Ronnie Lane heard about this. They had been with Immediate, and they said, "Don't sign. Don't go with Immediate." They said they were being screwed there as members of the Small Faces. Steve said, "Why don't you leave The Herd and form your own group?" And I said, "Good idea." And he said, "I've got this young drummer friend of mine named Jerry Shirley.[4] Why don't you get together?" So I took up with Jerry, and we needed either an organist or a guitarist and a bass player. Meanwhile, I did some sessions with the Small Faces in France with a singer named Johnny Halliday, the French Elvis Presley. When we got back to England, I was staying at Glyn Johns' house, and I got a phone call from Steve Marriott asking me, "Can I join your band? I've quit the Small Faces." I said, "Yes." And he said, "I've also got this great bass player from Spooky Tooth named Greg Ridley." We were born! And we decided to call ourselves Humble Pie. After that, we spent a month in a country cottage getting it together.

I just wanted to be in an exciting rock band for a change and be the guitarist rather than the front man. We wanted to get away from the teeny-boppers and play some serious rock music. To me,

[3] The record company responsible for recording The Nice.
[4] Now drummer for Natural Gas.

I thought Humble Pie would be an extension of *Ogden's Nutgone Flake,* which had been the Small Faces *Sgt. Pepper.* But we weren't. We didn't become that because we weren't the Small Faces. We never pretended to be them.

The first single we'd released in Europe was "Natural Born Boogie," which was a Top Three hit single. So we started our career by touring England and we were screamed at by the fans. We didn't want that; that's what we had tried to get away from. So we looked to America.

After our first American tour, we ended up on the West Coast and couldn't even afford to get home. The audiences weren't really that interested in us. There were a few people who had been staunch followers of the Small Faces, but we made a terrible name for ourselves. We played far too long for an opening act, and people would get bored stiff halfway through our set. We also didn't do any of our acoustic stuff from the albums. The American audiences wanted to hear our heavy stuff and that's the direction the group soon took. Besides playing too long, we thought we were the be-all and the end-all. We were English upstarts as far as the promoters were concerned.

SO I HAD TO LEAVE

I left Humble Pie because I was interested in leading my own band, and there wasn't really room for two leaders in one band. Steve and I just couldn't compete.

Musically, I just wasn't into heavy rock and roll anymore. Steve was going into more R&B stuff, and our music was just moving apart instead of moving even more tightly together. I wanted to do acoustic things that I'd written, and that wouldn't have worked out being a member of Humble Pie. So I had to leave. And wouldn't you know that the minute I left the group, the live album we had recorded got released, and I clutched my heart as I watched this thing shoot up to the top of the charts. It was a gold album within three weeks. I thought, "Uh oh, Pete's made a boo-boo." But in the end, it made me want to leave Humble Pie even more.

The rest of the group was upset and hurt that I wanted to leave. They felt that I was an integral member, a founding member, and that would signal to the fans or the press or whoever that all wasn't well with Humble Pie. All *wasn't* well with Humble Pie. But my leaving had to be. Jerry Shirley, who's now in Natural Gas, and I have had long talks about our days with Humble Pie, and he told me that leaving was the best decision I'd ever made— even though he didn't think so at the time.

THERE WAS MY FIRST LEGIT SESSION

I first recorded at the age of twelve. It was with a group called Denny Mitchell and the Soundsations, who actually appeared on TV. But my second session was more important. This time I went into the studio with a semiprofessional group called the Preachers, who were being managed by Bill Wyman. And the engineer was a man by the name of Glyn Johns. So there I was, my first legit recording session with Bill Wyman producing it and Glyn Johns engineering it. I was about fourteen then. Wyman was great. He's a very musical guy, very easygoing. After the session, he managed to get us on "Ready, Steady, Go," which was the big rock TV show in England. It was a live show, and in any one week you could see the Stones, the Who, and the Beatles—all on the same show! Then the Stones were given their own show called "Ready, Steady, Stoned." (Yecch!) I was on TV with the Stones when I was only fifteen. Each of the Stones was allowed to bring on his own guest. Well, we were Bill Wyman's guest.

Glyn Johns is basically an engineer and a producer second. He's definitely a style of engineer that is very unique. Especially with microphone techniques. I picked up more from Glyn Johns than from just about anybody. Musically, he's become very creative. He's even gotten into arrangements and everything. Whether or not to double-track something or not, things like that.

But Glyn likes to do things his way, and if your way doesn't work, he can be very difficult. But I respect him very much. He did all the great Eagles tracks, the Stones things, the Who's things, some of the Beatles things on the Abbey Road and the White albums. In the studio, he's capable of working fast if the artist can handle it. If you're recording something and you say, "I've got a verse for this. Let's stick it in here," he can do it in a flash. He's very quick. I need that when I record. I can work both ways, but I like speed. Only when I'm working out backing vocals can I take forever. Then I'll go over and over and over it again. I can really be quite difficult for the other people on the session when I'm doing that. But if I'm doing a lead vocal or a lead guitar, then I like to do it in one take. Otherwise it becomes mechanical. And Glyn's great for that.

SOCIALLY I'LL STAND
IN A CORNER AND SHAKE

People always assume that the group Frampton's Camel came next. Actually, all my records have been solo albums. It's just that I took a band on the road, and I wanted to give that particular band a name, an identity, rather than be a solo artist with a couple unknown guys behind me.

The first album that I did as a solo was called *Peter Frampton, Wind of Change*. The second album should have been called *Peter Frampton, Frampton's Camel*. But instead, it was just called *Frampton's Camel,* which turned out to be my tribute to my insecurity.

I'm not half as insecure as I used to be. The reason that my career didn't make it then, and I've made it now, is that I'm incredibly confident onstage now. Not about other things, though. Socially, I'll stand in a corner and shake. But onstage, I've really learned how to be comfortable and concentrate on my performance. I have a hard time when I'm introduced to people. I was never the sort of person who could be the center of attention at a party. I like to mingle, to be part of the crowd. Onstage, I'm different. Now it doesn't matter if I talk or I don't talk—if I walk into a room I become the center of attention because of my career. It makes me nervous when people get nervous meeting me. There's no reason they should feel that way. But I kind of understand, because that's the way I felt when I met George Harrison for the first time. I didn't know what to say, and I came out with something so inane that I thought I was an idiot. But I was imagining the whole thing. But I know how people feel. When it's you they're nervous meeting, you just have to kind of laugh at it.

I like being a celebrity, and I don't find it difficult coping with my success. I've sort of freaked out with enjoyment a couple of times, I've gotten "personality-drunk" a couple of times, but it's happened so gradually that I'm used to it. It's happened before, although not as intense, with Humble Pie and The Herd. I can relate to The Herd now more than ever before, because while with them it was mobbing and screaming and everything like that. Which is happening now. But now it's far more intense, and I'm now much more guarded from people, from the fans, than I've ever been before. We go out back doors and we take private planes just to avoid airport scenes. At hotels, if it's too close to the gig, then sometimes I have to be sent up a service elevator or out the back door running for the cover of a car. I've always read that things like that happen, but I never dreamed it would be happening to me. We've even had to use some decoys and police escorts. Incredible! Fabulous! It's so exciting.

AS A PRODUCER, I'M RELENTLESS

I love being with A&M Records. I could have been with any other label, and if I hadn't had a big album after my first or second, they would have dropped me. But A&M waited until the fifth album—the fifth!—which is very nice. Jerry Moss[5] and I both think exactly the same way. He's just one of those guys who tries, tries, tries again and even one more time. He won't give up if he believes in the project. And he believed in me.

Jerry and I really started getting close before the *Frampton* album when he said to me, "You've got to play more guitar on the albums." By the time we had done the live album, there was *too* much guitar on it. That's Jerry's favorite thing—he just *loves* the guitar playing. Which knocks me out. He's also encouraged me as a writer and producer.

I prepare for recording all the time because I'm always writing. I have a cassette player around me all the time, everywhere. I'm always putting ideas onto tape, because otherwise I'd never remember them. Then I get all the cassettes together, sift through

[5] Chairman of the Board of A&M Records with Herb Alpert, Jerry is more active in the day-to-day aspect of running the label and working with A&M's artists.

them, put them onto a reel-to-reel tape recorder and, maybe, join ideas together. That way, I'm writing all the time. It's my own little assembly line.

I don't do any rehearsal before I go into the studio to record. I hate rehearsal. I just like to go in and play everybody the song and have us all play it through until it feels right. Then we do it immediately so it's fresh. I love to record on location, like where the *Frampton* album was done—in the castle. Every instrument was in a different room linked together by close circuit TV from a mobile truck outside. That's very important for me soundwise. I hate dead studios. I hate studios that have carpet everywhere. I love the ambient sound of the instruments.

As a producer, I'm relentless. I'll go on and on and on. I remember doing "Baby I Love Your Way" so many times—and the one we kept was the very first take. I just didn't think it was good enough. We'd do two or three tracks a day, and then I'd say, "Well, let's try 'Baby I Love Your Way' quickly to see if we can get a better recording of it." And every day we'd try it again. Until one day, John Simos[6] came into the mobile truck. Now, I'd never seen him do this before because he's so patient. But he said, "Pete, I don't think I can ever play that song again—ever! The first one's a killer, Pete." And that's the one I kept.

THE ALBUMS

Each of my albums represents what was happening in my life at the time we recorded it. *Wind of Change* was about leaving Humble Pie. I was writing very obscure lyrics in those days. Musically, I love that album. The arrangements to "Jumpin' Jack Flash" and "The Fig Tree" and "Ode for Another Day" with the strings— well, I'm really happy with those.

Frampton's Camel was about the breakup of my marriage and being miserable. "Lines on My Face" came from that mood. It was about being jilted, which, people tell me, they can relate to. President Ford's son, Steven, told me that that was the album he had picked up on. He said it saw him through a terrible time. That album was recorded at Electric Lady in the Village. It was the

[6] John Simos is Peter's drummer.

only album recorded in America except for the live one. And I mixed it back in England.

Somethin's Happening represented my marriage getting back together—but not really. There was somebody else involved in my life at that time, and that's why the lyrics were very obscure. I was singing about all sorts of people whom I shouldn't have been singing about. If you listen to the track "Waterfall" you'll see what I mean. No one really knew what "Somethin's Happening" meant, but now it will all come clear. That album only had four tracks a side, and I hate albums with only four tracks a side. If the album is only eight songs, each one's got to be stupendous, otherwise there's no point in putting it out. And I thought there were a couple of weak songs on that album. "Somethin's Happening" and "Go to the Sun" are two of my favorites. But there are some other ones that just aren't up to par. Like my life at that time.

And *Frampton* represented the getting together of me and Penny. Every song is about her, and I like the album.

Because I wasn't having record success like I thought I should have done from the music of the studio albums, I had to go out and make the live show entertaining and involve the audience and become a showman. Dee Anthony, my manager—the best—really helped me with that. I was going down much better in front of a live audience than I was in front of a record-buying public or in front of the DJs or the listeners. It was like: here's his album, but *oh,* go out and *see* him. He's much better live. I heard that a couple of times. So I was given the opportunity to go out and do a live album. Because I had been doing the show for so long, the fans could come out, see the show, and then go out and buy the album, which duplicated the show note for note. *Frampton Comes Alive* is exactly that. Everything we do, apart from "White Sugar," is on the live album. Now there's no point in going out and doing all new material in front of an audience until a new album comes out. They want to hear what's on that album, and that's why I'm against doing any new material live until a new album is released. Because after my show in any city, the album sales jump sky high. If they like the show, they go out and buy the album because they can hear what they've just seen.

On the live album, the excitement is there because the audience is mixed so loud, they're right there. I've heard so many live albums this year, but you wouldn't know they were live until the end of the number when the engineer turns the audience up. You don't hear them whistling or screaming. I think that's another reason why *Frampton Comes Alive* has been so successful. You can hear if someone drops a bottle or a can.

The album has done the impossible for my career. I'm an extremely happy person. I love this new success, this new life I'm living. And I don't want anything to end it now. I'm ready for more.

Sid Bernstein

"What do you think about that?
Well, I think it's kinda nice.
Love is really out of sight,
I'm glad I took your advice."

F. CAVALIERE AND E. BRIGATI, JR.
The Rascals, *Love Is a Beautiful Thing*

Sid Bernstein is a true show business conceptualist born on inspiration and with a gypsy's sense of the future. He is one of a dying breed of magnificent entrepeneurs whose Barnumistic hype is more an agreeable rattle of charm than an overblown discourse of grandiloquence. He's got style.

There are few of us around today whose lives haven't been touched by one of Sid's ventures. He's been involved in the entertainment industry for nearly thirty years, supporting a musical cast that includes Judy Garland, Tony Bennett, the Beatles, the Rascals, the Blues Project, Laura Nyro, Phoebe Snow and the Bay City Rollers. He has acted as agent, manager, promoter, and publicist and, at every turn, has been successful. But more than any professional quality, Sid Bernstein is a gentleman whose guidance and loyalty to the people he's represented are an inspiration to the business of music.

Bernstein's past achievements reflect his sense of the success-to-be more so than his aesthetic understanding of the music itself. Sid

*knows people, he knows what they want in entertainment and,
most important, he knows how to package it for them. He is by no
means a connoisseur of rock and roll; however, he has a natural
instinct for evaluating performance potential. He had no idea that
the Beatles were excellent writers and musicians when he contracted them to perform for the first time in America. I'm not even
sure that he had heard one of their records. But he did realize that
a historical event was in the making, and he chose to become involved, to bank on it. Likewise, the Young Rascals were a Greenwich Village happening when he decided to affiliate himself
with their career. And, again, he repeated his former success with
the Bay City Rollers. To many people, Sid's affiliations may
appear on the surface to be a subtle form of opportunism. But in
almost every association he's had with artists, Sid Bernstein has
made monumental career moves in their favor, sometimes making
the proper decision between success and failure. Laura Nyro came
to him years after she achieved her recognition as one of
America's foremost writers. Today he is one of the most sought-
after advisers in rock management.*

*There are those who write off Sid Bernstein as a spokesman for
a fading era. This is due, in part, to Sid's quiet manner with people. He is not brash or loud, nor does he travel with the in-crowd
looking to be quoted or written about. Sid's publicity for his clients is selfless, and he chooses to allot his private time to his wife
and nine children. But that is not to undermine Sid's character as
a hustler. He is everywhere at once, utilizing personal, much-
guarded and cherished contacts such as Howard Cosell, New
York* Post *columnist Earl Wilson, the late Ed Sullivan, and others
who are out of reach to the better-known rock executives. These
friendships have been cultivated over the years through Sid's ability to deliver on his hype, to produce. It is this older-style method
of promoting which marks Sid Bernstein's* modus operandi; *reaching to the larger-than-life, going out on a limb,* legitimizing.

*As a promoter of concerts, Sid always backed his intuition to
the hilt after conceiving the event, again always expanding on the
situation to make it extraordinary. He was the first to promote
rock concerts at arenas such as Madison Square Garden and local
stadiums. He committed himself to putting the Beatles in a
50,000-plus seat situation even before they created a name*

*for themselves in the United States. Instinct, that necessary cata-
lyst. And yet, if there's one fault in Sid Bernstein's musical career
it is that he often loses confidence in his instincts even after they
have proved successful time and time again. He is by no means a
man of extreme wealth, although it was within his reach several
times. This is due, in part, to Sid's inability to capitalize on his instincts, to wring every last ounce of life out of a situation, to ex-
haust that spectrum within which he is working, be it concerts,
management, or publicity. However, it is probably that quality
which has enabled Sid to move so freely from area to area within
the confines of the rock music business, and to do so in an aura of
respectability. He has developed a reputation for just that flexibility, for being able to pick up and move to the next thing, the
next horizon.*

*Sid Bernstein isn't a tough guy and I seriously doubt that he
could ever exert the insolence so often mistaken as authority in
this business. He has a manner of making his associates believe in
a common cause and exercises that knack to organize all aspects
of a situation. One often develops a sense of personal guilt not
being able to deliver for him.*

*It's early yet. Even in this highly advanced technological age
where the young executives feel as though they have the business
in the palms of their hands, where the seemingly automated
publicists have it "seemingly" down by rote, Sid Bernstein is
devising some new approach, something for everybody. It's only a
matter of time until the public finds out what he's up to.*

THE DAYS THAT ARE NO MORE

Nobody in my family was musical. My father was a tailor in
Harlem, and then we moved to the East Bronx. No music at all in
my family. There wasn't time for it. I was going to Columbia University to become a writer and had a girl friend in Brooklyn. The
subways were hard from the Bronx to Brooklyn, so I took a job in
a Brooklyn neighborhood ballroom at night doing publicity. The
music in the ballroom was Latin—mambo was the rage—and I
got very caught up in the music. In fact, I completely forgot about
writing. I had found music. And a lot of young people came to the

ballroom: ethnic crowds—mostly Jewish and Puerto Rican—who were excellent dancers.

Not long afterward, I became manager of the ballroom and started to book the bands, and that's where I *really* acquired a taste for the music and the business. All the great Latin bands of that time played there: Noro Morales, his younger brother, Esy Morales (for whom I left the ballroom to become his manager), Ralph Font, Tito Rodriguez, Tito Puente, Marceleno Guera— every great Latin band played that ballroom and I booked them. It was extremely easy to book those bands then compared to today. We didn't have all the sound requirements, lighting, temperament, and egos the bands have today. The prices were reasonable. I didn't have to deal with road managers and writers. I made a deal on the phone and that was it.

I spent two very interesting years working for Esy Morales. He was a great flutist of world renown. He died at age thirty-five from diabetes after having abused his condition. But in those two years, I booked him into the Catskills for an entire summer, and part of the buildup was that I booked him into a popular hotel where he acquired a huge following and then brought him back to New York and got him a TV show with CBS and later NBC. That's where I began to get a feeling for promoting on television and a good working knowledge of the music business.

When Esy died, there was a big Latin booking agency called Mercury Artists, headed by Leonard Green, who seemed to have a corner on the Latin bands. He asked me to join him—which I did—and I found myself booking just about every important name I had been buying at the ballroom a few years earlier. I was with Mercury for about two years, and then I quit to work at the Latin Quarter for Lou Walters.[1] The girls were beautiful— America's most beautiful showgirls, a number of whom I was lucky enough to date. The acts were mainly foreign acts from Europe—acrobatic acts, as Lou was the Ed Sullivan of live entertainment. That was part of my education, too. Not in music, but in good showmanship. Lou Walters was one of the great showmen of all times and I learned a lot from him.

---

[1] Sid later related that Lou Walters used to bring his young daughter, Barbara, around to the club frequently.

I CLEANED UP

After two years at the Latin Quarter, I went to work for a black agency which booked mainly jazz and R&B acts. I was with Shaw Artists for four years working with such acts as Miles Davis, Fats Domino, Muddy Waters, Ray Charles, Stan Getz and Chris Connor. This was the beginning of the rock era, and everything was new and exciting.

The artists weren't really reliable, though. They had their hang-ups. They really didn't have good business judgment. They were musicians having a good time between gigs. There were a lot of no-shows or coming late, and there was a lot of drugs at that time, which was a real problem. But some of the people—the characters —were fantastic despite the traumas and the dramas.

I quit on New Year's Day, 1960, to become a promoter of some of the acts that I had been working with as an agent like Fats and Miles and Brook Benton and Ruth Brown—and I cleaned up! The business wasn't very competitive then. R&B was just beginning to cross over (to attract white audiences), jazz still had a very good audience—I think much larger than it has now—and I did both types of shows very successfully in my first year as a promoter.

Soon after, I blew all the money I had made on my R&B and jazz shows when I promoted a season of the Newport Jazz Festival. I had spent a fortune on security as there had been a riot there the year before, and I had booked Judy Garland to play there one afternoon at something like $16,000 for a single performance.

But at the same time, Alan Freed had gotten himself in trouble with the Government[2] and had been dislodged from his tremendous position of holding rock concerts at the Brooklyn and New York Paramount [Theatres]. He was a lovely guy, very warm. I

[2] In May 1958, Freed had promoted a rock show in Boston headlining Jerry Lee Lewis at which a riot broke out. Several children were stabbed and beaten, and the authorities held Freed responsible for inciting a riot. After that, he was disowned, and he soon declared bankruptcy to cover court costs. He died in 1965 at age forty-three.

grew even friendlier with him after the tragic disruption of his career. He became a very sad figure, very lonely. Later, after he had attained such great heights as a promoter of the music, he actually came around to me looking for a job and we had some long talks. I think he probably died of a broken heart. He was a very decent human being. But I saw my opportunity, and realized that jazz was very, very risky and the audience wasn't very large—and Freed had spread rock and roll to such great heights. So when he left the scene, I moved right into the Brooklyn and New York Paramounts and took over the rock shows. I introduced a young man named Murray The K as my MC. When I had made enough money from that, my interests changed and Murray took over. I was foolish to let it go, but I just walked away from it. I needed something new. I had made enough money and I was single then, and my needs weren't as great as they are now.

In 1962, I was broke, and I went to work for GAC,[3] which later became CMA,[4] which is now ICM.[5] I became the head of their young talent department. All the rock stars of the day were there. I worked with Bobby Darin, Bobby Rydell, Chubby Checker, Dion, and so many others. A lot of these people had worked for me at my previous rock shows, and I was very key in holding onto them for the agency—which is why they brought me in, as more of a public relations man than an agency booker. Recording acts at agencies had become *the* thing at that time when they saw the kind of numbers and dollars that were involved. The one-night thing was becoming very popular in weekend theaters. It hadn't yet reached places like Madison Square Garden or ball parks. But it was the Paramounts right across the nation that were paying big dollars. At that time, Ricky Nelson and the Everly Brothers were the biggest acts, and they were asking about fifteen or twenty thousand dollars for the week—four shows. That was heavy bread for those days.

[3] General Artists Corporation.
[4] Creative Management Associates.
[5] International Creative Management: all of these conglomerates evolved over the years through mergers with outside agencies and/or new principals.

TONY BENNETT

I worked at GAC for another year. During that time, Tony
Bennett called me for lunch one day. He was my favorite singer
and I freaked. I thought someone was putting me on, until I heard
that noticeable "s" that he lisped so well, then I was sure who it
was. He was a client at the agency, and he had read that I had
joined GAC after doing a series of Judy Garland concerts. He
thought that the same series type of concerts could be applied to
his career. And he was right.

After an hour-and-a-half lunch with Tony that day, I got the
feeling that I must do a Carnegie Hall concert for him to re-
stimulate his career. "The Ed Sullivan Show" was *the* show at that
time if you were making it. Tony hadn't been on for a couple of
years, and he hadn't had a hit record in three or four years. His
last record had been an unknown song called "(I Left My Heart
in) San Francisco" which had fallen off the charts. It went as far
as Number 85.

Tony called me later that evening and thanked me for the en-
joyable lunch. He was over at Columbia Studios rehearsing with
his then leader, Ralph Sharon, for a record session. That was
about three or four blocks from my office and I said, "I've got an
idea for you," He said, "I'll be right over." So I saw him twice that
day. At six-thirty he walked in my office, and I said, "Tony, listen,
I want to put you in Carnegie Hall." I had called Carnegie Hall
and got a Friday opening—June 8, 1962. "I want you to do your
own show. I'll get you all the musicians I got for Judy Garland—
twenty-nine men." He was thrilled but very scared. "But I'm a sa-
loon singer, Sid." And I said, "Then why did you call me today? I
don't book nightclubs." He asked me who would promote the
concert. I had already called the one chief guy, the master
promoter, Felix Gurstman, who started us all off in promotions.
He turned me down. He said that nothing was happening with
Tony; he was just good for a week at the Copacabana, and that
was all. But I didn't tell Tony that. Instead, I said to him, "You'll
have to put up your own money. It'll cost you about $10,000 to
advertise it well, to rent the hall, and to get the type of orchestra I
want you to get." He immediately asked me how much we would

make. "We won't make anything. We'll break even if we sell it out." And I actually got him to put up his own bucks, which wasn't easy.

I asked Tony to do something that hadn't been done in those days: to take three hundred tickets and give them to every executive and every kid at Columbia Records. The clerks, the secretaries, the switchboard girls, the shoeshine boy—they all got free tickets. Record companies weren't into buying tickets and supporting concerts in those days. I had also plastered Tony's face—that famous sketch of him—on every lamppost in New York and attacked the Italian neighborhoods with handbills, 100,000 of them. The concert was worked like no concert had ever been worked before. And the results paid off.

The next Monday, after the concert, all Columbia Records could talk about was the Tony Bennett concert the previous Friday. The entire staff had come out and had enjoyed themselves immensely. Ed Sullivan called him two days later after he read the reviews, and Tony was back on the Sullivan show. And then every executive, file clerk, and promotion man at Columbia went to work on Tony's last record, "San Francisco," and it became his greatest hit.

I'D BE A BALLAD SINGER

Judy Garland was one of my favorite singers—like Bennett was. Even though I was involved in rock and jazz, I loved the ballad singers. I guess, if I had my life to live over again I'd be a ballad singer. I respond emotionally to them. And I just *had* to play Garland.

I took her out on a series of tours, and we became tremendous friends. We danced after the concerts. But she had this unfortunate dependence on booze, and one of the requirements was that a big bottle of wine with a long stem and a branch had to be in her dressing room. That was her medicine, and she needed it to function. And by the time the show was over, I'd almost be supporting her on the dance floor. She was really a great woman, though, and a gifted artist. She cared a lot about people, but didn't care enough about herself.

One time, in Montreal at the Forum, we had an overflow

crowd, and she wasn't going on because she had laryngitis. And just an hour before, she had yelled across the huge lobby of our hotel—which was about a block long—"Hey, Sid, can I give you a lift?" So I just knew it couldn't be laryngitis. She called me at my little office from which I was working out of up there, and I went over to her dressing room. When I got there, she whispered to me, "Sid, I can't talk. I can't go on tonight." So I immediately picked up a phone in her dressing room which was only for *incoming* calls—one of those on which you can't dial out—and I feigned a phone call to her personal physician in New York. I said, "Dr. Som, you *must* fly up to Montreal right away. Judy's in concert and is about to go on shortly. And she's got laryngitis. I'll send a private plane for you. She can't go on unless you get here." I hung up the phone, and she looked at me, kissed me, and said, "Sid, you're the best." All of a sudden she found her voice back again, went on ten minutes later, and gave one of the great shows of all time. And she never even asked where Dr. Som was!

Judy was lonely as hell, looking for friends, needing people, insecure—as many stars are—but she never stood me up on a date during a time in her career when she was considered unreliable by most promoters. She always sang at her peak for me. I was one of the lucky ones.

In a lot of ways.

THE WORD "BEATLEMANIA" APPEARED

I was attending the New School in Greenwich Village taking some evening courses, and one of the courses was a lecture by Max Lerner, the noted news analyst, on American civilization. He would often give us books to read on government and, at one point, he said, "I'd like everyone in this class to read an English newspaper—one a week—to gain an insight into the English form of government." So I'd pick up an English paper or two each week.

After a while I started to see in the slim entertainment pages the name "Beatles" popping up in very small, fine print. After two or three months, the print, which had started out as 8-point light, became 34-point bold. The stories got bigger. And then the word

"Beatlemania" appeared. I watched it spread from Liverpool to London and just felt that this was where I had to go.

As an agent, I couldn't interest any of the heads of GAC, who were astute theatrical bookers, to take on this new group. They thought the name was crazy and gave me every excuse for not letting me go over to see them. So I decided to find out about the young manager whose name I had been reading about: Brian Epstein.

It took me three weeks of almost heavy detective work to get his phone number—LIverpool 6518. I believe it was the home of his parents. His mother answered, and she put Brian on the phone. Well, I hit him with my experience: Tony Bennett at Carnegie Hall, Judy Garland at Carnegie Hall. He told me that he had just seen the picture *Carnegie Hall*,[6] on BBC-TV. It was purely accidental; my timing just happened to be right. So he knew about the tradition of Carnegie, he knew about all the great artists who had appeared there, for he had seen the movie, and I sold him on [the Beatles] doing Carnegie Hall a year later. He said to me, "Mr. Bernstein, how do you know they'll fill it?" I just replied, "Brian, a year from now, they'll fill it. Let's make a deal." So we made a deal on the phone for sixty-five hundred bucks for two shows.

I picked February 12, figuring it was a holiday in the middle of the week—the weekends were reserved for the symphony—and luckily, after we had made the deal on the telephone, I called the hall and the date was available. The rest is history. Ed Sullivan happened to be going through the London airport that summer, and as he got off the plane he saw a couple thousand kids with signs saying, "I Love You Ringo, I Love You George." He asked some kids what it was all about, and they told him it was the Beatles. Well, Sullivan thought the Beatles was an animal act. Being the good showman he was, he booked them onto his show for just three days before my date, which just about insured my date, because there was still no record being played in America. But when I heard that he booked them *twice,* I knew I was home because, in those days, when you appeared twice on Sullivan you were a star.

Somewhere around November or December of 1963, their rec-

[6] Made in 1947 for Universal International.

ords broke in quick succession. By the time the doors opened, the Beatles had the number-one, two, and three records in *Cash Box* and *Billboard*. My tickets, which were priced at $3.50, $4.50, and $5.50, were selling on the streets for $75 and $100. I had never dreamt it would be anything like it was. Up went the barricades because we had three thousand kids inside [Carnegie Hall] and twenty thousand outside on Fifty-seventh Street.

The Carnegie Hall shows very firmly established the Beatles in America. And the following year, of course, I did them at Shea Stadium, which marked the first ball-park booking for a rock act. I knew they could fill it. It was a new challenge, a new vista. Brian and I always made a handshake agreement on the phone. He was a very serious, very straight, not warm but honest guy. He took good care of business, and never changed so much as a comma in our phone agreement. I think, without him, the group might never have flourished with all that talent. He was right for them at the time. When he died it was a very, very untimely passing for a man who I thought was a brilliant businessman. He was a great friend who changed my life by making that deal with me.

THE RASCALS ARE COMING!

My ambition, after doing a second concert with the Beatles at Shea Stadium, was to create an American Beatles. Everybody was now looking for that American pot of gold. So I moved in on a then unknown group called the Rascals.

I was invited up to see them at a barge which had been turned into a discothèque in Westhampton, New York. Actually, a friend of mine had shanghaied me in his car to see them. My friend wasn't into rock or even popular music, but he had been vacationing in the Hamptons and he had called me frantically for several nights in succession saying, "There's a young group up here wearing ridiculous costumes and they're great. People like Bette Davis are dancing up a storm to them. All of Westhampton is waiting in line to see these kids." Well, this was just prior to my first Shea Stadium concert with the Beatles, and I just didn't feel like going. But he coerced me, and I wound up at The Barge to see the Young Rascals.

The Rascals were street kids, tough kids, and when I went to

Westhampton to see them, they were dressed in stupid outfits: Buster Brown shoes like Pilgrims would wear, Buster Brown collars like little eight-year-old boys wore, flowing ties, and knicker pants. Awful. At the time, I wasn't a manager. In fact, in addition to being a promoter, I was being paid $300 a week as a consultant to a TV show on NBC called "Hullabaloo." And just the week before, Frankie Valli and the Four Seasons had been appearing on the show and had asked me to manage them. I turned them down because I didn't want to get into management. But when I heard the Rascals, I got goose bumps. I just knew I had to manage them. So I left promotion slowly.

I went after them against some pretty heavy record company competition. The reason I got them was because of my association with the Beatles—which ruled out other interested parties like Phil Spector and other very important names.

To kick off their careers, I used the electric sign during the first Beatles' Shea Stadium concert saying: "The Rascals Are Coming! The Rascals Are Coming!" We also handed out two thousand buttons that read: "I'm a Rascals Fan."

I was getting offers from record companies all over the world for the next week or two, and these companies had never even *heard* them. Atlantic Records had very few white acts—like Shaw Artists, whom I had worked for earlier—and I just felt we would be unique there being the only white group. It was my judgment that they would give us extra effort. And they were in the midst of signing another white act which I thought a lot of named Sonny and Cher.

Felix was the real soul and energy of the Rascals. He had an incredible amount of energy and a constant drive toward achieving success. Had the group not broken up, he and Eddie Brigati would probably still be writing magnificent songs. But who knows why groups break up? We had been together seven and a half years and they probably just got tired of working. Once Eddie left, though, it was never the same. Gene soon left thereafter, and the group was shot.

The five years on Atlantic were wonderful; the two years on Columbia without Eddie were not very meaningful. We loved being with Atlantic through the first five years. The company was small and they really got behind you. Now it's so big. But then everyone cared. We were a New York-based group; they were a New York-based company. And Jerry Wexler became a papa to the four boys. When we switched to Columbia, it was because we hadn't had a hit in the last year with Atlantic, so the contract renewal price wasn't significant enough, and Wexler gave us his blessing to find a much better offer. I did through Clive Davis at Columbia and we signed there. But Eddie quit on the eve of signing the Columbia contract.

I GOT SWEPT AWAY

As a result of my success with the Rascals, I was able to meet a lot of other singers, performers, and groups who called and romanced my services as a manager. One of those groups lived in the Village, where I lived. In fact, one of the guys in the group lived in my building, as did Jerry Schoenbaum[7] and Howie Solomon.[8]

I went to see this group one night at the Phone Booth, a club where I had played the Rascals to resounding success. It was a little place that seated only 120 people—so every night looked like New Year's Eve because the audiences numbered three or four hundred and took thirty days for everyone to get in. Because I went to see this new group at the Phone Booth, which had been the scene of such fond memories for me, I got swept away by them and decided to manage and promote them. They were the Blues Project.

Because they didn't have the advantage of a hit record, it wasn't as easy as it had been for me with the Rascals. But on the basis of my reputation, I was still able to book them across America. I took them from a $600-per-week figure at the Cafe Au Go Go to a $3,500-a-night situation. I was with the Blues Project almost a year until they broke up. Danny Kalb, the guitarist and leader of the group, had a few personal problems and without him it was useless to go on.

But the Blues Project and the Rascals helped to establish me as the peer in the United States at this time in terms of managing

7 Jerry Schoenbaum was president of Verve/Folkways Records then.

8 Howie Solomon was the owner of the Cafe Au Go Go, a Village club which played successful recording acts.

rock groups. Soon after my stint with the Blues Project, Nat Weiss,[9] who was Brian Epstein's closest friend in America at the time, asked me whether I would be interested in becoming a partner with Brian. Nat had met with Brian in New York with a new chap for whom Nat had this master plan of the three of us becoming partners in everything except the Beatles, and we would build an empire. On the advice of my accountants, I turned the deal down. This new chap turned out to be a guy named Robert Stigwood.

I WENT TO WORK WITH A VENGEANCE

After being the manager of the Blues Project, I spent a couple years working as president of Management III,[10] and it finally got to a point where I couldn't handle working for somebody else anymore. So, one morning while I was shaving, I just made up my mind and said, "That's it! No more!" I had to be my own boss, do or die. So I quit.

I didn't know what to do after that. I could have become an agent again, I could have gone back into management, I could have gone back to promoting concerts. But a friend of mine said, "Sid, why don't you go back to where you had your greatest success, the start of it all—England." I wasn't sure of what the musical scene was back in England, but I soon found out.

I heard about the Bay City Rollers from a young boy working in my office whose musical intuition I have yet to find a peer for. David Stein used to be a rock critic and worked for me for about four years, and it was David who told me about the Bay City Rollers. The next night I was on a plane to London to meet the manager in Edinburgh. They were delighted that I was interested because of my previous association with the Beatles. Well, I got carried away with them, and I said I would break them in America—and I did.

Larry Uttal, who was then the head of Bell Records [which is now Arista Records], had signed them when they were fifteen.

[9] A prominent music business attorney and president of Nemporer Records.
[10] Owned by Jerry Weintraub, Management III currently represents such diverse acts as John Denver and Frank Sinatra.

And when Larry left Bell, Clive Davis took over. Now Clive is a man of very particular tastes. And he also likes to have his stamp of approval on all his artists. The Bay City Rollers were not his, he had inherited them, and musically they were not his cup of tea.

Clive said, "The American kids are too sophisticated. You're putting your credibility on the line, Sid. Let it work for us on our label in England. I don't think the American kids will buy it." The next day I went to work with a vengeance—with an opinion of my own, with all the respect I do have for Clive Davis—and I broke the act.

They've sold more than four million records, and Clive couldn't be a happier man.

ON LAURA NYRO

Laura Nyro is an old friend of mine. I turned her down about nine years ago when I fell asleep while she auditioned for me for her first record. I fell asleep! Snored in her living room while she played for me. I was taken there by a kid who worked in the mail room at the William Morris Agency named David Geffen. He said that she was going to be a big star, and I slighted her by falling asleep. I was probably tired from running to the bank with Rascal money.

But Laura and I became pretty good friends, and Felix Cavaliere of the Rascals produced one of her albums, so I got to see her often in the studio.

Recently, we met over breakfast and made a deal for her to go back to work. She had a marriage that had lasted only a few years, had been out of the scene for four years while she lived up in Massachusetts, and when that ended she didn't know what to do with herself, so she went back into the studio to record. She did *Smile* for Columbia, and went on the road after finishing it. At this point, she's been working longer than she ever worked at one time and enjoying it, so I'm optimistic. She's probably the sweetest person I've ever worked with, but she has her rules which I find a little uncomfortable: no TV appearances, no interviews, no hustle —but this is her style. I can live with that because she's such a superb artist; I must compromise because this is her life, a private life, and I respect her for that. Even though it kills me!

THE MANAGER'S ROLE

A good manager's job can never be fully explained because it's endless. He has to be totally candid with his clients, let them know the truth as you see it, call the shots as you see them. If the performance is lacking or the show just doesn't make it, tell the act up front.

A manager has an incredible amount of responsibilities. They are being a nurse, being a doctor, being a philosopher, being a psychiatrist, being a banker—if you can afford to be one—being a friend and an ally, their wise man, their medicine, their public relations man, their troubleshooter, and, above all, a manager has to understand the group.

Today there is an overabundance of great talent, but I've found that the kind of personality it takes to be a manager plus know-how plus instinct to know what to do at a given time has caused a great deficiency in capable managers. A manager has to understand the needs of the artist plus temperament in addition to economics, and must be able to bridge all the problems that exist between artist and employer, between artist and audience, between artist and all other contacts he must make: media, record company, etc. So a manager has to be uniquely gifted to deal with all these other problems that result from handling an artist. This is the reason why there aren't many good managers. It looks like an easy business, but it's not—because you're dealing with human beings and it takes a lot of good judgment under pressure. In New York, it's hard to think of ten good managers. Or ten good managers across the United States.

You know, you can do fifty things right for an artist, but the minute you make your first error—whether or not it's an accident or something beyond your control—you're a bum.

My big weakness with management is that I allow myself to get very close to the people I represent. I expose myself. I'm not a tough guy, so once people find that out it doesn't take them too long to absolutely take advantage of me and my rather quiet personality. They mistake my gentleness for weakness. But I've been angry a few times lately and it's been working for me.

Maybe I'll lose some weight as a result.

Mary Martin: A&R

To a person unfamiliar with the responsibilities of the position, the role of the record company A&R (artists and repertoire) co-ordinator appears both glamorous and facile. Outwardly, they are the people who find new acts and sign them to their respective labels. In fact, the capacities of being an A&R person are expansive and vexatious and are composed of multiple subtexts ranging from the distinguishing of commercial music to corporate economics to interoffice finesse to relating to the public. For it is the A&R person who must be able to create a viable package of talent and assemble its facets with polish and precision.

Ultimately, an A&R person must be able to spot a great new talent. But those moments come far and few between and only after spending countless hours sifting through tape-recorded auditions and spending nights at any showcase club which has a reputation for turning up talented people. Once that initial signing has been undertaken, the star-making machinery must swing into full gear: the correct producer must be paired with the artist, complimentary songs are chosen and whittled down for inclusion in recording, the proper studio contracted, a realistic recording budget is established and adhered to—all these areas must be affected for the chemistry to occur.

Additionally, the A&R co-ordinator must convince everybody within the sphere of the record company that the artist is worthy of their efforts and rally them behind a carefully planned campaign. The money must come through, publicity has got to be effective, marketing must be directed at the correct audience, the promotion people in the field must be attuned to the music and the artist so they are able to transmit the excitement to the disc jockeys and the distributors.

Each time the A&R person signs a new act, he is putting his reputation on the line. Intuition and instinct are held up to cursory examinations at all levels. But a good A&R person is right too often to write off a new "find" to chance, and the extreme pressure of delivering the goods is an expendable component in return for the elation of making it all come together.

Mary Martin has both the "ears" and the ability which are an absolute necessity in her position as East Coast director of A&R for Warner Bros. Records. Beginning in management, she apprenticed with Albert Grossman and later assumed total managerial responsibilities for such celebrated music people as Leonard Cohen and Van Morrison.

As an A&R director, Mary works slowly and stubbornly over each detail which will ultimately affect her artist's career. She exercises her mind's eye in visions of finished product and audience response, and once she has that image, she works toward achieving it with unmitigated determination.

THE RESULT OF A BROKEN HEART

I was raised in Toronto, and I used to go out with a folk singer who is now married to Elizabeth Ashley. He was my first beau, a really good folk singer. But I soon discovered that he loved my best friend, and I decided it was time to leave Canada. So I got together my sixty bucks in American Express money, got on a bus, and came to New York, where I had a couple of friends. One of them worked for Albert Grossman and John Court—John Court

being the most negatively magnetic man on the face of the earth. I
got a job working as their receptionist: "PLaza 2-8715!" I had no
skills. I came to New York as the result of a broken heart.

Albert's office was an exciting place to be. This was about 1963.
Dylan was just lurking in the background at Gerde's Folk City.
He had made his first record. Peter, Paul and Mary were doing
well. Odetta was the grand lady of the office. Ian and Sylvia were
there. So it was all the primo folk artists. Working there was just
wonderful.

I was then shipped back to Canada because I was told that, perhaps, if I wanted to be successful, I should (a) take a vacation,
and (b) learn how to type. So I got my skills together, came back
to America, and worked for Stan Getz for a while. But I had to be
in the office at nine o'clock in the morning, and that was just completely against my code of ethics. Albert Grossman called me and
asked me to come back and work for him. I was flattered. So
when I went back, he was doing the same acts, but they were a
whole lot more successful. Peter, Paul and Mary were being
major, Dylan was about to break into the $2,500-a-night category,
and Odetta was still the grand lady of the office.

I learned a lot working for Albert. I learned about what it
means to have class and effort and being first and having pride. I
also learned other things that have become valuable. For instance,
every now and again Albert was "inaccessible" to promoters and
booking agents. I learned how to buff for him, and I became good
at it.

DYLAN AND THE HAWKS

At the time when the Byrds had their little Bob Dylan hit,[1]
Dylan came into the office to listen to it. He was sitting in Albert's
office, and it was the first time he heard what was then termed folk
rock. Well, Dylan was small in frame and every so often he would
hunch over just a bit. And he was hunched over Albert's desk listening to it, puzzled about where music was going and how he was
going to fit into all of this.

When I was young, I had spent many a day at the Friar's Tav-

[1] Mr. Tambourine Man.

ern in Toronto swooning over a group called Levon and the Hawks, and I became friends with the bass player, Rick Danko. And I had always remembered that group because they had played together so long and were so tight. Those lads were so fine.

I told Bob [Dylan] that perhaps what he should do is go up to Toronto and listen to these guys. He might be interested in what they did and incorporate it into his musical future. So, at one particular point, he did. And that was the Band way back then. And Dylan and the Band got along fine. But when he first heard them, they had never heard about Bob Dylan, they had never heard "Mr. Tambourine Man," and they didn't know much else. So there was a great deal of sharing of musical wealth.

LADIES AND GENTLEMEN, MR. LEONARD COHEN

I had for many years, as a Canadian, loved the works of Leonard Cohen—the printed page. And it was very important growing up that those books were held close to me so I just had a frame of reference with Leonard's poems. So, about 1966, I finally got to meet him. He was just finishing "Beautiful Losers" and had completed a speaking tour of Canadian universities, and he was real good. He had every single quality that a wonderful entertainer should have. He had a good sense of humor, a real flow to his material, and then he started to sing songs. He had also been offered the position of Minister of Tourism for the black power movement in London and was thinking that perhaps he could address himself to that. He might make some money. But he came to the decision that he owed it to himself to reach a broader audience and decided that his songs should be heard on record. When he asked me if I would do that—to help him get to artists and record himself—I said, "Dream come true!" I left Albert Grossman's office in a state of grace. I may not have had the space to grow within Albert's office, but he provided me with my own space to grow.

When I started to manage Leonard Cohen, I was basically real naïve. We made some tapes and initiated the going around with them to the record companies. Columbia, MGM/Verve, and Elektra. I wanted Leonard to be at Columbia really badly, because it was at that point that Dylan was seriously thinking about going to MGM, and I thought Leonard would fill in the void [left by Dylan at Columbia]. I had this film of Leonard called *Ladies and Gentlemen, Mr. Leonard Cohen,* done by the National Film Board of Canada, and after you saw the film you really understood the man. I showed the film to John Hammond, Sr., took John the poems, introduced him to Leonard, and they got along real well. Leonard went to Columbia Records with John Hammond as the antenna of what is new, of what is young. Leonard was trusting of John and, in turn, he was great with the Columbia Records people.

Jac Holtzman[2] was very anxious to record Leonard, but what always goes wrong when people in the record business think they're dealing with novices is that they get greedy. Elektra wanted his music publishing, and we took a pass on that. Jerry Schoenbaum, who *was* MGM/Verve in those days, wanted Leonard Cohen too. He had seen the film and liked it. But I started to tap dance when I realized we were hot, and Jerry got mad. He threatened us. He said, "If your artist doesn't sign with this label, I'll make sure he's never successful." This was surprising, because Jerry's not all that bad of a guy. And his instinct for artists were always dead-on accurate. I have a feeling that he said what he said out of frustration. So Leonard Cohen signed with Columbia.

John Hammond was such a supportive human being. There are not enough words to talk about how receptive he was. He stood up all the way for Leonard while still maintaining the dignity of a record executive. He was very much of a teacher to me. He drew a contract that allowed Leonard to have the same kind of royalty in Canada as he received in the United States—which was unheard of. Leonard was also the last person signed to Columbia to get free studio time. Columbia had always given that to their artists, and the more that Bob Dylan and the other artists recorded, the more Columbia saw that free studio time was silly.[3]

After Leonard signed, the most important thing I had to do was to create a mystique, because Leonard Cohen was just not the

---

[2] The founder of Elektra Records, Jac Holtzman was president of the company before he sold out to what is now Warner-Elektra-Atlantic.

[3] Elsewhere in this book, John Hammond recalls that Dylan's first album cost $408 dollars to make. Today, recording costs are upward of $35,000.

kind of man you turned out on the road. He only did a couple
concerts, and, on several of them, he wasn't prepared so he came
out and apologized to the audience and walked off. The first thing
I did was to put Leonard Cohen into my bathtub with my new
tape recorder, and I made demos of him singing his songs. Before
Leonard's first album came out, we had circulated the demos and
Judy Collins recorded "Suzanne" and "Dress Rehearsal Rag,"
which established Leonard as a singer/songwriter. Her next
album, *Wildflowers,* had three Leonard Cohen songs on it. So we
did manage to make a few bucks on his publishing and create an
image for Leonard.

Leonard was *my* teacher. I took a lot of council from what he
took as his council which was the *I Ching.* Leonard was fearless,
he was dedicated, and he was a sham. He found making records a
really painful experience, and that's why the first one took almost
a year and a half to make and there were so many changes of
producers between John Hammond and John Simon. Leonard
was always able to manipulate people in a righteous way and
sometimes in an evil way.

But every so often there are some people who really do have
the need to commit suicide in one way or another to either keep
themselves on the tightrope or to satisfy the need of inflicting
pain. And after Leonard decided my representation wasn't enough
for him, I really do believe Leonard had fulfilled his obligation to
himself through me. Because the *I Ching* said three years of gentle
penetration, and that's exactly what we did together—for three
years. And then Leonard committed his own form of suicide in his
own way.

THAT'S VAN MORRISON!

Van Morrison called me one day just as I was winding down
the Leonard Cohen affairs. So I was particularly traumatized, perhaps not all that receptive to anybody. And he said, "Richard
Manuel[4] said you'll take good care of me." And I said, "Sure—
why don't you come by? I'll listen to your record." It was *Moondance,* and I was no rock and roller and I didn't really know who

[4] Drummer for the Band.

Van Morrison was at all. Perhaps I had heard "Brown Eyed Girl" somewhere along the line, but not that I could recall.

So this dishrevelled (*sic*), curious little man with his odd sidekick came stumbling into my office and I thought, "Holy hell!" *That's* Van Morrison?! But then I *heard* the album *Moondance,* and I was really knocked out. I had met Mo Ostin[5] on several occasions, and Andy Wickham[6] was a friend of mine, and they all worked at Warner's, so I had to get the reading [on Van] from them. And the more I talked with people, the more it seemed that he had a really hard time coming to grips with the music business—responsibilities and so forth. The more I liked the challenge. Van never signed a management agreement with me. I felt that he had paid enough dues in his past that it was time for somebody to show him some good faith and support.

The first thing I did for Van was to get him out of a production contract with [Bob] Schwaid and [Lewis] Merenstein. The kind of contracts Van had with those people were rude. To my knowledge Van never received any royalties on his music publishing with them.

In addition to that, he was part of a deal that included several other, lesser known songwriters, and because he was the only substantial money-maker, he bore the lion's share of the recoupment. And he didn't even know this was the arrangement. That's mean, you know. Well, I introduced Van to a lawyer, Fabulous Fred Gershon, who got him out of those contracts and stood by him through the whole dirty business. It was scaring poor Van, very painful for him.

I was only with Van for a year and a half—*Moondance* through *Tupelo Honey.* I saw him move from Woodstock to California and I was glad. I felt that Woodstock was just a debilitating place for any creative person. And he and Richard Manuel, who lived in Woodstock, did carouse a little bit too often, jeopardizing both of their respective lives. They did like the sauce, and they were not particularly conscientious drivers around the hills of Woodstock. I got real worried in that respect, and one day I put the word out that I wanted a driver for Van. And this little boy showed up at Van's house one day and said, "Hello, my name is Larry and I'm your driver." And Van just loved that.

[5] Chairman of the board and president of Warner Bros. Records.
[6] Director of Warner Bros. Records country music division.

The one thing Van *didn't* like to do was going out to perform with a band. But he knew that he'd have to put the bit in his teeth and do it. Actually, working with Van wasn't any more painstaking for me than working with Leonard. I had a deep respect for Van Morrison's talent. I adored him, even though he was perhaps difficult at times.

After I got Van in the clear with that production contract, he called me up one day and said, "I've got all these people to take care of me, I've got records to make, and I just don't think there's any money for you." He was living in Northern California above San Francisco in Fairfax, and I sent him a telegram that said, "I quit! All good things. Love Mary." And that was the end of that.

Van Morrison had one quality that he will probably never lose, and that's the torment he goes through. When things are going well, he would push the destruct button. It's true, and it's really sad. But my fond memories of Van Morrison are that I saw him grow from a boy into a man. I think I had a lot to do with that, and that made me proud. I still like him a lot. He was in New York a couple years ago, at the Felt Forum, and he looked me dead in the eye and said, "How are you, Mary?" And I knew that he really meant it. He spiritually gave me a big hug. And I thought, Van, you're doing just fine.

I'M BORED

I went back to Canada after that and thought I'd just forget about Mary Martin Management, Inc. I got a job reading scripts for the Canada Film Development Association and did some radio shows about what was going on in America. I just flitted and farted about, but I got robbed four fucking times and got to the point where I said, "This is hogwash. Canada's full of shit."

One day, I called Mo Ostin and said, "I'm bored." And he told me to get on a plane and come to Burbank to discuss my boredom. *That day* I got on the airplane and was in Mo's office the next morning. And at lunch, he appointed me the director of A&R for Warner Bros. East Coast office. I mean, I had had good taste in the past, but this was *something else!* He wanted me to look for and discover new talent for the label and, perhaps, re-establish some of my contacts with my old pals who were artists so that when their contracts expired with other labels maybe they would come over to Warner's. The first letter I wrote was to Bob Dylan.

At that time, James Taylor was doing real well for the label, Randy Newman was beginning to emerge, Deep Purple was superlative, Alice Cooper was peaking, and I was really happy about coming back to New York because I like the city so much.

I'M ONLY A CATALYST

As an A&R person, my main function working with an artist is to make sure that the package is attractive to the record company. I always keep that at the forefront of my mind. Management must be there—compatible not only to Warner Bros., but to the artist —and a producer. And I help the artist select good management and production if they don't already have that.

I don't go searching for songs for artists. Many A&R people do, but I don't think I'm necessarily qualified to make that contribution. I feel that once a producer has become associated with a particular artist, it's a producer-artist relationship which must find the right material. They're the ones who should be talking music, and I don't trespass that bond. I did it once, though. When Anne Murray was floundering, I heard a song called "Danny's Song" and played it for about three days. Then I called up Brian Ahern, Anne's producer, and told him that he must record it with her. Sometimes I can hear things, but most times I can't. I don't profess to have the greatest ears. The producer and the arranger must set the style. I'm only a catalyst. I draw the forces together.

I've been trying very hard lately to be conscious of what is mass appeal. But usually I am drawn to an artist by my own sensibilities, and I think that is reflected by the people who I have signed, Commander Cody, Dory Previn, Chip Taylor, the Good Rats, and Emmylou Harris.

I MUST HAVE CHIP TAYLOR

When I was in Los Angeles after the Van Morrison episode, I listened to a lot of the great records a friend used to keep around his house. And one of those records was by a boy named Chip Taylor. When I heard it, it was another case of my swooning. I just thought that this was one of the most crafted musicians that I had ever heard. I'm a real fall guy for low, growling voices. And I thought, "I must have Chip Taylor. I absolutely must if that is my job—to get artists."

Well, Chip was about to sever his relationship with Buddah Records and I was there. And one day someone said they would introduce him to me. This was my chance. I had this extremely large desk with a big hole in the middle of it. And when Chip came in, I was under the desk. I mean, that was the only place I could think of to go. Well, he finally signed to Warner Bros.

He made a really nice first record. When I first heard it, though, I thought, Oh my goodness, there's only one song on the album the people in Burbank [Warner Bros. West Coast office] will understand. And that was "The Likes of Louise." Warner's really did apply a great deal of money, effort, and time into Chip Taylor. The promotion campaign was really well thought out, and then it was up to the artist. But Chip Taylor really let himself down. He had no management. He made a second record and then renegotiated his contract and was signed to our country division. But his records just never sold.

I believed it was very important to Chip Taylor to have a producer, but he never wanted that. He's with Columbia now, and I hope he addresses himself to making better records—records more viable to the general public. He has to choose a producer who allows the roughness to surface because that's one of the charms of Chip Taylor.

My day begins at night. I spend an awful lot of time going to the clubs on the East Coast, mostly in New York. What I hope to do is come across someone real interesting—a virgin: an artist who hasn't been ravaged by the music business, who hasn't been ill-advised by a lousy manager, someone who hasn't been done dirty in another record deal. Gee, what a fantasy, but I guess there are a few artists out there with those qualities. I usually get home about two in the morning, so I'm never really very serious about getting up at nine o'clock in the morning. I get into the office at about noon and spend most of my day on the phone.

I never listen to tapes during the day. Never. There are just too many distractions in the office. Can you imagine my putting on your tape, being halfway through the first song, and then be interrupted by a half-dozen phone calls or my secretary? How exasperating that would be for a musician. By the time I got back to listening I would either have forgotten completely about what I had heard in bits and pieces the first time around or be so sick of hearing the opening song again. I take a bagful of material home over the weekend and listen to them with the headphones on.

I also employ three or four free-lancers, listeners who help with the mail that comes in—the unsolicited tapes. They sort through that for me and, if anything catches their ears, then I listen to it. And I encourage all my free-lancers to find somebody to whom I can say, "I'll back you!" But they haven't done that yet.

One of my jobs is putting artists with the right producer. You see, marriages work, and the best example of that is Emmylou Harris and Brian Ahern.

I had been told that I should go see Emmylou Harris by Don Schmitzerle, one of the general managers in Burbank who is a wonderful man. So I thought, "Uggh! Another artiste." But I went to Washington twice to see Emmylou, and she was great. I loved her slightly unabashed brazenness. She was playing for a particularly rough audience—all drunk—and Emmy had absolutely no compunction about telling the people to shut up. That she didn't want to play "Orange Blossom Special."

The whole exercise for me was that I had learned, by virtue of the Chip Taylor episode, that unless there was a producer of certain merit and track record, it would be really silly to present someone like Emmylou Harris to Warner Bros. because they wouldn't understand her. The package had to be complete. Enter Brian Ahern. Then it was real easy to tell Warner Bros. "This is going to be your Anne Murray." And Emmylou Harris is certainly *not* an Anne Murray. But those are the kind of graphic terms with which I have to communicate. Luckily Brian Ahern came to see her and just fell in love with Emmy.[7] And they make nice records. I'm really proud of that.

WE WILL HELP YOU

It's a very curious thing, but whenever I'm interested in signing someone to the label, I have to sell him or her to the rest of the record company as well. I start with the other A&R people and

[7] Literally. They married in January 1977.

the promotion people because I feel they are the most important people there [to get behind an artist]. I think that if I had spent more time with them on Chip Taylor, that album might have surfaced a whole bunch better. I would play a demo for them and talk about the artist to get their ideas. There must also be a commitment from the people in the branch offices. They have to say, "Yes, we will help you," if that artist is to get his or her fair shake. But then the artist cannot blame the record company if the company lives up to all those commitments and the record is not terrific.

I can also sign an artist by going straight to Mo Ostin and saying, "I've got an artist I want to sign right now." And Mo says, "Fine." But that's a privilege which I don't abuse very often. But I do believe that the people I sign deserve a shot, and if it's necessary I see Mo, then I do.

TWO CULTURES

Our West Coast office has started to broaden itself a whole lot. They've hired a few additional in-house producers like Steve Barri who just finished a Dion album[8] and Gary Katz, who produces Steely Dan. But even though they've begun to broaden their outlook on music, we have two extremely different cultures between our East and West Coast offices.

I had three years ago suggested to Lenny (Waronker)[9] that we might try and do some serious investigating of Bruce Springsteen. That came from the East Coast. Bruce was one of the best performers I had ever seen. And if there was anybody who could ever assume the role of King, I do believe it is Springsteen. There has never been a rock and roll performer who gives as much to his audience as Bruce. I would go to see him and I would cry and I would laugh and I would get real angry. But [our West Coast office] could never hear it. They couldn't understand his music. They thought he was not an innovator and that his songs were not any good. But, you know, I don't think any of them fucking *listened* to his records. Just the name Bruce Springsteen *East Coast* turned them off. I may be a little bit paranoid, but there is a real

[8] *Streetheart.*
[9] Director of A&R and staff producer for Warner Bros. Records.

cultural difference and in that lies the real reason why I never per-
severed hard with Patti Smith. She would not have made it at
Warner Bros. Records. They wouldn't have understood what she
was trying to do.

And that's a serious drawback about being associated with
Warner Bros. and being on the East Coast. The guys out there [in
Burbank] look at me real funny when I try to interest them in an
Eastern act. So, as an A&R person, it takes me a lot longer to get
something accomplished because I have to spend so much of my
time spoon-feeding it to the West Coast. I've gotten some goodies
past them in spite of their cement headedness.

RARE RECORDS

I really believe that the artist's responsibility to the record company is delivering the best possible product, and by *best,* I mean
accessible to the airwaves for the media within the talent's perspective. Not all this self-indulgent bullshit that's being written to
mesmerize little teenagers' minds. That's a lot of bull. Commer-
ciality should be truly born in mind.

Leon Redbone, for instance, is a good example of the opposite
of that. His album was not commercial. It received very little
airplay, and Warner Bros. did not make a lot of money from it.
But when Leon Redbone went off to do his gigs, the album sold as
a result of him being in a particular area. There was sporadic met-
ropolitan airplay in places like Seattle and Philadelphia, but I
don't think that the record company capitalized on it. But it was
such a rare record that I don't think any of the people in sales or
promotion really understood what the record was. You see, it was
unique.

Dory Previn is another example of a rare record. Her first one
for the company lived up to that accessibility and responsibility an
artist should have, but Warner Bros. did not live up to their responsibilities and promises which they had given to her. I think
Warner Bros. was intimidated a little bit because I think if they
had, in fact, *listened* to Dory's album, the words were so clearly
defined that there was very little room for their particular thoughts
of what it was. It was so definitive. It was humorous, it was musical, and it was well done. You see, a record company can also
fuck up the process as well.

MO

Mo Ostin has saved my life on more than one occasion. There was a time when I could not get the wheels functioning at Columbia Records for Leonard Cohen, and I just thought the best thing I could do was to ask Mo to buy up Leonard's contract. So I called him up and he told me that the most important thing for me to do was to make sure a record—*any* record—comes out. Too much time had already gone by and Leonard was losing his credibility as an artist. Straight ahead advice. I've got to respect that.

He's a very busy man. And the complexion of Warner Bros. has changed over the last seven years because of the Warner Communications setup, whereby we are not a family company so much anymore as we are an enormous corporation. So Mo isn't quite as accessible as he once was because his concerns are more bottom line than they are creative. But Mo has always believed that his nurtured department is the A&R department and he has built—through Lenny Waronker, Russ Titleman, Teddy Templeman, and now Steve Barri and Gary Katz—an incredibly productive A&R department. When, at a time, it was just not fashionable to have in-house producers, Mo Ostin always believed that the backbone of his company was going to be the A&R department. So Mo purported that particular style, and he was right.

And Joe Smith,[10] when he was with Warner Bros. had the completely opposite style, which was fast, quick productions with outside independent producers—and that was why we had such a good balance. The stuff that Mo involved himself in was the Gordon Lightfoots, the Maria Muldaurs, the Randy Newmans, and that gave Warner Bros. a really class reputation, a reputation of caring. And Mo always has and always will care.

IT'S MURDER FOR A WOMAN

When I was managing people, I had—physically, mentally, spiritually—a concept of the differences of a woman being an executive in the music business. But I also had an intense belief in what I was doing and what I wanted to contribute to American

[10] Joe Smith is currently president of Elektra/Asylum Records.

music. If there was any kind of backstabbing, whimpering, or whining by executives in the music business against women, I was not cognizant of it.

However, the more I sit in a record company, the more I believe there is a serious backlash going on of ladies who make a great deal of sense, whose logic is impeccable, whose ideas are valid, and, if given the power to execute, they're just as thorough as any man could be. But it's murder for a woman to achieve that position where she can make those decisions.

Warner Bros. is set up with various departments. There is an area which is called the general management. And these general managers are buffers. They represent the artist and their management to the various departments in Warner Bros. And there was a lady who worked at Warner's and had been there for quite a few years working for a general manager. And that particular general manager left to assume a vice-presidency at Capricorn Records, leaving his lady at Warner Bros. She suggested to the department head that she was capable of assuming the vacant general manager's position. She was. She participated almost as an equal with the man who had left. She was doing half his work. But when it came down to whether or not she would get the position, one of the other general managers said, "I don't believe a lady could do my job." Then the head of the department said to her, "Perhaps you'll type the artist roster." And she left. Now she's managing Fleetwood Mac, and hooray!

I think the discrimination is worse today than it has been, but that's because I'm a little more frustrated. Lenny Waronker—my sweet, wonderful, cowardly boss, ineffective administrator, terrific human being—when I was out in Burbank recently, we were having this discussion about how I thought I had been a conscientious A&R person. I listen to the tapes, I go to the gigs, I spend a lot of time on the road—and he did take a chance on me when he first hired me because I didn't have that kind of experience. And I was a *woman,* and women weren't being handed A&R positions left and right. And Lenny said, "Yes, it *was* very *liberal* of us to give you that job, wasn't it?" He said it in jest, but if I hadn't been as well brought up as I am, I would have boxed his fucking ears!

Barry White

"I've got so much to give . . .
It's gonna take my lifetime,
It's gonna take years and years."

B. WHITE, *I've Got So Much to Give*

Recorded rock and roll has always been a collaborative art, a liberal channeling of creative input drawn together by the perspicacious ear. But in its early years, most of the movement was dictated by the president of the record company, the money man. Recording artists were basically vocalists who cared for little more than putting forth the most dynamic rendition of the song; they couldn't have cared less about recording technique as long as their music came out on a respectable label and was given an honest push. Frequently, by the time the group came into the studio, arrangements of the material had already been written and the studio musicians had been selected. In most cases, even the songs had been chosen before the vocalists had ever been considered. And rehearsals were merely sessions during which the artist was taught the song as the company intended to have it go down.

Over the years, of course, all that has changed. Technical sophistication has been implemented in every phase of recording, brought on by the ever-increasing quality of the music and the discriminating ears of all concerned: the artist, the producer, the en-

gineer, the record company executives, and, most important, the record-buying public. Their fastidiousness has not only refined the recording arts, but has placed demands on the industry requiring constant exploration and experimentation. It has also encouraged persons once celebrated in only a single phase of the business to expand their resources and to become versatile in other areas as well. Hence, we have seen the emergence of the singer-songwriter, the artist-producer, and any number of other hyphenates eager to have a more decisive hand in their careers. One such artist is Barry White. He has not only explored other avenues of creativity, he has assumed unmitigated control of his talents with complete success, alone, comfortable in his private world of music.

Call him the Maestro, call him the Chief, or call him any one of the half-dozen or so titles of musical royalty bestowed upon him by his fans, Barry White remains the soul of rock and roll—a versatile composer-arranger-musician-producer-performer deserving of the éclat which has followed his career at every turn. He has revived the sound of disco music which has renewed the spirit of dancing among young people and has revitalized the sound of self-unconscious, commercial black music.

White's emergence as the auteur came at a time when he, like so many of his musical counterparts, felt that he was being taken advantage of by the rock establishment. Unable to accept their improvidence toward black music, he abandoned the "set" way of giving up control to a major record company and made his own deal which gave him exclusivity of product. He had a basic understanding of the business of music and was able to successfully tackle his aspirations. And as each new level of success came to him, he improved upon it and, subsequently, improved upon his deal.

But aside from White's business and technological acumen, his unique blend of vocals and music remains the essence of his popularity. He is the master of melodic dialogue—half-spoken, half-sung—spinning tales and choruses around his compositions in a whimsical self-satisfaction. That crawling, gravelly voice which he has made his trademark over the course of his hits becomes so much a part of the temperament of the material; it assumes both an I-told-you-so manner and, yet, can beg for forgiveness without changing the timbre of the lyric. Meanwhile, White's orchestrations continue to weave in and out of whatever he chooses to purvey lyrically. His string section—oversized and overpowered—whips around rows of horns, percussion, and a continuous high-hat, not to mention his ladies: the background choir composed of Love Unlimited, who he produces under their own label. Collectively, Barry White's music spells excitement, albeit a touch of imperiousness not usually conveyed so magnanimously in music.

Barry communicates his many directions with a master's hand. His style is not to hint about what he wants to hear but rather to command. There is very little outside contribution other than his own in his sessions and, therefore, one of the many reasons his name is so prevalently displayed on everything he touches. This is not done so much to show himself off as it is to say, "This is what I have to offer. Be the judge of my work and either accept it as I would like you to, or reject it—but on my terms which I have set forth." And that is the same way White has always entered into business arrangements, with a touch of the innovator's arrogance and a vengeance to deliver.

Often a critic discussing a Barry White song will imply that it sounds the same as his previous numbers. Although, for all the sameness of the material—and there is a lot of sameness in the flavor of the song—he manages to capture the listener's interest again and again. He maneuvers you into a lyric or into a beat or into an emotion—he illustrates his feelings through this creative sculpturing of a song—and charges any similarity with a new attitude, be it through music or verse. And these attitudes, these musical statements, are what restore the vitality to each new Barry White offering. Statements of love, statements of hurt, statements of hope.

I CUT EVERYTHING LOOSE

I fell in love with the piano when I was very young. There was just something about it that got to me, and I got into it right away. My mother played quite a bit, and I started playing when I was six years old. I never took lessons. My mother *could* have taught it to

me, but I was too impatient. Now I wish she had. But I wanted to
play the damn thing right away, get into it and *go!*

I really got involved in music through the church when I was
eight. I went from singing in choirs to directing choirs when I was
nine, and when I was ten, I started playing organ there. I had the
piano down pretty good, so I wanted to go to the next best thing
that was handy. My mother kept a piano, but outside of that, we
couldn't afford anything else. I came from a very poor family.
Very poor. As far as bread, we had nothing. We were always
moving because we couldn't afford to stay in one place. But as far
as love and understanding and things like that—we had *plenty* of
that.

I was the only teenager in my area who listened to jazz music.
Now when I talk about an area, I mean twenty-five miles square.
Everybody was listening to rock and roll, but I knew all the rock
and roll tunes. You see, jazz had an adultness to it. It had sub-
stance. And with my mother playing classical music all the time
and my developing an ear for and understanding the classics,
picking up jazz was no problem. I listened to people like Ahmad
Jamal, Miles Davis, Thelonious Monk, Cal Tjader, Hank Craw-
ford, John Coltrane—*yeah* Coltrane!—Coleman Hawkins and
Milt Jackson. I was *really into it!*

It's unusual my liking jazz because my friends weren't into it,
no, sir. But I was always an independent teenager. I never did
what anybody else did. I played a lot of basketball and probably
would have ended up in basketball if I hadn't been drawn so
deeply into music. And you needed an education, you had to go to
college to play basketball, and I didn't have that. I dropped out of
school during my last six months in high school to pursue music.
On my seventeenth birthday, I cut school loose. I cut church
loose. I cut my friends loose. I cut *everything* loose. I decided I
was going to look at the world like it is, and deal with it on that
level. Just me and the world.

HIS NAME IS BARRY WHITE

I was invited to Hollywood by a friend of mine, and decided to
see what was happening out there. It was to a session, the first
recording date I had ever been to. When I got there a group of

people were in the studio clapping their hands to a song called "Tossing an Ice Cube." The song was never a hit, but it belonged to a man named Leon Renee, who owned Class Records, the label that had Bobby Day's "Rockin' Robin." I was sitting on the other side of the glass window watching the union people they had hired try to clap their hands. It was a tricky timing, and they couldn't get it right. So I said to my friend, "I can do it." They had tried fifteen people just to clap to this timing, and Renee was paying fifty dollars. Fifty dollars to me, at that time, was quite a bit of bread. So I said again, "I can do it." And my friend ran into the studio shouting, "My friend can do it!" And Renee said, "Who is he?" 'Cause nobody knew who the hell I was. "His name is Barry White. That's who *he* is." And so, I went in there and did it on one take. And it amazed the man so much that he gave me two hundred dollars. You see, clapping is one of my best talents, and that's one of the secrets to Barry White's success—rhythm.

Anyway, it was 1961, and I started doing this and that for a lot of sessions in California. I used to do all the arranging for people like Jackie De Shannon and a Bob and Earl session called "The Harlem Shuffle," which was a big hit. But most of the things I did then I never got credit for. That was when I was playing the game: you do this for me and I'll do this for you. Shit, I even gave my royalties away without knowing it. But it gave me exposure as an arranger and to the business, and I got to know the right people.

I SWORE I'D NEVER WORK FOR ANYBODY AGAIN

I started producing in 1965. In 1966, I produced a girl named Felice Taylor, who was on Mustang/Bronco Records. I was an A&R man there. I got the job through a friend of mine. I had never been an A&R man, but this friend of mine said, "I'll give you a shot, Barry, if you'll do it." So I had to pretend I knew what an A&R man did. But I always believed that if a man wants to do things bad enough, strange things happen. I started off at forty dollars a week there, and six months later I was making four hundred dollars a week as their vice-president. So it was a very creative thing for me.

I got to work with Bobby Fuller, the man who did "I Fought

the Law," which I produced. Then I did Felice Taylor again and had three number-one records in a row in England with her, the last of which was "Under the Influence of Love." Then, in 1967, Mustang/Bronco went bankrupt, and Bobby Fuller killed himself. The strange thing about it was that nobody knew why Fuller did it. We had been in the studio five nights and five days straight. I was dropping bennies to stay awake because this was my chance to prove that I had the endurance as an A&R man to hang in there. I wanted to prove it to the president of the company. And it was that session that eventually launched me. I was gone—all over the place.

I had so much of me involved in Mustang/Bronco. It hurt me so bad when they went bankrupt. I swore I'd never work for anybody again. Nobody in the record business. And that's when I started Soul Unlimited.

LOVE UNLIMITED

I met my three babies, Love Unlimited, in 1969, and immediately began working on their first album. The first thing a producer learns is that you never become personally involved with your artist. It's bad business. You've got to keep it on a business level, because if something happens you can cut it off just like that, no sweat, no hard feelings, goodbye! There are always more artists. But with Love Unlimited, it was a lot different. Mainly because they had never been in the business before, they had never been hurt by anybody. They were such sweet ladies, and they still are. They wanted to sing professionally, but they were scared. But one day, Linda finally asked me if I was interested in them, and I said, "Yes." We got together, we made certain vows to each other, and they've never been broken. Staying together was one of them. From that came "Walkin' in the Rain with the One I Love"—my first million seller, their first million seller.

After I finished "Walkin' in the Rain," I took the master over to Uni Records. We never got any further than Uni. I didn't want to go there, but I had a partner at the time, Larry Noone, who wanted to go to Uni. I tried to fight it, but we went, and that was my first mistake. Uni wasn't into black music. They were Elton John-oriented, Olivia Newton-John-oriented, they could do won-

ders in that area. But when it came down to what people call
black music—I hate to label it that way, but that's the only way I
can describe it—they couldn't handle it. And they couldn't handle
my girls. But they wanted them very badly and they paid a lot of
money for them.

But they lost the album. We needed from them concentration, a
campaign, promotion, marketing and merchandising, and a will
that they weren't going to lose—they were going to win. Especially after they had had a million seller with the single. There's
no way you're going to lose after that. But they didn't feel that
way. And when a company doesn't get in back of my records,
there's not much I can do besides cussin' the shit out of them and
threatening to jump on a few of them. I try real hard to be
businessfied, but . . . It's real hard to do that when you're from
the ghetto. You're used to when a person's stepping all over you,
getting him off of you—*fast!* You have to learn to develop business tactics as opposed to violence. So I used my power as a
producer, and pulled the album from Uni.

After that, I went on the road with Love Unlimited and discovered a lot of problems. We couldn't get into that lucrative concert
area. We had to work in nightclubs. I tried to figure out what big
star I could go to to let my girls work with, to open the show for
them so that we could get to some bigger money. And up popped
the man! Yes, sir—Barry White! It was a matter of seven months
from when I was looking for it to when it happened. It was the
most incredible thing. And it never even dawned on me that we
could get to concerts through me.

THIS WON'T MISS

I was going to do an album on an artist of mine named Jay
Dee.[1] While I was on the road with Love Unlimited, he got involved in some problems with a writer—fighting and all—and I
released both of them from our agreements. I just cut them loose.
I had rearranged "Standing in the Shadow of Love" for him. Everything except the intro. There was a whole vocal arrangement,

[1] White was under contract to produce Jay Dee independently for Warner
Bros. Records.

but it needed an intro desperately. So I said, "I'm going to see what I can do about that." And I also kept writing for other artists. Later on, I wrote "I Found Someone" and "I've Got So Much to Give" and "Bring Back My Yesterday," and when I played it back on the cassette with me singing on it, it sounded very commercial. So I polished it up, put it together, called Russ Regan[2] and told him that I had a concept for Barry White. I said, "This won't miss, Russ." He listened to me and said, "I think you're right, Barry." He hadn't heard anything, but it was a gut feeling.

So I went into the studio and recorded the concept, and when I came out [and played it for Russ] he shook he was so scared to death. There were only five tracks on the tape. Each was something like eight minutes long, and he wasn't used to that. He was used to nine songs, three minutes each. I told him, "You just put it out." He wasn't going to do it, so I started negotiating with Columbia Records for the album. In between my dealing with Columbia, Elton John heard the album. He stole Russ's copy and took it back to England with him. And that convinced Russ. So Russ called me on the phone pleading with me, "Please bring the album back here. We want to do a job on it." And he put the album out. The rest is history.

ON RUSS REGAN

I first met Russ Regan in 1964. He was a promotion man for Motown [Records] and was working on the Supremes and Marvin Gaye. And he was damned good. In fact, Russ was the best promotion man I ever knew. He was *dangerous!* And he always liked my talents. Russ was a producer, too, but he never had a hit. *And* he used to sing. People didn't know that. But he couldn't make it either as a singer or a producer, and I think I showed Russ a side of himself in me that he always wanted [for himself]. I was always honest with him, and he was always honest with me. We just got together naturally and developed a relationship.

[2] Regan was the president of Uni Records when White signed Love Unlimited there. He is currently the president of 20th Century Records and brought the Barry White deal in as White describes it.

Then, when he became president of Uni Records, I used to go by there with my masters that I was cutting on different people, and he would always sit and analyze them with me. I never tried to sell Russ anything—we just talked and talked and talked, all the time. But he happened to be president of Uni when I took my girls there. And when he heard them, he went crazy for them. He said, "There's no way they're not going to happen. Platinum album time." We bickered and fought until we reached an agreement and put the deal over at [Uni] with him.

Russ is a beautiful human being when people just leave him alone. The man can't stand a lot of executive bullshit. Russ believed in Elton John when everybody over [at Uni] told him he was full of shit, that he didn't know what the fuck he was doing—and that big ol' English superstar just came rolling through there for them. Thanks to Russ. And he also signed Neil Diamond while he was there.

When the decision came up for me to go with a record company, I knew I wanted to be with that man. I knew if he believed in me as an artist, the gears would start rolling, it would happen there. It was only a matter of making him a believer. And he's *certainly* that now. Yes sir!

PEOPLE SAID WE WEREN'T GOING TO MAKE IT

When I decided I was going to perform as Barry White the artist, I had a concept. First, I didn't want to go out on the road with what's *not* on the record. If you make a record with ninety thousand people on it, you'd better take ninety thousand people out there to the audience. That is one of the biggest capitalized movements in the record industry: they cut with violins and horns, and when you pay to see the act they have a little rhythm section backing them up. That's bullshit! To actually put it together is another thing. My managers and I fought and fought to do it. People said we weren't going to make it. We couldn't make it without television. Russ Regan was one who said that. Nobody was going to pay for thirty men to back me up. Now we have sixty pieces in the show. It's all in what a man believes.

We put three minds together to create our concept. We all came up with a lot of ideas, then we pieced them together into an overall picture, and that is what made it a hell of a concept. But we had a problem making it work—especially with black promoters. They said, "We don't want to hear that shit." Soul Train didn't want us on there. They said, "What the fuck do you mean you have twenty-four pieces? Are you crazy?" Well, we finally went on there with forty pieces. "We've never done a show that big in our life." I said, "Fuck that." That was in 1973, and in 1975 we were sitting on there with fifty pieces. People talk shit, but you've got to stick with what you believe.

There was a lot of money involved in getting it off the ground. I miss a lot of money because of that. All the money that the orchestra is getting would go into my pocket. But image is more important to me than the money. You see, there's nobody who could do it this way—*nobody!*

I HAVE TO BE ABLE TO TALK MY MUSIC

I'm just another person completely when I step into the studio —a Jekyll and Hyde. I'm a firm believer that without those hit records, there is no stage. When I get into the studio, I'm very precise, very direct. I'll tell a man what I want and if he can't play it, I show him how to play it or goodbye. But I guess I'm a nice producer to work for. We don't drink, we don't bullshit. We go in, cut the album, and come out to good times and hit records.

I don't rehearse at all before a session. I have five guitar players who I use at once, a drummer, a bass man, me on piano, a conga man, a vibes man, and we get in there and everybody loves each other because there's a creative force that occurs when I record. Musicians play differently when they play on a Barry White session. Then, other producers who use my musicians on their dates bring my records to their sessions and tell the musicians, "I want *this* on my date." But people don't realize that it's not my musicians—it's Barry White the arranger giving them those vibes. That's the difference.

The work begins before I ever get to the studio. *Oh my God, is there work!* Creating it, and then trying to remember it all. The drum groove where the drummer is going to make his roll, what's

going to happen when he makes that roll and how it goes to the
third guitar to accent the first guitar. Nothing gets written down,
and that's the hardest part—remembering, because I can't read
music. I have to be able to talk my music. I had to develop my
own style of communicating my music in the studio, of dealing
with it in my head, of speaking it to the musicians. And believe
me, it comes off. I can walk in, and inside of three hours I can do
a whole album.

My albums are expensive [to record] because of all the pieces I
use, but they would be more expensive if I couldn't get things
down so quickly. We use twenty violins, eight violas, eight cellos,
six French horns—that shit gets up there in cost. When I go in to
mix the tracks onto a master tape, I spend three to four hours on
Barry White and three to four hours on the Love Unlimited Orchestra. If you spend a lot of time on the mix—like most
producers do—you can't get many albums done. I've done over
fifty gold records in four years. So I'm moving! I just finished the
new Barry White album and the new Love Unlimited album, and
I cut twenty-one songs for those in five days. *Music Maestro,
Please*—I did the whole album in a week: cut, mixed, and
mastered. Russ said he needed it quickly.

That pressure and an inner feeling are what really motivate me
to create. I could be anywhere and feel the urge, and I just sit
down to that piano whenever that feeling hits me. I was just in
London and it was about three o'clock in the morning when I got
a *real* feeling. I woke everybody up and said, "Get your asses over
here and listen to this."

MUSIC UNLIMITED

I don't know anything about the state of black music today. I
write music for the world. I'm not into this black music. I don't
know what black music is doing.

I *do* know there aren't a lot of black superstars in any of the
foreign countries—or even in America—and that bothers me. But
we do a tremendous business in foreign countries. The music that
I make is not limited to one nation or color of people. Everybody
can get into it—and everybody does!

I'M STILL CONNECTING

I think I deal with my success very well. I've still got enough
sense to know that a humble man is a man who will get further in
the world than a bigoted or boastful man. I can't act like a rich
man who comes on with that bullshit. I like Barry White the way
he used to be. That's why I'm still that way.

I can still understand somebody struggling over hurdles in life.
I've always admired that. I'm still connecting, man. Some businessmen feel that they're not supposed to help anybody but themselves. I don't believe in that. My mother used to tell me that if
you do something, you should expect to get paid for it. But don't
be surprised if you come out on the long end. And my mother's
always been right.

Grace Slick

"We're something new, We don't quite
    know what it is, or particularly care
We just do it—You gotta do it!
Open your eyes there's a new world a-comin'
Open your eyes there's a new world today
Open your hearts people are lovin'
Open it all we're here to stay!"

P. KANTNER, G. SLICK, J. COVINGTON,
Mau Mau (*Amerikon*)

The urgency of rock is dependent upon its ability to maintain a musical-cultural equilibrium. It (both the music and the culture) is a whirlwind of what is immediate, what is changing, what is necessary, and what is future. Accordingly, rock creates and moves within its evolutionary lifestyles and has, for the last twenty years, been the spokesman for modern society. This society has, of course, been punctuated by staccatoed philosophical face-lifts which have carried its youth, the prime movers of the culture, from passivity to revolution back to passivity. This same fickleness is prevalent in the music. We have moved rhythmically through periods of street-corner doo-wop, Liverpool hysteria, San Francisco-styled rebellion, singer/songwriter self-indulgence, and we are currently resting in a melting pot of musical transience.

Grace Slick—as a member of the Great Society, the Jefferson Airplane, and, currently, the Jefferson Starship—has come through those transitions as a major force in the music culture, a rock and roll revolutionary hell-bent on vibrance and purpose-

fulness and people's rights and music. Most of all music. Few rock enthusiasts will ever forget the image of Grace, head thrown back, eyes closed tightly, wailing the final notes of "Somebody to Love" or "White Rabbit." Or arrogantly encouraging the audience to get up off their posteriors and shake their fists in anger and frustration. Those images have become permanent metaphors of rock and roll history, like Lennon and McCartney sharing a microphone and Peter Townshend smashing his guitar to smithereens on the stage. And trying to recapture them as a part of today would defy all that we shook those fists for. Instead, Grace Slick has continued to be meaningful to today's music by launching phase two of the Starship's time travels, with new ideals, new songs, and new excitement.

Our culture owes much of its electricity to its proponents such as Grace. With the Airplane's rise to prominence in the middle-1960s, we were introduced to a new type of music and thinking called (wishfully) mind-expansion. Musically, it encouraged the exploration of instruments and motifs; philosophically, it stressed freedom and love. The Starship, five years later, are resigned (or neutralized) to the complications of society and have endeavored to reach their people through an updated version of their previous music. Having taken us through our formative stage, they seem satisfied that our minds will function independently and have devoted themselves almost entirely to the music. Still immediate, still changing, still necessary, still looking to the future.

Grace sings as part of a group. Her voice is neither unusual nor extraordinary, yet it provides the group with a reserved identity, a fulcrum on which to shift its many musical styles. Coincidentally, neither does her ego try to dominate the Starship. Onstage, she wanders from member to member joining in harmonies or blending in with a lead vocal. There has always been an intentional defiance in Grace's stage presence, an arrogance which she has gone out of her way to project. Offstage, she exhibits a toughness and sometimes tries to be downright fulsome, but people who know her claim the shield is a defense mechanism and that she is a sensitive woman often caught with her emotional guards down.

For the first time, we are seeing our rock stars age. Danny and the Juniors were sixteen when they went on the road, the Beatles,

*were in their early twenties. Elvis Presley has passed forty. Rock
and roll is no longer a teenage music. Grace Slick has been performing on the road for over a decade. She no longer shakes her
fist or throws objects into the crowd. Nor does she look like a
young girl. But, like all people who possess true talent, she has developed both as an entertainer and a singer—she has matured—
and intends to keep singing what's relevant, what's exciting, what's
rock and roll for a long time to come.*

A REAL PRECOCIOUS KID

Most of my musical influence came from my mother. She was a
performer back in 1930, 1932 and played some radio stuff and a
few hotels. But she wasn't any kind of virtuoso. And her career
didn't last a hell of a long time. When I came along it was take-
care-of-the-kid time, and that was that. But some of her desire to
perform rubbed off on me as a little kid. When I was little, I used
to dress up all the time—all sorts of costumes—and sing and play
the piano for my parents. And I'd dance a little, too. Nothing real
great. I mean, Jesus, I was just a five-year-old kid. A real preco-
cious kid. I never performed in public. My parents weren't like
that, and there was no public when you were that young unless
your parents took you by the neck and pushed you out into show
business. Some kids enjoy that, and some kids are shoved into it.
But not this kid. Believe it or not, I grew up as a normal little kid.

My parents had a windup record player in the house, one of
those contraptions you had to crank to play. And my first songs
were duds like "Say It with Music" and *Peer Gynt Suite,* which,
by the way, is not a dud. I think those were the only records I can
remember being around our house. Records weren't a big item
there. But I did hear a lot of radio. And the music that I listened
to wasn't popular—it was classical. I remember my mother taking
me to see *Fantasia,* and I asked her, "What kind of music is
that?" She said, "Classical." And I said, "Fine, let's buy a bunch
of classical music." Popular records didn't come until later, and
then it was stuff like "No Other Love of Mine," by Perry Como,
and "Stranger in Paradise." I was hooked on that stuff.

I did okay in school. Not a goddamn genius, but not a poor

dumb slob. I got grades based upon what I was taking. If it was something I was interested in, I got A's and B's, and if it was something I was bored with I got C's and D's. There was no in-between. I was so damn stubborn. Like with mathematics, you can bet it was the C's and D's. Couldn't stand it. But in writing and English, it was A's all the way.

While I was in school, I didn't pay much attention to popular music. I couldn't get into the Fifties' rock at all—didn't like it. I'll never forget, a girl friend of mine called me up one night and said, "You ought to see this guy on television named Elvis Presley. He's great." Well, I turned on our set and saw this greaser sliding all over the screen who made me sick. I didn't like him. I think he's an interesting figure right now because I've had a chance to watch the whole rock musical process. But I never cared for that "Be Bop-A-Lula She's My Baby" shit.

YOU'RE OUT!

After school, I did anything I could to support myself. I was a receptionist for two days, but I lost two thousand dollars for the company in two days, so they fired me. Actually, I left people on hold too long. Then I'd get back on the phone and they would get mad at me. I'd say, "I'm terribly sorry, but Mr. So-and-So is busy." And finally I'd say, "I don't care how long you had this account. The guy's busy." What I didn't know was that the chick who used to have the job before me was listening in on the other line to see how my progress was going. And when she heard how I talked to these idiots on the phone, she said, "You're out!" And she was right. I'm not trained for things like that, things like slavery. So I decided to become a model.

To be a model, all I had to do was make up my face—I'd been doing that for years anyway—and lose ten pounds. That wasn't too hard. I thought, This is for me! I modeled for a photographer and did some live stuff, but the job became boring and was full of a lot of boring people. I imagine if you work in New York City and are six feet tall and weigh 105 pounds and are incredibly gorgeous you can have some fun in it. Then they take you to Jamaica for two weeks to do some exotic shots. Great! But in San Francisco, walking up and down on a runway for hours on end was no great shakes. And I soon said aloha to that.

But while I was modeling, music was changing into Joan Baez and a little Bob Dylan and I started listening more seriously. Well, not seriously. I don't think I ever took music that way. But I started listening more and enjoying it. I sort of wanted to sing like Joan Baez, but I had such a low voice that all I could do was crack when I got up that high. All I was doing then was yelling.

THE GREAT SOCIETY

I got into professional music by going to see the Jefferson Airplane play. They played all over San Francisco, and I saw them dozens of times. It looked as though playing for a living might be fun, so we started our own band. The Great Society was formed by any of the kids we knew who had instruments. Jerry Slick had a set of drums, so we said, "Okay, you're the drummer." Whoever had a guitar was our guitar player, and that was that. We tried to do all original songs. Jerry wrote, everybody wrote, as a matter of fact. I was writing too, and the songs "Somebody to Love" and "White Rabbit" came from the Great Society. I had been writing songs since I was little—songs like "Poor Dead Robin," one of my great piano songs. But the stuff I wrote for the Great Society were the first things I had ever written which were performed. The first time I ever went onstage with the Great Society, it was terrifying. I was so scared that I couldn't remember any of the words and nothing came out of my mouth. But that's the only time I've ever been terrified on a stage.

We played everywhere with the Jefferson Airplane. In those days, the club scene was very big and every week kids would pack into them just to listen to the music. We played places like the Fillmore West and the Matrix and the same people would come every week. And a little place called Mother's that has since changed names about fifty times. It changes every week, in fact. At the time, the clientele was about five sailors a night, a couple fags, an old lady drunk, and maybe two more sailors. But we played because we were having fun and we really needed the money. It was during a time, when you could have gone to any number of clubs in San Francisco and seen groups like us, the Grateful Dead, the Jefferson Airplane, Big Brother and the Holding Company and Quicksilver. Now that I think back on it, it was fantastic for music.

THE JEFFERSON AIRPLANE

We had been playing with the Airplane on and off at the clubs
around the city. At that time, the group consisted of Jorma
Kaukonen, Jack Casady, Bob Harvey, Skip Spence, Paul Kantner,
Marty Balin, and Signe Anderson. Then Signe went off to have a
baby and a couple other guys left to study the sitar in India. Signe
also had a lot of other pressures on her, too. So it was a natural
cross. I knew all the guys and I knew the songs, so I became the
chick vocalist with the Jefferson Airplane.

When we became an influence on the kids in San Francisco
when we started out, the band was actually talking among themselves about what was going on and our transmitting it to the kids.
We were just saying to them, "Wake up, dammit!" A lot of people
back then were not awake because they were told not to be awake.
What a waste. They were told, "Don't read this because it's bad
for you." What do you mean, *bad* for me? *I'll* make that decision.
We told them that they would have to be aware more of what they
were doing. The same thing went for drugs. They heard a lot of
songs about drugs and never bothered to understand what they
were hearing. A lot of the songs should have said, "Look, before
you dump this shit, find out about it." Instead, they heard "acid"
and bam! they're in the nuthouses now. When we said, "Feed
your head," it did not necessarily mean: Put drugs into your head.
It meant: Open up your mind. Look around. Learn. But people
are too quick to say we woke the kids up. If they hadn't found it
through listening to some of Kantner's songs, they would have
done it by reading literature or reading newspapers or other musicians. But we were definitely part of what the kids learned about
when they started to look around themselves.

"HI, I'M SLY STONE"

While we were the Great Society, Tom Donahue[1] set up a record deal for us with Autumn Records. But everything happened
so damn quickly, I don't remember how the thing came about. We

[1] Sometimes called "The Father of Progressive Radio," he was the first
disc jockey to use that format on a San Francisco FM station: KSAN.

really didn't record the first album. It was just some old tapes that some guy made off a stereo system. And it wasn't even done in a recording studio. I think we did it live at the Matrix. And then, this guy who was managing us at the time decided he was going to put it out as a record. One of the *great* business decisions of all time! It was a piece of shit.

We also made a demo that Sly Stone produced, but it was never released. Sly was a producer for Autumn Records at the time. He was performing too, but mostly just producing and that end of it. We had never met him before, and he came in and said, "Hi, I'm Sly Stone and I'm going to produce your new record." Just like that! And we said, "Well, here's the song we're going to do, and this is how it goes." And he said, "No—*this* is how it goes," and he proceeded to go around and play every instrument in the room better than any one of us could play. So we—or Sly—made a whole LP in an hour, and it was never released. They probably couldn't decide whether to call it *The Great Society* or *An Afternoon with Sly Stone.* But it turned out to be a practice thing for us, a demo tape to find out how we sounded on record and then go on from there.

Really, I'm glad it never came out as an album because soon after we finished it—or Sly finished it (I can never get that straight)—Autumn Records kind of folded. And I joined the Jefferson Airplane before the Great Society ever got off the ground.

ON BILL GRAHAM

I first met Bill Graham through my husband at the time, Jerry Slick. Jerry was a cinematographer and he was filming some stuff with the San Francisco Mime Troupe, a group of actors from the city who were fairly well known. Bill Graham was more or less running the Mime Troupe, and at that time he didn't have anything to do with rock and roll. I don't know if he even liked it.

A little later, Bill opened the Fillmore West and started bringing in all the local bands and really rejuvenated a dying rock scene. The Airplane was one of the groups that played there all the time, and he became manager of the group—which never really worked out. We let him become our manager because we saw him all the time. I mean, we were always playing his place and it became like a full-time gig. A manager should be a guy who's always around, and Graham was always around—and looking out for us. So it was more or less logical. But Bill did a little more booking of the group than we liked to do. In fact, we were working *all* the time and that's not where we're at. We prefer to work slower: every other day, not that long and not that hard. Bill's a much harder worker. Very few bands can stand that pressure, and that's why most of them split up. We're one of the only groups that are still together after ten years. The Who is still together, but they take different planes and don't like each other too much. But I think it's stupid working like that. You see, we'd rather be happy thousandaires than psychotic millionaires. That's the deal. And because Bill wanted us on the road all the time, we just decided to become friends rather than partners. And we're still friends after ten years.

Bill is the same type of guy now that he was ten years ago. He's extremely bright and funny. I don't think anyone else could have organized the San Francisco sound like he did. He's very organized and unbelievably determined. He was determined to make the San Francisco sound *the* sound, and there was no stopping him once he put his mind to it. He's a great public relations guy and he just spread the word. As a promoter, he always makes sure we have everything we need. When we get to one of his gigs, everything's together. He's real fussy. Everything has to be just perfect. That's why he's so good.

THE STARSHIP

For two years, there wasn't any group. Jorma and Jack had to do Hot Tuna, and Paul and I were waiting for them to get their shit together. We'd continuously say, "Are you guys ready to come back with us?" And they'd say, "Yes," and go out on another [Hot Tuna] tour. We *really* thought they'd come back. So Paul and I just kept making albums and didn't do any live dates. What a waste of time, waiting. When we finally got it through our thick skulls that they really weren't coming back, we formed the Jefferson Starship.

The Airplane wasn't working out anyway. Everybody was

fighting—a lot of yelling and screaming at each other. No fun. Jorma and Jack had gotten down on Marty's writing, and Marty wasn't feeling too good about that. So he left, pulled out and went home and wrote a screenplay and formed a group called Bodacious which never really happened. (David) Freiberg just got real good and pissed and went home. Also, everyone was so stoned out all the time that no one ever really knew what was going on.

The idea behind the Starship was Kantner's. Something about an idea he and [David] Crosby had about space travel. But it's little more than an extension of the Jefferson Airplane.

I wasn't really concerned about not working after I really thought about it. Because I never started out saying: I-am-a-singer. I-have-to-have-a-career. I-have-to-be-the-best-singer-in-the-whole-world. I don't care about that. And if it all stops now, I'd be very satisfied. I'd go into movies or do some writing for other people.

But it was great to re-emerge as a top group and to play for a whole new bunch of kids. The music business just goes around and around and around. While we weren't performing, I had some time to watch the process. And it's fascinating to watch everybody clawing for that top spot.

YOU'VE GOT TO BE ABLE TO MOVE

I've never been a good singer. I took a few voice lessons, but hell, I'm just a screaming rock and roll singer. I made up any excuse I could to get out of singing lessons; finally I convinced myself that [my voice teacher] was too far away for me to get to and that was that. No more lessons. I'm a great one for talking myself into something I've always wanted to do anyway.

I'm still not in love with my voice. The chick [the Airplane] had before me, Signe Anderson, was a hell of a better singer than I was. She had great tubes. Real boring onstage, but she had great tubes. Well shit, that just ain't enough anymore. You've got to be able to move and do more than just sing the notes to rock and roll. You just can't stand there and pat your thigh and expect people to get off on it. No way. I've learned how to supplement my weak voice by moving onstage. It gets the kids going and they get into the performance as well as into the music. If you can't do that, you don't belong onstage.

Most of what I do onstage is spontaneous. People think I do things just for the effect, but when you're singing music at that volume, you have to lean over and push like that, like I do. That movement eases you into the notes that are next to impossible to hit. Especially with my voice. There's no way I can get notes out at that volume just by standing there. But I don't do any planned posturing. Can you imagine me rehearsing that shit? Now, we're all moving onstage and I think it makes for a much more exciting show. There's no other way to get it across as effectively.

THE RECORD COMPANY

The record company doesn't place so many restrictions on us anymore, but when we started it was like they were coming down on every other word that came out of our mouths. Jesus, it was like pulling fucking teeth to get an album out. After we had recorded, we had to arbitrate our goddamn lives away compromising over what was on the records. Everybody was scared stiff for their corporate asses. RCA Records, our parent company, has changed a hell of a lot. Four years ago they were real weird and had a changeover of presidents about every two weeks. Gray suits and all. But now they're really behind us, and it's been real good for our heads. We know they're going to support whatever we do rather than fight us and I can't say how much a group needs that. The last thing we want to do now is to waste our time fighting with our record company.

And most of all, we've learned how to rephrase things so we don't cause grief. Like, I've got a song that talks about nothing but dicks and fucking and that kind of stuff, but the record company doesn't know that because I've phrased it as if I'm talking about a gun. I did that on purpose just to avoid any record company hassle. "Seven inches of pleasure/seven inches going home/ somebody must have measured/around the old bone." Now, a bone-handled gun is about seven inches long. That was fun, and I may do it again, but not right now. That kind of stuff isn't that important to me anymore. I had a lot of fun, though, playing with the English language and, as you can see, that song is blatantly dirty. But it was just to get around a corporate problem.

Now, the only problems we have with the record company are over our contracts. That's where they're doing it to us now. They screw us around every which way. It took us a long time to sign this past contract because we kept finding little clauses thrown in all over the place. They think we're stupid and that we don't know what they're doing. But we do. But we've got the contract problem ironed out now. Shit, what are they going to do? We've had two best-selling albums for them in the last two years. They've got to start seeing things our way after that. And if they're going to play with us, we're going to do it with them. We won't do it so much with lyrics anymore 'cause I've already done that, but we'll come up with something. We'll come up with something.

THE ALBUMS

I really enjoy recording. It's a release of having all this music and words and stuff down in your gut and then going into a room with electronic gizmos all over the place and letting it all out. And it comes out on this little tape and you can work on it and work on it until it's the way you want it to be.

I do about three weeks of preparation—actually longer if you count all the time that I'm scribbling down lyrics. I do *that* all the time and I've got a whole book of them. Anywhere I go, if something inspires me—bam! into the book. I don't really know what inspires me; it could be anything. But if it does anything to me at all, I write it down. As far as the actual preparation for recording goes, though, it's only about three weeks. I'll come in with an idea, play it or sing it for the rest of the group, and they'll just play along until we've got it down. Then, we add things, subtract things, until it's fucking tight. Then we'll put it down on tape. Everybody contributes to the process.

Each album that we've recorded represents an era in our existence, something particular. Otherwise, what's the use of recording? It's got to say something as well as just your being able to drum your fingers along to it. That's been one of the main reasons for our success. We just don't make a hell of a lot of noise, we say something as well. And it could mean a lot of different things to a lot of different people.

Bathing at Baxter's was rather nutty. We wanted to experiment and decided to try out all new dials and different electronic sounds. Maybe the music wasn't as important on that album as the sound—at least to us. Experimental madness! But it turned out okay. *Surrealistic Pillow* was like a standard echo backup Phil Spector-type trip. A freaked-out Philly sound. It was real exciting for me. I had never been in a big studio before, and here we are at RCA in Los Angeles, a monster studio with great sound. We took over that fucking studio and had a ball. That was probably one of our best received albums and it sold real well. One of my favorites. *Manhole* was sort of weird. It was a too much liquor, too much darkness album. That's what I remember from recording it: darkness and booze. I was drinking a lot then. And I think the music was dark too. Not really our best thing. Too fucking moody. And *Long John Silver*—you know, I can't even remember doing one track on that album. I was totally gone. There were some other albums we did, too, that I really don't care much about.

I like the Starship albums a lot. *Dragonfly* and *Red Octopus* and *Spitfire*—yeah, they're real good albums and it was nice making them. There's a lot of music on there that all the kids can identify with. And I think we really cared about making them more than ever before. I mean, shit, we have grown up a little, and we have matured musically. I think you can hear that on those albums. I stopped drinking and doing drugs and that allowed me to really get into the creative aspects of making the albums. I'm real happy with them. But we never had any idea that *Red Octopus* was going to sell the way it did. We just go in and make every record the best we can and hope to hell we make some bucks off it. That's the name of the game.

THAT'S THE WAY I AM

Being mobbed and all that star shit doesn't really affect me anymore. We've been around and have learned how to deal with it. At concerts, I try to move at an even pace, because if I stop anywhere around the place we're playing ten people try to talk to me at the same time and that's plain silly. So I don't stop. I used to, but then I'd stand there like a dumb motherfucker not knowing anything that was being said; it was all a jumble. I usually only reply to the comments that I can hear clearly, and to those I only reply with one short sentence so that I don't get caught up in some chaotic affair.

Being a celebrity is part of the whole thing that a rock group must contend with. It really hasn't affected me adversely in any way because when I was little and dressed up and came out and sang, my parents would go crazy clapping and singing. And that hasn't stopped. Only the characters have changed. So I'm used to that part of being an entertainer and I like it. If this group falls apart tomorrow, I will still be the attention-getter at parties. I need that. That's the way I am.

You know, I've always lived in a fantasy world. When I was little, I always thought of myself as a princess and I guess that I've never moved out of my childhood. I've never outgrown it. I still live in a fantasy world where everything works out and is fun. Yeah—I like being a part of all this, whether it's history or whatever people want to call it. It's great.

Mike Klenfner: Record Promotion

In 1975, approximately two thousand pop record albums were released. The number of those records that makes back the negative (artist advance, recording, promotional) costs is very small. One of the reasons is that these albums all vie on an equal basis for airplay on the radio; because radio is a highly commercial medium and relies on advertising revenue for survival, the majority of stations are restricted to a tight playlist of records—popular records which attract the most listeners. Needless to say, the fewer records played over and over and over again, the more familiar a listener becomes with a particular artist or song or sound and a better chance is created for generating sales. So when a new record is released, only one thought runs through the mind of the record executive: Get Airplay!

Getting airplay is the main function of the record company promotion man. Creating awareness, getting the product to the people, cultivating excitement. Causing sales. All of these qualities are a direct result of airplay. Without it, the record stands still. But getting airplay is the final result of a very long process that begins with loving music and ends with encouraging a large population of the country to feel the same way.

Mike Klenfner has been in love with rock music since he was a young boy growing up in Brooklyn from where much of the early doo-wop sound originated. As a teenager, he was a permanent fixture in the Greenwich Village music clubs—as an enthusiast—pouring over the likes of the Lovin' Spoonful, the Rascals, Mountain, and just about any other important group passing through New York City. Later on, to get his foot in the door of the music business, he left a job on Wall Street to sweep the floor at the Fillmore East, where he later became part of the stage crew and a close friend of owner Bill Graham. This led to a short stay as an announcer on New York's leading progressive FM station before joining Columbia Records as the director of FM album promotion. Today, while still in his twenties, Mike Klenfner has been vice-president of album promotion at Arista Records, is currently vice-president of Atlantic Records and is considered a taste-maker among company executives.

Klenfner's approach to getting a record on the air is very basic: if the record delivers the sound it has a fighting chance. And that's when Mike Klenfner begins to fight. He's on the phone for several hours a day conversing with disc jockeys across the nation about everything from the weather to an update on the condition of their sick dog. He's cultivated friendships over the years and he allows them to work for him in as unobtrusive a manner as possible. He knows that his credibility is on the line every time he recommends a record for the playlist, so his discretion plays an important role in his life. And his reputation bears out the reliability of his intuition.

PAYING DUES

I'm still a kid. How could anyone be in the business that I am and not be a kid. Not possible! I've grown up on the music which I'm promoting today. I'm from Brooklyn—Brighton Beach—which is a very Jewish neighborhood. I think I was the first person in the neighborhood to have a stereo and probably the first one to have components. I had to have them. You don't think I'd let some other schmuck have them before I did, do you?

I think the first records I bought were by the Platters. I loved Ritchie Valens, Paul Anka. In fact, I even managed to get a Canadian import of "Diana" before it was released here. God, I was a music junkie. I could never get enough. I even think I exposed most of my friends to rock and roll. Look, I'm twenty-nine years old. Ten years ago I was nineteen and the music that we're listening to today was relatively just starting.

I went to Brooklyn College for a little while and had to drop out because I had to work. I studied anything to keep me out of—well, you know. I liked school, but it was not for me. If I could have done it in a year it would have been okay.

In 1966, I went to Wall Street. I was a finance major in school, so I stayed down there for a few years and worked on the floor of the New York Stock Exchange. I was there the day Abbie Hoffman tossed money onto the floor from the balcony. Everyone else was standing around laughing, but I was scurrying like a rat. I think I made seven dollars that day; I wanted the fucking money and was happy to take it.

Wall Street prepared me very well for the music business. It gave me a good business sense, but I had to leave. Music was killing me. I just loved rock and roll too much. I was spending every Friday night at the Fillmore and went to every show I could get into. I didn't care who was there. Really! And when the Fillmore wasn't in progress, I went to every other show at places like the Au Go Go and the Anderson Theatre and all the Village clubs. I legitimately remember putting money in the hat when Dylan sang. I mean, I saw the Lovin' Spoonful so many times that I thought I was able to sing along with Sebastian probably as well as he could.

One day I just walked into the Fillmore East and got a job as an outside security man. I was always a big boy, and they figured that no one was going to mess around with me. It was a tough job because there was this gang called the Motherfuckers who tried to break in all the time. I remember one time when they tried, and Bill Graham got hit in the face with a chain that they were swinging. That was during the era of "We're going to take over the world; we want the world and we want it now." There was a lot of fracas, but mostly they were good times.

While I worked at the Fillmore, I was still holding down another job. I knew Scott Muni and he was now the big man at WNEW-FM[1] when it was just starting to happen. They needed a music director—somebody who was in tune to this music. So I got this call asking me if I wanted to be the music director for WNEW. I mean, does a wild boar shit in the woods? No problem. So here I was in a unique situation as the music director and on Friday nights I was on the stage crew of the Fillmore East. And the promotion men who came to see me at the station were the old line guys who were used to working the AM stations. And they'd come in and hype me and say that this or that act is sensational and I'd say, "You're fucking crazy. I was there for four shows this weekend and they *stunk!*" I became notorious for knowing what was going down. All these promotion men wanted to take me out to lunch and, at the time, I was trying to keep my weight down, so I'd refuse. And they all thought I was a snob. Hell, I was just into the music. I didn't know about promotion, that they were just trying to do their job.

THE BIG FACE-LIFT

FM rock radio was brand new in those days. We were breaking people like Elton John and Joe Cocker and Ten Years After. So radio was real exciting. It got the big face-lift, and things will never be the same. You see, radio is breaking new acts now, but back then we broke people who we *knew* were going to be around for a long time when rock stars came and went without notice.

But progressive radio has totally changed. It's not as progressive anymore. The stations are still playing brand-new Fleetwood Mac albums like they did ten years ago, but back then it was *all* brand new. Radio has gotten a little smarter and a little slicker. They've had their ups and downs and they realize that they can actually make a lot of money—a fucking fortune. And the kids have gotten smarter too. You can't pull the wool over their eyes anymore. They know all the names of the members in a particular

[1] New York City's leading FM progressive format radio station.

group as well as the producer of the album and probably the names of the individual writers. I used to pay two, two and a half bucks for an album. But these kids are paying four and five bucks and they deserve to know everything for that kind of money.

I ACCEPTED COLUMBIA'S OFFER

Kip Cohen, who managed the Fillmore East for Bill Graham, went to work for CBS[2] when the Fillmore closed. Kip and I were good friends, and he brought my name up to Clive Davis, who was then president of Columbia Records. Clive had heard of me, and he subsequently wanted to interview me for a possible position at CBS. Now, I had a pretty good job with the radio station. I was only a young guy, and I figured I had a lot more to learn about radio before I decided to move on to a position with a record company. But a tough decision arose: Columbia offered to double my salary. That's a tough thing to turn down. So I walked into Scott Muni's office, told him about it flat out, and asked his advice. He told me that I *had* to leave radio for that kind of a job. It was a once-in-a-lifetime thing. And when he sanctioned it, I accepted Columbia's offer.

Well, I went to my interview with Clive and I was scared shitless. He had me—right away—come to a singles meeting and that shocked me. I mean, everything that went on at those meetings was astounding. All facets of music and records were discussed in *very* realistic terms. I was absolutely fascinated. I thought I knew everything about music, but I found out that you really don't know anything until you've sat through singles meetings. That's where you learn. I saw a whole other side of the business, and I *had* to get my teeth into it.

CBS created a special position for me. I was the first director of FM promotion. Before that, there was never a great need for a special department covering FM stations because FM was just beginning to happen. And my job was to stay in close contact with the network of FM stations and introduce them to the new related product we were releasing. To become friends with the jocks and to talk music with them.

[2] As East Coast director of A&R.

I loved working for CBS. I was pretty low down on the corporate totem pole there, so I wasn't supposed to have that much direct contact with Clive, but I *did* because I pushed myself to him. I wanted to learn from a guy who I watched operate in the most magnificent manner. I went to all the concerts and got backstage before he got there. I knew all these artists from the Fillmore days. Hell, I knew Carlos Santana when Graham flew him in to jam for the first time. I remember getting so drunk with Janis Joplin that we couldn't stand up. I was friendly with Alvin Lee. But working with Clive was hard. He's very demanding. Still is. It was like working for Bill Graham, but in a more polished way. Bill was more guttural, while Clive's approach is more Harvard. Neither one is stupider or smarter than the other, but both are very demanding.

PROMOTION CAME EASY

I became a promotion man because I'm a mouth. I can turn a person onto a great piece of music faster than almost anybody I know. And I learned all the ropes from Steve Popovich, who is the best,[3] like Dom Perignon champagne. He's probably done more effective promotion than anyone I know of, a guy who will be in his office until ten o'clock at night on the phones with the jocks. And I'm a *tummler*. I like to create excitement. If there's nothing happening, I'll do something. I'll turn the table over to get something going. When I was in public school, it was the same thing. When I thought it was too hot, I used to take the pole and open the windows. And if there was nothing particularly exciting going on in the class, I'd occasionally break a window. So being a promotion man came easy.

Promotion is the same thing—creating excitement. It's my first love. And it's the essence of rock and roll—excitement. Without it, there's no music, no electricity. Promotion is the spark which lights some fires. It's a crazy profession, and sometimes you have to resort to some pretty crazy things to get attention. When I was with Columbia, we had a group called the Wombles. And [another promotion man] and I dressed up as Wombles and started walking

[3] Former director of promotion for Columbia Records.

through Manhattan. I started directing traffic at Fifty-seventh Street and Sixth Avenue. Then we walked into a bank and they thought it was going to be a holdup. Jesus, I've done a lot of crazy things, but the truth is that I've loved doing every one of them.

But one of the keys to promotion is that if you don't get good records to work on, you're not going to break anything. I was fortunate at Columbia. I got a lot of good records to start with; I got Loggins and Messina, Blue Oyster Cult, Bruce Springsteen.

A NEW RECORD COMPANY

(*In 1975, Mike Klenfner left his position at Columbia Records to join his old boss, Clive Davis, at Arista Records.*)

When I came here in 1975, it was still Bell Records, and I had some job ahead of me. Bell was known primarily as a singles company. They weren't able to break many acts onto the FM airwaves. So I had to do something to let the radio stations know that we weren't going to maintain the same image as [Bell had]. So I took a road trip across the country and let people know that we were now Arista—no longer Bell—and we were a *new* record company. The image was not going to be the Archies, the Monkees, or the Partridge Family. A lot of people listened to me and said, "Yeah, sure!" but the majority said, "Yep, we know the people involved and we *know* you're going to do what you say."

The next step was our coming with releases that showed the stations and the buying public what kind of a record company we were going to be. It was *so* important to come with the right things, and I think we did. We came with a progressive group called Gryphon and Barry Manilow and Gil Scott-Heron. Barry took a while but outdid our wildest dreams by becoming a superstar. Gryphon was good for the image we were trying to project, but they were not particularly successful. But Gil came pretty close to our expectations. He got involved in some management problems which have since been worked out, and I think he's going to become one of music's prime spokesmen. Besides being great musically, he's a bright guy—a teacher in Washington, D.C. —and is social-minded.

THE GUYS IN THE FIELD

A record company promotion department is as good as its men in the field. We have branch offices in every major city across the United States, and in those offices we have our local salesmen, local marketing men, and local promotion men who work with radio stations, writers, stores, and artists when they come into their city. It's a simple operation, much like a General Motors distributorship. Our local promotion men are catchall operatives: promotion men, salesmen, baby-sitters, the eyes and ears of the artist. They know what's right for their market. It's a twenty-four-hour job, and good local men live, breathe, eat, and shit their jobs. Regional promotion men are a little different. They are, more or less, the papa bears of the field team. The regional man will cover the local men in several large cities and, mostly, several states.

I work with my field men as much as possible. We have conference calls every Monday morning after I'm finished with the singles meeting in New York, and these calls encompass everything: Top Forty, R&B, FM progressive, the works. And about once every three or four weeks I have a separate call only on FM product. Then occasionally I'll go out on the road and visit with my men or fly them into New York for conferences. You see, I have to promote them before I can rely on them to promote our product to stations. I have to sell the music to them, because when they go out to cover the stations in their territory, they have to be excited. That's my job—creating the excitement.

I try to get stuff to the men in the field as early as possible so they can listen to it and learn what it's all about. I have certain men who I know I can get excited about a new Outlaws album before I can get them excited about, say, a Movies album. Then, they in turn will excite the salespeople, the store people, and, most of all, the radio people. I encourage them to hype, but you can only hype acts so much. Otherwise, you just blow your ass right out the door. After you hype so much, you lose your credibility. Then you become a hypemeister, and then blow it.

I also work with independent promotion men. These are professional promotion men who work for a few record companies at the same time. They can be an incredible asset. When we're busy and have eight, nine, ten singles released and the same amount of albums, an independent man who's powerful in his market can really take some of the load off your hands. We have a few of them who we keep on a year-round retainer. And these guys help us get a record started in an area where we might not be too strong. And they can finish it off, too.

There are very few FM promotion men because you don't break a record FM like you do Top Forty. FM stations don't have playlists. Top Forty stations all have playlists. On FM, you have six different program directors (if there are six different disc jockeys): you have to talk to each jock separately because they're not bound to a uniform playlist like with Top Forty. Promoting Top Forty, all you do is talk to one guy at each station—the program director—and pray he adds your record to the playlist. So it's very intangible.

YOU TRY TO SET UP A BATTLE PLAN

There is a system for breaking an artist, but each act is totally different. There's no two alike. First, I'll listen to a record from a new act and try to figure out what area of the country might be strongest for it. I mean, with Patti Smith, we obviously decided to break her in the larger cities and hoped her music spread from there. With the Outlaws, we concentrated in the south, but they broke out of Los Angeles. I goofed, but I'll take that kind of goof all day long because they became a major act for the label. You try to set up a battle plan, and then you go out and fight the battle. And, hopefully, you have an act with singles potential. That always makes the job easier.

Singles get albums to the people. If you hear a single you like again and again, you're likely to buy the album. So we're always looking for acts with hit single potential.

I disagree with: "No hype is the best hype." It doesn't carry any content. In Patti Smith's case, we hyped a little bit differently but it worked. First of all, there was a lot of word of mouth on her. She had put a single out herself (before signing with Arista). As head of promotion for the company, my job is to get people to hear about the artist and get the record played. Well, I sent letters to stations around the country that I knew weren't playing Patti Smith, and I got back vehement replies like: "What do you *mean* hyping me on Patti Smith? I knew about her before you were ever in the music business." We tried to underplay the hype on Patti and let the music speak for itself. Patti Smith made a *good* album and is capable of making a *great* album. And that will break her wide open. She'll promote herself.

PUSH RECORDS

Push records are records you know you've *got* to break. If in one month you're coming out with a four-album release, you're hyping yourself if you think they're all going to be hits. That's bullshit, because they're not all going to happen. So you take your shot.

When you walk into a program director's office with five albums, you know damn well he's not going to listen to all five. The attention span doesn't last that long. So you pick the albums which you think have a shot and you hope you're right. You probably have two good shots. The third one is straining. The fourth is nonexistent. Otherwise, you come back in a second time.

A lot of what we "push" comes from direction from Clive. We sign the other acts [that don't become push acts] because we really do have a belief in them. Even if they don't happen big, we and they still make money being on the label. And a lot of the smaller acts give us a well-rounded image and add a lot of prestige to the label.

There might be one record in your monthly release that you really like yourself and that you're not getting pressure from the company to break. So you say to yourself, "Okay, let's take this one and bust this fucker." And you do it.

I'm paid to get a record played. Sometimes I may hate the record or get turned off by the artists (when I meet them), but I just grit my teeth and, without jeopardizing my credibility, try to get it played. But I won't let a record haunt me. If I hate it, I'm not going to go down saying I love it. I'll find one of my men who is really tuned into it and let him spearhead the promotion of that particular record.

CREATIVE PROMOTION

We do a lot of promotion with more than just records. We try to get our artists to visit radio stations [when they're on the road]. It helps an awful lot. Especially if you have a very vocal artist who's good with people. A Paul Simon is not the most personable person to have talk to a disc jockey where a Barry Manilow is or somebody like Jimmy Messina is wonderful. A Bruce Springsteen, unless he knows somebody there, is not that good with radio stations. So if the artist is good with people, a good promotion department will take advantage of the situation.

More important, we'll use the artist with stores—which is an untapped resource. You walk someone like Barry Manilow into a store and forget about it! It will probably do him more good than having a hit single. And that's not regular day-to-day promotion. It's above and beyond, but it makes the difference between being successful and being a fucking star. If you walk an artist into a store in a shopping center or a big J. C. Penny's or a Sears Roebuck that has a record department, the results are amazing. The buyers and the general managers of the stores freak. It's a happening event. It only takes ten minutes, but it really works.

Most people think that the only promotional play you get is radio play, but there is what's known as "in-store" play, which is very important. And a personal appearance by the artist might just generate some good in-store play. A good example is a record chain in Georgia known as Peaches, which is a huge store that's set up for the record buyer. When you go in there, if you didn't intend to buy a record you're going to buy one, and if you intended to buy one, you'll walk out with two. It's set up so well and so easy to browse that it actually encourages you to buy. Now, if you go into the store to buy the new Lynyrd Skynyrd album and you hear the new Outlaws album coming over the store sound system, you become hooked—and that's exactly how a record company will use in-store play to sell records.

You can also use artists in other creative and social ways. We took the Bay City Rollers up to a children's hospital. People don't usually think of promotion in terms of things like that. But it generates publicity and good will. The kids will all, God willing, get out of the hospital. Can you imagine if you were a kid and you're laying in the hospital after a tonsillectomy and the Bay City Rollers walk in! If you're thirteen years old, you're going to freak. And, of course, when you get discharged you're going to buy their newest record.

All you need is the co-operation of your artist and your local promotion man. And a little thought.

M-O-R

The current M-O-R situation is totally asleep. M-O-R stations don't break records; parents don't buy records anymore. Leading M-O-R stations like WNEW-AM (in New York City) and WIP (in Philadelphia) don't really motivate people to buy records—albums or singles.

But you promote M-O-R stations just like you'd promote any other station. And I'll promote any vehicle that has a signal. I'd be a fool not to. M-O-R stations won't break records, but they will sustain records that are selling.

But M-O-R stations have gotten a lot smarter in the last few years. Now, in addition to the latest Andy Williams record or Jerry Vale record, they will play an America tune or something by Crosby, Stills and Nash. They have to broaden their audience because the M-O-R stations were dying on the vine. There are very hip Elton John cuts that can be played M-O-R as well as Eric Carmen cuts that can go the same way.

A MUSIC JUNKIE

I think the bottom line to being a successful promotion man is living rock and roll. I love it and wouldn't have it any other way—even if it meant going back to the stage crew at the Fillmore. I'm a music junkie. I'm addicted. It's the only way to fly.

Jerry Wexler

"I need you, to see me through,
Someone to hold my hand
Try to make me understand . . ."

B. BURNS, S. BURKE, and J. WEXLER
Everybody Needs Somebody to Love

During a series of lunches and meetings which were the foundation for this chapter, Jerry Wexler not only reminisced about his previous years in rock and roll but also spoke eagerly about the days ahead. He had just turned sixty and was entering a new era of creativity. Only days before, he had begun learning how to play squash, he was in between recording sessions, and he had begun musical direction on Louis Malle's film Pretty Baby—*a task which had taken him on preproduction research to New Orleans swamps and the Mississippi delta in search of some musical heritage which exasperated him. He also talked about a book—several books— he intended to write out of his need to capture eras of music which he felt would escape the attention of younger generations. Jerry's need to stay busy and to achieve is obsessive, partly because of the self-invested caricature by which so many men of his accomplishment measure themselves when they feel their activity is limited by age. But, more so, I think, because Jerry's innovative contributions to popular music are inexhaustible and he is driven by an impulse to bring them all to life.*

Jerry resembles a real-life archetype for a character in a Hemingway novel, a man whose chiseled features portray a certain robust quality, an outward sagaciousness which attracts others to him. He is uncannily youthful in manner and speech.

Jerry grew up on the streets of New York City where he hung out wherever music was happening: in the neighborhood record shops where he befriended the owners and in the jazz establishments which made Fifty-second Street both celebrated and notorious. However, unlike so many of his associates in the rock music business, Jerry was afforded extensive formal education, most notably in journalism, in which he holds a master's degree. It is that side of Jerry Wexler which is constantly at odds with his street sense. He is most dignified and consciously makes use of a complicated vocabulary which at times becomes profoundly confusing; he is coincidentally both charming and guttural. This is further exemplified in Jerry's home—a spacious Manhattan apartment whose rooms reflect ultramodern and Victorian décor.

Not so ironically, his personality finds its most logical personification in the music that he has produced over the years. This stems not so much from Wexler's unquestionable taste but, rather, from his intrinsic understanding of music itself. That knowledge has allowed him the mobility of recording various artists and capturing their regional styles: the urban sound of the early Atlantic artists like the Drifters and the Clovers, the gospel and blues roots of Aretha Franklin, the Tex-Mex derivation of Doug Sahm, Dr. John's Cajun traditions, Memphis, Muscle Shoals, Macon, Broadway—the distinctions are mind-boggling. But his knowledge extends even beyond musical dialect. Ask him about the artists he produced in Memphis and he begins with a history of the region that includes W. C. Handy, Furry Lewis, the famous Blues Carnival that featured Bill Barth and the great Sun revival before working his way to his arrival on the scene. So, in analyzing Jerry's recordings, one must also take into consideration his interpretation of feelings, spirit, and social temperament.

Jerry's life is governed by organization. His projects are timed so that he can move from one to another with relative ease; they are well researched and planned in advance. I would guess that this comes from his having been a journalist, from structuring his thoughts before committing them to posterity—that trait unique to writers who expose their thoughts to public scrutiny. If this is the case, Jerry exemplifies it early in his career by the technique of arduously rehearsing a group before taking it into the studio to put it on the tape. His personal preparation for a particular session is reflected in the over-all sound for which his records are most noted: sharp contrast, depth, musical quality, honing in on the heart of the song and exploiting its full potential. It is the quality of perfection, of pride in one's work.

They say that a person's office is an extension of that person. Looking around Jerry Wexler's office, one can tell many things about his extraordinary life, a life which he undoubtedly treasures. Alphabetized bins stuffed with record albums line the upper reaches of the walls. His catalogue is enormous but tastefully selected. Always close at hand. Below the records are mementos: scores of gold records proudly displayed among achievement awards and laminated press clippings. But most important are the pictures—pictures of true friendships born of his years in the music business, of people who have placed their trust and love in him, of peoples whose love and admiration he returns selflessly. That's the kind of person Jerry Wexler is all about. His reputation among the artists he has worked closely with is untarnished; ultimately, most of those artist friendships still exist even though the professional ties have long passed.

I've learned a lot about Jerry Wexler's legacy, about how many rock historians consider him to be the father of popular rhythm and blues. I am familiar with the incredible discography for which he is responsible. I admire him truly for those contributions. But there is much more to Jerry than merely musical ties. There is another feeling with which he leaves me. And now, when I hear Aretha Franklin singing, "R-E-S-P-E-C-T, that's how much you mean to me," I can't help picturing her standing at the microphone looking at Jerry at the controls in the glass booth and feeling the same as I do.

IN THOSE DAYS

Classical music was the only thing that was played in my house while I was growing up. My mother played classical piano. She didn't have a great gift for it, but she had good taste and a good ear. She wore out six piano teachers on me but, somehow, in those very early years, I glommed onto pop music.

My going to pop was very strange, because in those days the demographics were different. Kids were not only not record buyers, they didn't even *hear* records. There weren't any pop radio stations. There were no records on the air, but there were live musical programs. One of the first things that turned me on was Bing Crosby. He used to come on the radio for fifteen minutes in the evening. There was only one radio in the house, and my mother had to listen to "Easy Aces." So a buddy and I always had to run down to a store that had a radio in the vestibule so I could listen to Bing. And he was backed by Paul Whiteman's orchestra or a bunch of jazzmen. That's where I learned about music.

My interest in music really became heightened when I went to college and started listening to the bands which broadcast live from the Reno Club. It was a short-wave station, but it managed to creep onto the radio and we always managed to find it. I used to save up my money and do weekends in Kansas City just to hear all the music. It was a ninety-mile hitchhike from my school, but I don't think that ever entered my mind. I had to get to the music. And I invariably did.

If there was one midwife for me between journalism and music, it was Milt Gabler. The jam sessions he used to run on Fifty-second Street in New York were incredible. He kept jazz alive almost singlehandedly by sponsoring Fats Waller, Jimmy Sullivan, Red Allen, and a host of others. I originally met him in 1938. A bunch of us used to hang around his Commodore Record Shop. We were record collectors—an art that is no more—and we'd spend the day at his store. Then he'd close up and we'd get high and start playing all these rare records he had. Milt also kept us liquid because when we needed to sell off records for money, he would buy them from us.

GUT MUSIC

What got me into R&B was the Ravens. You'd be surprised how seminal the Ravens were for a lot of people. I'll never forget: one of my jazz-collecting buddies said, "You gotta listen to the

Ravens." I said, "Hey, man, that's a vocal quartet. Who are you kidding?" But I gave it a try anyway. They were probably the first successful R&B act in the Forties. And the Forties was when it really all began. The Ravens, Billy Eckstine, Savannah Churchill, Dinah Washington—a matrix of R&B and jazz which is still being carried on today.

There was no category called R&B then. It was called "Hot in Harlem," race records. Modern Records was the leader of the genre along with others like King and Federal. This is the kind of new world I walked into when I came to Atlantic Records. R&B today represents the rising aspirations of the ghetto. It's got symphonic arrangements with strings and it's not the same thing as when I got into the business. There were no rising aspirations of the ghetto then. It was gut music.

A GREAT BIG FERMENT ON THE STREET

I began in the music business by working at BMI—not very long, but long enough to get a feeling for the industry. I heard about an opening at *Billboard* and a friend got me an "in" there. I had a degree in journalism. I didn't know that much about the music trade then—but what I *could* do was write a grammatical English paragraph. So I became a quick and prolific rewrite man. Suddenly, their stories began appearing in English.

A lot of exciting things were happening then in the trade: the emergence of BMI, which meant throwing off the old shackles of ASCAP for the new music—R&B, country, and rock, which ASCAP gave short shrift to; the emergence of the independent record companies, those Eleventh Avenue brigands—companies like King, Savoy, Aladin, Specialty, Miracle, Apollo, and Atlantic began emerging via the efforts of people with diverse motivations. Most of the people who headed those companies became record executives because they had access to compound-plastics men who used to make toilet seats and as such had access to the materials from which records were made, so they said, "Okay—we'll make records, too." It was very exciting, and black music was the matrix—a combination of R&B and jazz. There was a great big ferment on the street.

A FRANTIC SCUFFLE

While working for *Billboard,* I used to do something no one does anymore. I used shanks' mare: I used to walk. I went out and covered a beat. I'd go to the Brill Building, start at the top floor, and cover every office—walk into all those dingy little offices. A lot of the people who claimed to work there used to lurk in the hallways and give out business cards with a number of the public phone booth in the lobby hoping to hop onto a deal; they didn't even have offices there. But you could rent a cubicle in the Brill Building for a fish cake and a guy would declare himself a music publisher by putting a sign on the door.

Someone would knock on a door with a lead sheet and the little publisher would grab the rights. Things were so close by and loose then that the guy could go over to BMI and get an immediate advance[1] and cross the street to RCA and pay off an A&R man to record it with someone like Perry Como. It was a frantic scuffle.

Most of the men there, though, had been brought up on Tin Pan Alley ballads and were afraid of the new music. And so it passed them right by. There were so many characters there. Some of the great song pluggers were there and had a gift for getting a deal for anything they could connive for. They were flashy, lived a night life, dressed well, and spoke all the lingo. It's an era gone by.

"GO ON—BE A RECORD MAN"

In 1952, I was working for Robbins Music, a large music publisher, doing publicity, promotion, and hustling songs to A&R men at record companies. I was separate from the rest of their professionals who were still concerned with bringing songs to Guy Lombardo. And I ran songs to some of the independent companies. So I met Ahmet Ertegun and Herb Abramson, the principals at Atlantic Records, and we began hanging out together.

In 1952, Herb had to go to Europe to do some detached duty in

[1] Publishers still give songwriters advances on royalties based upon a projected earning of that particular song.

the service; he was a dentist in the Army Reserve. There were three principals in Atlantic Records at that time: Ahmet, Herb, and Herb's wife, Miriam, who actually made the company hum. Ahmet and Herb were jazz fans—they weren't businessmen, and the whole company was totally chaotic. They had a lot of ideas about records they wanted to make. In fact, they almost went broke a few times trying to make them. But pressing plants, shipments, and collections were not exactly their bag. Somehow, they had a notion I could help in that area even though I hadn't any experience. That demonstrates what prejudice a friendship can produce.

So, in 1952, they offered me a job of coming in to run the publishing company and to do some marginal work in the record company. I said, "No. I've got a job." But I had the balls to say, "If you want me in with you, give me a chance to acquire a piece of the company." And they kindly invited me to get lost.

But we remained good friends.

A year later, Herb had to report to camp. So they called me again, and this time it was arranged that I could buy into the company. I got a piece of Atlantic for a nominal amount of money, like they were actually giving it to me. This time I said, "Yes."

They moved me right in. The first day I got in early, they dumped all the mail on my desk and said, "Go on—be a record man." Of course, Herb's wife taught me a lot about the administrative end of the business. Then, almost immediately, I started recording with Ahmet. I did business all day, and at night I made records. During those first sessions with Ahmet, he trained me; I watched what he did carefully and learned as much as he did— and, I must say, in those days it wasn't very much. Both of us were in the rock music business on a pass. But the two things we had going for us were taste and good ears.

MY VERY FIRST SESSION

My very first session was with Clyde McPhatter and the Drifters. We cut "Money Honey," and I'll never forget it because we had to recut the session. That was in September of 1953. Clyde had just formed the group after breaking off from his former group, the Dominoes, and he never sounded better. He was a great artist with a great ear.

When we cut groups like the Drifters, we had a lot of rehearsal and always used an arranger. We rehearsed the group for weeks as opposed to the practice of most of our colleagues. They would run a group into the studio and say, "Okay—you're up next. Sing!" The group never saw the backing band before, and the piano player would invariably say, "What key is the song in?" The record executive would answer, "We don't study keys, mother-fucker. Play the music!" As a consequence, if people listen today to the records we made then, they'll hear records that are in tune, that sound good, that are balanced. Because we rehearsed and we prepared. And we had fabulous engineers like Tommy Dowd at the control board mixing the records. We didn't know much about music, but we knew if a guy was hitting a bad note, and we'd stop the session and do it again. People should listen to the other records—what they refer to the "Golden Age of A Cappella." It's totally shit, worthless. But people have a sentimental attachment to it because it's the first time they got a "feel"—purely condition-ing. They were listening to it on the radio when they got their first handful of tit at the drive-in. Listen to the Drifters' records when making a comparison. Listen to the background harmonies, the intonations—they're so full, the chords are so rich and blended well. Instrumentally, those records are great too.

We did a record with the Drifters called "What You Gonna Do?"—a little-known record that Ahmet wrote and "surprisingly" sounds exactly like "The Twist." Actually, I think it was *stolen* from the Drifters and used as a foundation for that later record. A few years ago, I ran into Hank Ballard from the Midnighters at a delicatessen. He had written "The Twist." He was in New York working for James Brown. And I said, "Hank—didn't you steal 'The Twist' from 'What You Gonna Do?'?" He said, "Did I *steal* it? Man, Mr. Nathan and I are still waiting for the lawsuit!"

AHMET

Ahmet Ertegun was a totally creative guy. He was the best R&B producer of his era. He used to write all the songs we recorded, tons of songs. The reason being was in those days, if you didn't

have an artist who wrote all his own songs, there were no
songwriters writing songs for rhythm and blues artists. That whole
genre sprang up later. Ahmet wrote all the songs for the Clovers,
he wrote a lot of the songs for Ruth Brown, a lot of songs for the
Drifters—not all under his own name; he made up a lot of pseu-
donyms under which he wrote. But you see, Ahmet drew on his
experience with the blues. Not being a musician, he would take a
line from here and a lick from there and put it together—which,
in effect, is what Irving Berlin and George Gershwin also did. But
Ahmet had a great feel for combining blues licks with rhyming
couplets. All he had to do after that was put a great backbeat to it
and he had a terrific R&B record.

People don't think of Ahmet Ertegun as a creative guy because
sometime in the early Sixties he stopped doing that and stopped
recording. He got more heavily involved with bringing the company into a major offer—which he did. If he had kept recording
and writing, then he wouldn't have had time to travel around the
world with Mick Jagger or to take care of the coddling of all those
big white acts and their managers, which he did. I signed a lot of
those white acts, but Ahmet signed more of them.

THE ATLANTIC SOUND

White people began buying Atlantic Records in the early Fifties
mainly in the Carolinas and along the Eastern seaboard. They
called them "beach records." White high-school and college kids
would go to the beach with their portable tube radios and, by mistake, they'd listen to the black radio stations. Suddenly, a record
like "Money Honey" of "Tweedle De Dee" was born. We'd always get a call from our distributor in Charlotte saying, "There's a
beach record happening here." Then we'd madly try to get product there in time to catch the wave.

Southern white people of both the educated and uneducated
classes were very responsive to our music and, in my opinion, they
still are the more sophisticated listening audience because they
have such strong roots, so much knowledge of what went before.
That's how they started listening to the records we were making.

Then the cover records started. Bill Haley covered "Shake Rattle and Roll,[2] Georgia Gibbs had her hit that way.[3] It was maddening to us because if we took a Ruth Brown record or a Lavern Baker record to a white radio station, they'd laugh. It was unthinkable. It was plain, out-and-out prejudice. They wouldn't play a song by a black artist. They'd say, "Bring it back with a white singer doing it and we'll play it." Our publishing firm owned the copyrights on the songs, and that was the only consolation in having our songs covered.

People in the music business were always listening to our original recordings and stealing them to cover before we got ours out. Reports would come back to me from other sessions that they would have *our* record in *their* session, playing it over the loudspeakers for their musicians to pick up all the licks and rhythm changes. And they would use our records whether they were recording one of our songs or not. They'd say, "Take a sound like this . . ." It was called the Atlantic sound. It was a mystique that we generated a sound which no one else could. Now everybody knows how to do it. It was our own particular brand of clean funk which we knew how to create using our feeling and knowledge of blues, jazz, and old race records.

RAY CHARLES

Ray Charles was originally on a label called Swingtime and was represented by an agent named Billy Shaw of Shaw Artists, which was one of the last of the agencies that had anything to do with nurturing talent. It's a different scene today; maybe, if you "happen" with a record, an agency will sign you. But, in those days, agents used to go out and find the talent, finance it, nurse it, and bring it to a record company. Billy Shaw was able to effect the purchase of Ray Charles's contract and Ahmet bought it from Swingtime for $2,000 in 1952. I joined the company in 1953 and among the other talent I recorded with Ahmet was Ray Charles.

He was a beautiful guy, extremely certain and set about what he wanted in his music—as he should have been. What the hell could

---

[2] The original black version of the song was recorded by Joe Turner before it was "covered" by Haley.

[3] The original black version was recorded by Ruth Brown.

we tell Ray Charles about making music? We could only tell him
things like: we had to raise the volume on his mike, little things.
But when it came to things like arrangements and licks and ideas
and vocal styling, what in the world could we have possibly found
to say to Ray Charles? We'd just go into the studio, open up the
mikes, and pray—and sit there and learn! Ray Charles was certainly a learning experience for me. I learned how to make a *real*
record.

I can recall recording Ray Charles at WGST, the radio station
of Georgia Tech in Atlanta. We recorded "I Got a Woman" in
that session. I'll never forget—there was a doddering old engineer
who had never done any recording before. And we had to stop the
session every hour because that's when they gave the news. Then
we couldn't get a sound again for three hours. In those days, we
had to record monophonically and mix "on the fly." We couldn't
go back to redo the mistakes; there was no overdubbing. That
meant we had to achieve a balance "on the fly" too. A lot of people still feel those old balances are still the best sounds in popular
music.

With Ray, we did "I Got a Woman," "Halleluah," "Green-
backs," "This Little Girl of Mine," "Swanee River Rock," and
"Yes Indeed." Ray is responsible for bringing the gospel form into
popular music—eight- and sixteen-bar gospel forms. The other
acts had been using either twelve-bar blues figures or standard
thirty-two-bar songs, but Ray took gospel songs and substituted
popular lyrics for sacred lyrics. Instead of bringing people into the
church, he brought them into the studio. Ray's last big hit on Atlantic was "What'd I Say?" and his last album for us was *The
Genius of Ray Charles.*

LEIBER & STOLLER

Leiber and Stoller had such a great sense of music. It was as if
they'd gotten together and said, "Let's invent rock and roll on Friday." Jerry and Mike came to Atlantic because their own Spark
Records was failing. They had this label in California, and their
principal artist was the Robins, who were the forerunners of the
Coasters. But they weren't making it distributing their own records, and they made a deal for us to distribute them.

First they made their Coasters records in California and mailed them to us. Can you imagine receiving great records like those in plain brown envelopes? That's how beautiful the business was back then. Then they moved here to New York and began making the Coasters with King Curtis and Atlantic's rhythm section. We had a handshake deal with them; there was no contract for several years.

Leiber and Stoller began by only recording the Coasters. Then, one day, I was so burdened down by sessions and other work, I said to Ahmet, "Why don't we let them do a Drifters record?" It was a good risk then, because we were in between the real Drifters. We didn't have a star lead singer. Clyde McPhatter had left and we had not yet found Rudy Lewis or Ben E. King. So we said, "Make a record of the Drifters with no lead singer." And they *sure* did.

Leiber and Stoller were good guys and became our very close friends. They were intelligent, they were literate, they had a sense of humor about what they were doing, and they had no "cosmic" significance. Their musical style typified the point of view of the ghetto looking at the establishment, the Man, that prison, at gin mills, hustlers, pimps—but through the sardonic twist of *their* minds. Jerry had been raised on that type of music in a Baltimore ghetto and he filtered it through his own gentle cynicism.

BLACK AND WHITE: THE TRANSITION

The genesis of how we came from being a pure black company is very traceable. It actually started with and was precipitated by Bobby Darin. Bobby was signed by Herb Abramson, and Herb began producing his records. I used to hear this little skinny white kid in the studio next door to my office playing Ray Charles licks on the piano and I was really amazed. He and Donnie Kirshner, his manager, were kids at the time and would come up to our offices in their sneakers.

Bobby made a gang of records for us that were all flops. He had previously recorded on Decca Records and flopped. Then he came up with a song called "Splish Splash," and the only person who believed in it was Ahmet. I thought it was a piece of crap. But Bob insisted it was a hit and Ahmet made the record. That started it. And the next record was "Mack the Knife" and then "Queen of the Hop," and we were into white music.

We originally signed Bobby because he sounded black, fitted our idea of a white artist, and was subsequently the only white artist we had for years. We didn't sign white artists because we didn't want to compete with RCA and Decca. They would have wiped us out. So, instead, we had a little specialty. When we started, our music only sold to black people and white artists wouldn't sell to black people. We were a demographic record company. I made records by black artists to sell to black people. Period. But Darin was our notable exception. And we really didn't think that white people would buy Bobby Darin's records.

As Bobby became extremely successful, and while he became a major force in popular music, he started recording in California which drew Ahmet there. Ahmet started recording with California orchestras. Well, an important session man on Bobby's dates was Nino Tempo, the saxophone player. As a consequence, Ahmet signed Nino and recorded him with April Stevens—and they were our second big white act.

On the Nino and April dates, there was a little Italian kid named Sonny Bono, and that led to our signing Sonny and Cher. Through Sonny and Cher, we became friends with Charlie Greene and Brian Stone, their managers. One day, Charlie called me from California about a terrific group there that we *must* see, must rush out and look at. That group was Buffalo Springfield. Ahmet happened to be in Mexico at the time and I said, "Ahmet, before you come back to New York, run up to California and see Charlie's group." And that led to our signing Buffalo Springfield. So the tree, the flow, is Bobby Darin to Nino Tempo to Sonny Bono to Buffalo Springfield, which opened us up to white music as well as black.

At the same time, we were starting to take records from England and we signed both Acker Bilk and the Shadows. Ahmet wasn't the businessman at that time—I was. I carried the business and made records, too. But somebody had to be free to travel around and bring us the next musical phase, and that was Ahmet.

In the early Sixties, even before the Beatles, the English groups started to explode—Gerry & The Pacemakers, Herman's Hermits

—and it was falling all around us. We had the Who—they recorded "Substitute" on Atlantic—we had Arthur Brown, but, the fact is, we couldn't seem to bring a British record home, we couldn't make it a hit. We got to be known as a jinx label with the British music world. Then along came the Beatles, and if you didn't have the Beatles or the *next* Beatles in 1964, you didn't know if you were in the record business or not. But we still had R&B. There was always a market for that. And it kept us in the ball park.

"CALL THIS NUMBER, NOW!"

In 1967, I had heard through the grapevine that Aretha Franklin's five-year contract with Columbia Records was about up. She had made some great records for Columbia, but they hadn't found her essence. Her R&B and gospel roots hadn't been touched. And she wanted to find a new label who could make her a star.

Actually, I had been tipped off about her dissatisfaction by a friend. Jimmy Bishop, one of Philadelphia's leading disc jockeys, had a wife named Louise Williams, who was a very good gospel disc jockey. We were good friends and Louise was close to Aretha in those simpler, less complicated days when that gospel crowd was like one big family. And Louise was the listening post; she knew everything that was going on with Clara Ward, Aretha, and Sam Cooke. And she used to keep me posted.

One day, I happened to be in Muscle Shoals doing a Wilson Pickett session, and I got a call from Louise in Philadelphia. All she said was, "Call this number, *now!*" It was Aretha. I had never spoken to her, but I called her and that was it. She said, "I like what you're saying, but you'll have to speak to my husband," who was Ted White at that time. I spoke to Ted, they came to New York for the meeting, and we made the deal.

Aretha's been in different states of mind over the years, she's been at various degrees of peace with herself. If somebody's troubled by personal affairs, then it's difficult to generate the energy to set up a recording session. Once Aretha was in the studio, almost invariably she'd be fabulous singing, playing, and contributing. It was getting her *into* the studio. Once that occurred, we would barrel through and get great stuff. I can hardly remember a time we started a session with Aretha that we didn't get something out of it. She's still the consummate R&B artist.

HOW I GOT TO MEMPHIS

There was a man from Detroit named Robert West, who had a group called the Falcons. They had originally been a gospel group: Wilson Pickett, Mac Rice, and some other people were in the group. Robert called me and asked me if I'd underwrite a $500 session at King Studios in Cincinnati for this group. That was a lot of money in those days to record two sides. He said, "We have a terrific song called 'The Swim,' which is going to be a new dance sensation." So I said, "Okay, I'll back it for $500," and we made a deal. He made the record, I listened to it, and it was awful. I said, "Bob, I can't use it." He asked for the tape rights back and I gladly gave them to him. But I never listened to the other side. And I forgot about that fiasco.

About six months later, I got a call from a disc jockey from Buffalo who said that there was a song raising hell in that city by the Falcons called "I Found a Love." And that had been the flip side of "The Swim." Here I had given the rights away—even after I had originally paid for it. So I got hold of Robert West and said, "I hear the record is breaking." He said, "I've been waiting to hear from you. Leonard Chess and Lew Chudd have been calling, but I waited for you." So I had to buy back the master that I had paid for at premium prices and had to guarantee them a heavy royalty on top of it all. And after that, the Falcons never had anything as good—a few moderate sellers, but no big hits.

That gradually faded out. The next thing I know, I receive a tape from a guy in Detroit with eight songs on it—one of which was "If You Need Me," again with Wilson Pickett singing. At that time, I was producing Solomon Burke with Burt Berns, and we were looking for songs. "If You Need Me" stood out. I played it for Burt and he said, "There's no use covering it with Solomon. The demo's too good." And I said, "We'll do it with Solomon anyhow," because I always had a policy of supporting the artist I was working with. It was very common in R&B to take whatever came in the mail and put it out as a record. There were a lot of one-shot records as a result of that; people would have one hit song and no follow-up. Our policy was to try to get the song, save it, and build the artist. We at Atlantic were fabulous at building artists. So I paid $1,000 for the publishing rights to "If You Need Me," which was a fortune in those days. I had already cut it with Solomon Burke and knew the record was good, so I would be protecting that investment. But I neglected to deal for Pickett's master.

I'm sitting on the Solomon Burke record, and I get a call from a disc jockey one morning who says, "Man, I played this record fourteen times in a row, and the phones are jumping. It's called 'If You Need Me' by Wilson Pickett." I rushed into the office and I found out that they had sold Pickett's demo to a guy named Harold Logan, who was a partner of Lloyd Price's. They had a label called Double-L Records, which was distributed by Liberty Records. I'm trying to figure out what to do. Solomon's a big star and Wilson's a nobody. Nothing would work. There were no angles that Logan and Price would accept other than for me to suppress Solomon Burke's record—and I wasn't about to do that. The meeting got a little heated, and we never came to any conclusions. Actually, their record was better than Solomon Burke's. But we went to work and started promoting the hell out of Solomon. It was a big battle and we won just on general record company size and promotion skill. Of course, though, I made an enemy out of Wilson Pickett.

A couple years later, Wilson came walking into my office with a tape under his arm. He said, "I want to be on Atlantic." I asked him, "Aren't you mad at us?" And he said, "Nah—I forgot all about that." So I put out that tape he brought in, "Too Late," which he had produced. It wasn't a bad record, but it only sold about forty thousand singles. Then I had an obligation of doing something bigger with him. By now, Burt Berns was a heavyweight producer, and I gave Wilson Pickett to Burt. They made an interesting, weird record with a New Orleans singer named Tammi Lynn that was a total stiff and cost $6,000 to make, which was an unbelievable price for 1963.

So Wilson Pickett bounced back into my lap. I had faced circumstances like this many times: signing an artist either based on an understanding of who was going to produce him or a producer would bring him into me; the next thing, they have a falling out and I'm stuck with the artist and no producer—which means *I* have to produce him. Wilson and I dickered around for a year. If I found a song, he didn't like it; if he found a song, I didn't like it. Finally his manager called and said, "Look, either do something or let my boy go."

At this time, Atlantic was recording in New York, still using the same old studio musicians and arrangers, and our string of hits was running out. We had been having hits with the same type of arrangements since 1953. And you could hear it in the records we were making. They were getting very tired, and our stature in the industry started to slip. In the meantime, I had begun an association with Stax Records in Memphis through the president, Jim Stewart, to release their records. They had Carla Thomas, Rufus Thomas, Otis Redding, and Sam and Dave (who I signed and gave to Jim Stewart to produce). I called Jim and said, "I'd like to bring Wilson Pickett down to Memphis and use your studio and band to produce him." He said, "Fine." And that's how I got to Memphis.

I sent Wilson there ahead of me, and for three days he laid around with Steve Cropper and they wrote "Midnight Hour," "Don't Fight It," and a few more things. We produced a gang of good records through that session. I left Pickett there and Cropper and Stewart produced some more sides. So Wilson got a base in Memphis. Then I brought Don Covay down there and we did very well. But we soon reached the point that either Pickett had made himself a *persona non grata* or the people down there resented his success. But, either way, I wound up selling his contract to RCA. I sold a lot of artists' contracts on their decline. I made a business out of it. In fact, it's a *good* business selling artists that are finished—before the other companies find out they're finished. Pretty soon, other companies got spooky about doing business with me. I sold Delaney and Bonnie's contract to Columbia for $600,000 and they never had anything else worthwhile on record.

But the Pickett experience had gotten me involved with the Southern style of recording—which was "head" arrangements. A set band comes in and works out the rhythm section *during* the date. They just happen to have a horn section on hand, and that's all you need.

THE MEMPHIS SOUND

Jim Stewart had been a fiddler in a hillbilly band and worked in a bank. But he wanted to make records. He had a sister named Estelle Axton. They got a little money together and they bought an old movie theater. In the front, they put a little R&B record store and they started cutting records in the theater. It was a large, funky theater. The whole situation was just so *real*.

They used a mixed band: Steve Cropper, Al Jackson, Booker T. and Duck Dunn. Other people hung around like Chips Moman, a great guitar player named Charlie Freeman, and Willie Mitchell, who played great trumpet for many years. I started to record with Chips Moman, too. He had a great band: Tommy Cogbill on bass, Chips on guitar, Bobby Woods and Bobby Emmons on keyboards, Reggie Young on guitar, and Gene Krisman on drums. With this band, I recorded *Dusty in Memphis,* King Curtis's *Memphis Soul Stew, The Sweet Inspirations,* and Wilson Pickett's "I'm in Love" and "Stack-O-Lee"

But suddenly the Stax people barred the door. They didn't want any other outside productions done there. I don't know what their reason was. But I've always had this thing in the South, a strange ambivalence. I'm a father figure for a lot of people and, because of that, they always have a great affection and an equally great dislike for me. Maybe they think I'm patronizing them or I'm too strong or . . . I don't know what it is. But it happened with a lot of people: Rick Hall, Chips Moman, Jim Stewart. See, I've always come along at a time when my arrival on the scene is very significant for these people. And I'm sure that has something to do with it. I remind them of the days when they weren't doing as well as the present.

MUSCLE SHOALS

I went to Muscle Shoals because I had been distributing Rick Hall's records for a couple years. He was making his own records with a fabulous band: Roger Hawkins on drums, Spooner Oldham on keyboards, Jimmy Johnson played one guitar, Tommy Cogbill and Chips Moman played second and third guitars, and

Junior Lowe played bass. I brought Wilson Pickett down to work with this band and we had nothing but hits: "Land of 1,000 Dances," "Everybody Needs Somebody to Love," "Mustang Sally," that bunch of records. They're different from the Stax Records. They're hotter, and Pickett really put out. I recorded Ronnie Hawkins there, Lulu, and a few other artists. Muscle Shoals became my favorite place to record. And the reason was the band—that's the only reason. The mystique of studios was nonexistent. Today, the studio is more important based on the sophistication of electronics. In those days, you could record in a barn if you had the right band. And I still feel that way.

What happened in Muscle Shoals was after several years at Fame—Rick Hall's studio—his band started complaining to me that they were being mistreated by Rick. I said that I couldn't get involved. So one day they all came to see me and said, "We're quitting. We want you to be with us." I told Rick Hall, "Your band's quitting," and he said, "Who gives a fuck?" So Ahmet and I helped the band set up their own studio. We underwrote them without interest. And I still record there to this day. It's going on nineteen years that I've been working with the same band.

WHY I LEFT ATLANTIC

In 1975, I left Atlantic. I did it basically for one reason: I was getting bored. I was tired of working all day on administrative matters and still having to worry about making good records. I was the one responsible for making certain that Atlantic was running smoothly. I hired the people who are now head of promotion, sales, and marketing. I hired Jerry Greenberg, who is now president of Atlantic. I was monitoring the sales, promotion, everything else. And finally I said, "This has got to stop. I'm tired of all this." Hell, I'd been doing it since 1953. Now, it's someone else's turn. And I've still got a lot of records to make.

Forum: Producers

The difference between a producer and a person who merely supervises a recording session is most fundamentally demonstrated by dropping the needle on a record. From there, it is a matter of the listener's "getting off" on what's coming through the speakers. If the particular artist is one of your favorites or even one of your not-so-favorites but has a reputation for making exciting records and the music just sits there, chances are the so-called producer missed the boat. He failed to create the spark needed to take that particular artist over the threshold, to make the music come alive. In essence, he merely walked through the production of the album making certain the tracks were being laid down and the final product would be delivered on time. That is not a creative task. As extraordinary as it seems, a good producer will make the music "happen" whether or not the talent was there in the first place. If it means exorcising the artist to discover a hidden potential or concentrating specifically on the instrumentation or any number of other ploys, the good producer will find the key that unlocks the magic. The distinction is as simple as that.

However, the producer's job is not as simple as that. It involves many hours spent formulating a concept that begins long before a note is ever put on tape, often before an artist has selected or writ-

ten the song they intend to record. For many producers, it involves going through tedious legal negotiations with the artist and the record company to establish the financial ground rules for an association. And an indeterminable amount of picayune details in between, such as where the artist will rehearse, selecting a studio, hiring studio musicians (after the initial decision has been made to use them), booking studio time around everyone's existing schedules, preparing a budget, maintaining a psychological "high," and many more. Not to mention the making of music. It is an overwhelming responsibility and requires a person capable of undertaking such an effort. Consequently, today there is only a handful of producers who consistently make good records.

Every producer has a style of his own which he adapts to the artist being produced. That style begins with a psychological approach to the music and carries over to the laying down of the tracks. Some work for every minute detail, while others move rapidly through the session relying on spontaneity. Even others will assign themselves to several concurrent sessions and walk from studio to studio, adding their suggestions and cross-pollinating musical ideas.

This forum presents a wide range of production styles of some of the top producers of the day.

JIMMY IENNER

(Jimmy Ienner began his career in music at the age of twelve singing background for many of the doo-wop stars. He was the deep voice that sang: "Duke-duke-duke, Duke of Earl, duke, duke, Duke of Earl, etc.," the harmonies for the Dion hits and the Dovells, among others. Today, he is probably one of America's most successful rock and roll producers, having recorded hits for Lighthouse, Three Dog Night, The Raspberries, Grand Funk Railroad, Eric Carmen and the Bay City Rollers. In 1977, he decided to launch his own record company, Millennium Records.)

Choosing the Act

I'm not sure exactly how I go about selecting an act to record. It probably varies from act to act. But I think I choose a group I like, from having heard previous things they've done or from having been knocked out by listening to a tape which they submitted. Any number of combinations. Sometimes a group will fall into my lap unexpectedly. That's great.

It was very ironic how I picked the Bay City Rollers. I thought they were a great challenge. I liked what they did because I felt they filled a tremendous void. Why shouldn't the kids of today have their exciting idols? I saw my own kids loving them, and I thought that we desperately needed a group like the Rollers.

From listening to their earlier recorded material, I thought I heard them trying to take a more mature step in their music. I told my assistant, "Get me every review on the Rollers that you can." Well, one was worse than the other; it got horrendous. Critics weren't reviewing the group—they were letting out their venom. So I said, "I'll do it! I love it!" And that probably sums up my reasons for choosing a group: 1) that I love the sound, and 2) that it is a challenge.

The one thing I'll never do is approach an opportunity on a dollar level—although I am known as one of the three most expensive producers. One of the reasons I have that reputation is that instead of making a group feel badly by choosing not to make a record with them—I refuse seven or eight top groups my services per week—is that I always use the ploy "It's gonna cost you." I know in advance that most of the groups can't afford my price. If I really wanted to produce the group, I would alter the price to suit them. Otherwise, I use that line. I hate to turn a group down. It's so uncomfortable. So I take the chicken's way out. That's why, at times, my reputation for being expensive isn't real as much as it is taking the easy way out.

Preproduction

The first thing I try to do after selecting an act to record is to go through a feeling-out process, a testing ground. The Christians versus the lions, so to speak. Except at the end of the battle, everybody goes in and does a great album. But at times, there are winners and losers. I'm a winner; I've never lost.

Establishing a dialogue is the first thing I try to do. It sets the ground rules. Then the group will give me some feedback and I'll know where their head is at toward recording. After that, I start on the particulars. This song is good and that song isn't good because . . . This arrangement is good, but you used it on your last two albums. Then, when I give them enough to think about, I start with the actual work—who plays too much, who doesn't play enough. I take apart every inch of their past recordings—every note—and I homogenize it. The group doesn't feel it outright, but it's a case of: crush/let up/crush/let up. So that when that recording light goes on and we're ready to lay down tracks, the group isn't thinking anymore. That's why their recording performances breathe.

Rehearsals, for me, are extremely painstaking. It is the setup and conditioning for what will be in the studio. It makes life in the studio easier because the group has been through it already. I always try to give a group the impression that the studio will be one step harder than rehearsals—which the group can't fathom. But, in essence, it's easier. So, in the studio, the group just keeps giving and giving and cooks more.

The Wrath of Jimmy Ienner

There is a so-called wrath of Jimmy Ienner. The first time a group will feel it is in preproduction. The picking of material to be included on the album will, from me, be a constant barrage of "Why? Why do you like that?" I will put a group through mental exercises so that by the time they're ready to do the tunes, they won't think about why they like them or whether or not they made a mistake. They'll be past that. It's almost like shock treatment so that when they get into the studio it's an accepted procedure and the group knows they're not going to get away with anything, that they won't incur my "vicious" wrath. If they follow the preproduction to the tee, it will show up on the album because I'll capture it. And, if they don't, it won't go on the record.

I always make sure the group knows that there is a delineation, a thin line, between me and them. It's them against me. Not in any negative sense. But they depend on each other more instead of depending on me, the producer. And they give to each other more often. I become only a voice. They can see me through the glass, but I don't play on the session. It's all them.

There's just an incredible amount of psychology involved and some of my approaches, to the groups, become some spooky "wrath."

Hit Singles

I always look for a hit single, but it doesn't mean that I'll bastardize the work of the act if it isn't there. One of my favorite albums is J. F. Murphy and Salt's *The Last Illusion*. Critically, it was very well received. But I think it only sold 170,000 copies and was one of the worst disasters of my career. No hit singles, but it captures everything I set out to do. It is a personal hit, which, at times, is more important than a commercial success.

Today, there are other elements involved that make an album successful other than hit singles. For a group like Z Z Top, hit singles don't apply anymore. A group like Grand Funk doesn't need a hit single, but they certainly *want* one and could use it to enhance their sales. On the other hand, Three Dog Night's audience came to see them at concerts specifically to hear the hits. It's funny. It depends solely on the group and their audience. It didn't used to, but the times are a-changing. I'll still go for the hit, though, if it's there. Believe me, the group will only thank me for it later.

Approaches

I approach groups many different ways. With Lighthouse, I approached them as a group that made songs not nearly as good as their playing expertise. With Grand Funk, I tried to capture the feeling of their heavy-metal reputation and tried to work within that framework because they always had a certain feeling when they were ready to begin work on an album. They were a talented group which everybody knocked. I had to approach Three Dog Night on purely a song level: "You three are *it,* this song is for you, and here's how it will shine."

Eric Carmen I approached in two different ways. Firstly, as a writer. I think he's one of the best and someday just how great he is will become evident. But Eric can fool you. He'll send me a demo of a new song that's better than 90 per cent of the masters made today. But if I let him get away with that, then there would be a lot of tunes and constructions on the album that would fall short of Eric's potential. So I also approach him as one would approach an acrobat doing a balancing act. I let him be real busy and do all he has to do to get it out of his system. Then I will completely take him to another extreme, an opposite sound. I frighten him a little bit so that he thinks his song is being cut and turned inside out. That way, he makes a compromise and, instead of being extreme in one direction or another, he meets his artistry somewhere in the middle. He'll want to do forty-three strings and have lush lines throughout the songs. So I'll tell him, "I'd rather not hear any strings or lush lines." And it will end up somewhere in the middle. So Eric feels like he's getting more than what I had intended in the first place.

What They Don't Want to Hear

I always talk to an artist about his insecurities because they *always* exist. I don't beat around the bush; otherwise those insecurities will take over the recording of an album. The first thing I do is figure out if his problem is real. If it is, we deal with it; if it is not, you have to make him understand why it's not real—but not just by employing rhetoric. An artist bases his life on his own creativity and is therefore self-indulgent; there's no way that he cannot be. In order to be able to put yourself out and expose yourself every time within the pains of writing and performing, an artist must be self-indulgent. And it becomes very difficult for an artist to view what is real and what isn't. So it is up to me to tell him. That's why it's important that the artists I produce have confidence in me, know that I'll be honest and tell them what they *don't* want to hear as much as what they *do* want to hear.

I've been known to say to some of the biggest acts in the world, "Hey, that's good, man, but why don't you just go into the bathroom and use your left hand because I don't want to be stroked and I don't want to stroke you." It'll shock them, they'll put their heads down and sit there quietly like a little two-year-old being caught. But it's my way. It's the only way. And it's the way it's gotta be.

JON LANDAU

(Jon Landau began his professional career in music while still in college in the Boston area as a musician and as a critic for one of the local periodicals. After graduation, he produced records for the MC5 and Livingston Taylor and joined the staff of Rolling Stone, *where he established himself as one of the foremost rock critics in the country. In 1975, Bruce Springsteen asked Jon for some recording advice, and he, once again, donned the hat of a producer. In the next year alone, he was awarded gold and platinum albums for his productions of* Born to Run *and* The Pretender.*)*

The Producer's Job

In my opinion, the producer's job is the following. He and the artist agree to work together. Then, it is the producer's job to supply that knowledge, insight, and perspective that will ensure a successful record for the artist. Not necessarily a commercially successful record, but an artistically successful record.

If a producer is working with an artist who doesn't write songs, it may be his job to help the artist find songs. If he's working with an artist who does write good songs, he has no work in that area. Then his job may be primarily to work developing the artist's sound.

Producers like Dennis Lambert and Brian Potter write an album for their artist; their imput is musical whereas others specialize more in the over-all sound of an album. Jerry Wexler has half perspective in each of those areas without having certifiable technical expertise. I'm more in that mold. Phil Spector and Thom Bell have a minute step-by-step perception of every single aspect of the record and the artist is there basically to act out a role.

My job is to "make a difference." I sit with Bruce Springsteen or Jackson Browne or whoever it may be and get to know the artist and form a sense of what the album will be about. I have a dialogue with the artist about all that and help him achieve his goals.

The Dialogue

With both Bruce and Jackson, the dialogue process took months of communication before the album ever began. When I first started discussing *The Pretender* with Jackson Browne, he was not even sure he was going to make an album. We spent a good amount of time arriving at the conclusion that there was an album to be made. When he played me the song "The Pretender," I said, "You're ready to start an album. You have your title song —a song that will sum up the album, will be the guts of the album." When you have that, it implies what the tone of the rest of the album will be. It puts into perspective the album that needed to be made.

Bruce and I became extremely good friends before it ever occurred to me that I'd work with him. When we finally started talking, I said, "Look, it must be aggravating for you to be reading over and over again that your shows are better than your records." He said, "Yeah, but that's because it's true." So I said, "Bruce, now that I've gotten to know you and listened to all your tapes and listened to you recount your entire career—you're a rocker. You got cast as a singer/songwriter, a folkie. But what I get from you, above everything else, is that you're into rock and roll. You haven't made a rock album yet. You've been making singer/songwriter albums." He cracked up. He said, "I was a singer/songwriter for about eight months. I've been a rocker for eleven years." I said, "You put a picture of yourself looking like a poet on the cover of your second album.[1] That just throws people off. There's a big gap between what you're doing in your show and doing on record." That dialogue wasn't designed to bring down his writing—he's the greatest. It was done to bring forward this other dimension that had somehow gotten lost. And that's how our association began.

What's Happening?

My approach to production is to find the key to the solution. The problem, the album, is *there* in the artist's hands. It's the

---

[1] *The Wild, the Innocent and the E Street Shuffle.*

producer's job to unlock different areas. What's happening? Where is this song turning me on? Where is it just treading water? You have to find the focus and close in on it.

In "Jungleland," the whole production leads up to Bruce's singing: "The street's on fire in a real death waltz/between what's flesh and what's fantasy." The whole thing is set up so when he hits those lines your ear is so totally focused on them. On "The Pretender," when Jackson hits the line, "Out into the cool of the evening strolls the Pretender"—I always thought that was the big moment and, to bring it more forward, everything else in the production falls away dramatically: only light bass, drums, piano, and guitar highlight the close-up. This is the type of thought process, the way I relate to approach the work.

The Voice of Reason

Sometimes the exceedingly detailed aspect of recording drives me nuts, but it's part of the gig. Often, I become impatient, but I realize that the only reason the artist keeps bringing ideas up is because he's trying to make a record sound better. If I never lose sight of that, I can cope with the impatience. Of course, sometimes recording conflicts with tours, scheduling, and practical considerations on which it is my job to maintain a perspective and to keep the whole experimental process from deteriorating to formless search. Anything can be carried to an extreme.

It's my job to say, "Okay, we've considered this, we've considered that—we're trying things again that we've already tried and rejected. We're going backward. It's time to make a decision." I have to be the voice of reason, to try and allow a certain amount to happen on a free basis and then organize it, shape it into something that will advance the album.

"Born to Run"

Bruce had been at work on the album and had completed only a single, "Born to Run," which appears on the album in the form in which he made it. The album then became stalled. He couldn't progress. There were ideas in his head which he wasn't getting on tape. I had written some articles about him when I was still a critic, and we met and became friends. Soon after, he came to the conclusion that I might be able to help him. I agreed.

He had problems for which he didn't have solutions: what is the album all about, why aren't we getting there, how are we going to get there? I have an analytical perspective concerning rock bands —their music, arrangement, and production—which I was able to share with Bruce. And part of what I did for his production had a lot to do with the work I did as an editor at *Rolling Stone*. When Bruce first played me "Thunder Road," it was seven minutes long —too long for its own good as some rough drafts of Bruce's songs frequently are. He has too many ideas prepared to be included in one song. By working together, we were able to cut it down and make it a much more effective song.

Bruce is very demanding in the studio, and he requires a great deal of patience, dedication, and faith in him. He comes up with a lot of unorthodox ideas which invite skepticism but which, many times, prove to be the key to something very exciting. I try to discipline that. But I've found out, when the budget is there and I'm working with an artist of exceptional caliber, there's no substitute for trying any idea that artist may propose. I will put it on tape and can better evaluate it that way. People say to me, "Isn't that an inefficient way to make a record?" Well, it's an inefficient way to make a hack record, but not to make an experimental record. I go into the studio trying to act out and develop new approaches with these artists. Bruce and Jackson satisfy their artistic talents *in the studio*.

"The Pretender"

If *Born to Run* took four or five months to record, *The Pretender* took six. Jackson and I learned so much on *The Pretender* that, ideally, on our next album it will go much faster. Jackson has developed his own particular brand of recording and has established a certain stylistic thing that he likes. I think that his first three albums sound a certain way, and *The Pretender* sounds another way, more musical. Those six months were very difficult, very slow and very demanding. It took a lot out of me. Jackson is a very emotional, demanding person. There was a lot of discussion, a lot of disagreements and a lot of redoing songs searching for still a better way. Hell, with Jackson, we cut some songs three, four, and five times to carry out the intention which we had devised for them.

I'm not too much into authority, though. So the only authority that I strive for in a Jackson Browne session is to persuade him that I'm right via the fact that I've got a good idea. I could never say to him, "All right, this is how I want to do it, this is what you are going to do, where you are going to stand, what you are going to sing." That's not my thing. And it is the only way I can work with an artist like Jackson Browne—without all that simple-minded direction.

But even though it goes so slow, the outcome is something I can really be proud of. Hell, I'm *real* proud of *Born to Run* and *The Pretender*. They were real adventures and I loved doing them. I love producing albums.

TED TEMPLEMAN

(Ted Templeman was an artist before he was a producer, having been the lead singer for a successful group called Harper's Bizarre. Since then, he has become a highly respected producer in the Warner Bros. Records team of in-house producers and has produced albums for Van Morrison, the Doobie Brothers, Carly Simon, and Little Feat.)

The First Album I Ever Produced

In 1970, when Harper's Bizarre had run its course, Lenny Waronker offered me a job working with him in A&R. He had been producer of most of our recorded material, and he knew of my desire to become involved with production. I was an A&R assistant for a long time and spent all day listening to tapes which had been submitted for our consideration. That's how I found the Doobie Brothers. I heard the tape, auditioned them, got Lenny to hear them, we signed them, and with Lenny I produced their first album. That was the first album I ever produced. It wasn't really successful. I was blundering around in the studio and so were they. I found out that thinking I was a producer and actually producing were two different things. I didn't understand the psychology of working with four or five guys in a studio, nor did I realize that although something recorded may not be perfect, it may still have the right feel, the soul. It was a period of growing pains for me. A lot of things went wrong. We were locked into a production deal and had to record at a studio which we didn't like and where we weren't able to get a good enough sound. It was a painful first lesson.

Primary Function

I think my over-all responsibility is producing a record that's going to represent the artist, appeal to him and a lot of other people, but not necessarily be commercial. I just did a record with Little Feat. I came across a tune that I knew would have sounded like a smash tune with them doing it, but it wouldn't have been right for their image. I want to make a nice record. If a group is in need of a hit single, it should come from them or else it should be something an artist can interpret naturally.

As far as a primary function of mine, I have to expose properly what the artist has got, try to get that talent out. Sometimes that means my getting involved in the arrangement, laying tunes on them, sometimes it means my shutting up—my sitting back in the studio and allowing them to do what they've got to do. It is a matter of my forgetting my ego and, especially, my participation *not* being recognized on the record. I would hate it if somebody said, "Ah—that's a Ted Templeman production." I try to create a recording environment rather than create a sound like Richard Perry or Phil Spector does, because I believe that even though the production is a creative process, it is still facilitating what talent was there in the first place.

Preproduction

Preproduction always depends on the group I'm producing. If I'm working with a touring group, it is hard. Many times they'll go into the studio right off the road and we have to get to work immediately. With a group like Little Feat, I take a lot of time. They'll come into my office, I'll make suggestions about their song structure, we'll work on the tunes together, and I'll attend their rehearsals. Whenever possible, I'll spend a lot of time rehearsing an act in a hall. I don't rehearse them to death. Instead, I get them to a point where the structure feels good and then take them into the studio while they're still hot. But a lot of the preproduction determines how the rest of the recording will go.

Creating a dialogue depends, again, on the individual artist. It is important for me to have good communications in terms of where the artist wants to go musically. And I'm not a "yes" man. So we have to talk a lot. That helps me through difficult moments. My records with Van Morrison are good examples of successful communication. He is a great guy, but it gets rough in the studio with Van. Luckily, I can talk to him. If you don't have a sense of communication with the artist, you cannot sort out the rough moments.

Time and Money

It takes me anywhere from three to six months to complete a project. It involves getting together with the artist and going over the proposed tunes. If there's something missing, we keep going over the songs until we determine what's wrong. That takes time. Then we begin rehearsal, cut some tracks to see how it's going. If it is a new artist, we take a little bit longer because we have to develop a feeling for each other in the studio. That involves me laying down demos for a week or so to get used to the way he plays and his dynamics. After that, we go in to do the tracks. It takes weeks to do that—working on the tunes, determining the arrangements, sweetening, trying things that may not turn out the way we envisioned them, and recutting. Then I begin to mix. I mix for long periods of time; I get heavily involved with mixing.

The cost of making a record album varies. If it is a rock and roll band, I can do it for between $50,000 and $75,000 because there is no sweetening involved. Otherwise, it may cost between $75,000 to $130,000. Rehearsing cuts the cost a bit. A lot of things can be done to keep costs down. I abhor drugs in the studio. Cocaine is a big waste of money and time. A producer owes it to his artist to outlaw drugs in the studio. I know a lot of producers who feel they have to "get down" with their artists. That's a load of shit. I don't care how rock and rolly a band may be, when it comes to recording they *don't* want you to "get down" with them. They want you to produce the damn record.

Studio Discipline

I only employ a few rules in the studio. I do not allow anyone to visit the session except the artists on the date. The old ladies, the friends, even the roadies—out! I just lock the doors. It's a private situation. That way, everybody is relaxed. It is hard for me to say to an artist, "Hey—you're fucking up," if his friend from out of town is sitting there in the booth. An artist might not level with me for the same reason. Also, I don't like any outsiders throwing ideas around. It just confuses everybody.

The Doobie Brothers

The Doobie Brothers were originally a beer bar band that played for Hell's Angels' parties. There is a lot of that still in them, so when we go into the studio, I try to get something exciting happening. We lay down a couple tracks and sit with them for a few days. Then we come back and work some more.

When I work with the Doobies, the sessions are not precise, but I've found that the group will work until they get the sound right. They're a real easy band to get along with. Sometimes it's difficult because I have to work with two drummers and it's hard to record two sets of drums and a lot of complications arise. But the band has no studio ego—none whatsoever.

Tom Johnson is always prepared for the session ahead of time, while Pat Simmons is more creative in the studio. Pat comes up with some amazing stuff there. "Long Train Runnin'" was originally a piece of junk called "Osborne." They didn't even want to record it. But Tommy had a line in there about "down along the tracks." So I said, "Make it into a train song." And he did. Then Pat came in and put an incredible guitar lick over what we already had. He does this all the time. Then I'll let things go and let them be creative as all hell. I'll sit back and not even interrupt.

Carly Simon

Carly is creative vocally in the studio; she is always coming up with unusual vocal ideas. When that happens, I just clam up. She takes over. Her sessions are fairly easy for me except that we have to use different musicians for every song.

My initial goal is to get Carly to play and sing along on every track. That helps to convey her feeling for the song to the band. Otherwise, she's easy and flexible to work with.

Van Morrison

There have been very difficult times in the studio with Van. He's got a certain fix on something when he arrives with new material, we rehearse it, go into the studio, and he immediately changes direction. Sometimes I could just scream! Mainly, it causes sound problems for me.

Our sessions got real bumpy because he'd bring in some last-minute drummer and we'd have to wait until this new musician learned the song. Musicians, in general, stand in awe of Van; it's an interesting thing to observe. He goes into a session, sings his guts out, and drives everybody insane. I'm most proud of the records I've made with him. I think he's the best singer in the world.

The In-house Group

A lot of the producers at Warner Bros. have known each other for years. Lenny Waronker is responsible for getting us all there. Lenny brought me in, then Russ Titleman joined and he brought Little Feat to the label. Russ produces Randy Newman. Then Tommy LaPuma came and he's had so much success with artists like George Benson. Steve Barri is real pop-oriented and Gary Katz knows how to make an excellent progressive album. We have an extraordinarily well-rounded producing staff.

The reason for our success is that Mo Ostin lets us all do what we want to do. It's a very loose situation. We all hang out and bang ideas around all day. A real creative atmosphere.

This morning, I listened to a Doobie Brothers track I had just completed. It sounded a little shaky to me, but I knew the feel was there. So I took it to Steve Barri and said, "Whaddya think?" and he offered his suggestions. Then Gary Katz came in. He had been working with Gregg Allman and wanted to know what I thought he should do with the drum track and I offered my advice. Each one of us knows things the others do not readily have a fix on. It's an exciting way to work.

Forum: Publicists

Next to music, image is perhaps the most important aspect of a recording artist's career. The way a particular artist looks and feels, thinks and reacts to situations plays heavily upon the way the public views that person and, many times, creates an appeal equally as important as the music. But unless the artist is so unique a talent or a personality before embarking on a recording career, it is up to the publicist to create an image that will catch the public eye and lure them into giving this artist a chance to be heard.

Publicity is an art in itself, distinguished by those in the profession who have achieved credibility by creatively formulating image within the bounds of reality from those who merely "hype" false praise. The profession begins long before publicists even take on their first clients. Actually, a prerequisite to becoming a publicist is the acquiring of contacts, avenues among the media for the purpose of exposure of one's clients. These contacts are delicately cultivated and maintained through trust; each time the publicist calls upon one of these contacts for a favor, that trust is put on the line and is a revolving process of building one's credibility for delivering exciting artists as newsworthy prospects.

But publicists also have another type of credibility which they must build, one even more important than their media associations, and that is the bond which they must establish between themselves and their clients. A rock artist puts his public image in the hands of a publicist and must feel secure in relying on that person's judgment in representing that image honestly. That is quite an act of faith. However, the artist must concentrate on making music and touring and a hundred other aspects of his career and cannot be bothered with the scheduling of interviews, parties, reviews, and other assorted ploys to keep him in the public eye. So that bond is established, again on trust, again on the principle that the publicist has an understanding of the psyche and character of the artist.

There are two very distinct types of publicists: those who work for a record company and who the artist inherits when signing a recording contract, and those who have companies independent of the diskeries who are hired either by the recording artist or by the record company when they feel an extra push is needed to generate excitement. In this forum, both types of publicists are represented and they offer their viewpoints on the fostering of images essential to the Making of Superstars.

C. J. STRAUSS

(Carol Strauss Klenfner has, all her professional life, been involved in publicity. She began touting books, did work for labor relations, and, finally, moved into rock music where her clients have included the Who, the Rolling Stones, the Jefferson Starship, the Doors, Joe Cocker, Janis Ian, Black Sabbath, Bill Graham, Santana, and the Bay City Rollers. She heads her own agency, C. J. Strauss & Co., in New York City, where she lives with her husband, Mike Klenfner.)

I'm Concerned with a Career

The pace in rock publicity is incredibly fast. Things happen before I ever have a chance to set up for them. That's what I like, though. It's in the music, too. The frenzy, the raw emotion. There is pretty much an urgency to all phases of the rock business and publicity keeps up with the pace.

For example, we are usually hired by the record company or artist two or three weeks before an act goes on tour when, ideally, it should be, minimally, six weeks in advance. During that time, we write a useful bio of the artist. I find that most record companies don't take the time to do that properly. They write a bio for record purposes rather than artist purposes. That's the difference between an independent publicist and a record company publicity department—"us" and "them." I'm concerned more with a career, while they're concerned more with a record. I also put together a press kit that makes a lot of sense, one that is useful, and, since magazines have a lot of lead time—sometimes as much as three months—we get the artist immediately doing interviews. Then the story will break when they are on tour rather than a month afterward when they're vacationing in Hawaii.

Responsibility

My responsibility to my clients is to represent them accurately and to better translate their interesting points to the public. An artist does not know what makes him interesting to a magazine or to the public and that's what I'm there to tell him. For example: the press loves you when you wear red, or the fact that you collect Japanese art is really interesting and you ought to bring that out more, or that you're doing entire interviews without mentioning that your album's coming out next week. I give the artist guidelines to what the press is looking for and how he or she should respond.

There are some acts where interviews are the heaviest thing they have that generates press. Some artists go to parties, some get arrested, some are busy throwing pies in people's faces—doing something that generates press for them. Others need interviews desperately to keep the word on the street that they're still alive and well and have a record for the public to buy.

I think even the big acts need press all the time. A career should build. It's very hard for an artist to get a record company behind them when their record is five months old and they won't have another one coming out for three or four months. But that doesn't mean that their career is over or that no one cares about them. And that's why they need me. I care about them. And I try to create situations whereby others will care about them equally as much as I.

Twisting Arms

It's difficult getting publications and other people to conduct interviews with unknown artists, but it's one of the most important functions of my job. If these new artists do not get press, it takes longer and longer for their records to be heard by the public. Getting those initial interviews is what's known in the business as "twisting arms." And it can be done. These journalists or interviewers will take a chance for a number of reasons; they'll do it because they've heard good things through the grapevine about the artist or because I can play them a record that strikes their fancy or because I've given them a shot in the past with an unknown who's turned out to be very big, and they "go" with my credibility.

Credibility is perhaps the most useful quality which a publicist can develop. I maintain my credibility by trying never to lie about the proportions of the act I'm publicizing. Once I do that, I've blown it; an interviewer will probably never take a chance with a new act again. I also maintain it by keeping my client list small and select enough so that I only publicize people in whom I believe, that I can get behind. Whether I listen to their records when I get home at night is not the point; the point is whether or not I believe they have some validity in the music scene.

Egos

All artists have egos and, somehow, these egoes all have to be contended with by me. Flexibility is the key. I try to get away from the ego thing, pretend it never exists. I certainly refuse to feed it. Instead, I try to appeal to the artists' reason. I tell them that I know what I'm doing; I've been in publicity for over a decade and I know what is right for them. I have to appeal to the artists on that level to keep their ego simmering but down.

I've dealt with an egomaniacal artist who's a wonderful performer. I've given her an entire list of interviews knowing that she likes to cancel them at the last minute. She does this because she likes to feel she's very exclusive. A lot of artists like to feel that way. So now I give her an inflated list of interviews and point out to her the ones that are truly the most important. As a result, she let's them go on as scheduled and eliminates the ones which I put there for her to eliminate. It's a little game, but if I have to use those devices, I will. Hell, it works. This particular performer does her interviews. That's the name of the game.

Why Hire an Independent Publicist?

Most record companies cannot give an act the kind of attention an independent can give them. For example, on a twenty-six-city tour, a record company is unable to set up interviews in some of the smaller but important press cities; a city like St. Louis is a good example. Record companies also fail to do a lot of the advance work. We always try to set up things in advance of tours or record releases so stories break at the right time for the artist to benefit from them. Record companies have fifty other acts that are working, that need their individual attention. So they will hire me for a certain length of time.

It's Part of the Act

When Janis Ian decided to resume her career, we were faced with the fact that she had been unproductive for many years and people associated her with what she had done before. At first, we exploited the "comeback" feature just to get people interested. Then we got the press to listen to her current material. She hadn't had a hit in years, but her new songs were beautiful and we had a lot to work with. Janis didn't want to rest on or be known by her "Society's Child" stuff, so we turned away from it completely. We stayed within her guidelines. That was a case where sheer talent broke the artist. We just got the right people to recognize it. Now everyone wants to interview Janis. It is relatively easy getting press for her.

With the Jefferson Starship, it's very difficult getting them to do any publicity things. They have a real San Francisco attitude of,

"Hey, man—do we have to go through with this?" The most important aspect of my working with people like that is to make sure they know what they're doing [in regard to press] and why they're doing it. I keep it to a minimum, to the essentials, and work with them intelligently.

Both Grace Slick and Janis can be arrogant with the press, but I have to maintain a certain distance. My client's attitude with the press cannot be *my* attitude. All I can do is try to smooth it as much as possible. If I tell Janis and Grace what they're doing is an important interview or that the interviewer is not an easy person to talk to, they understand. I have to cajole them a little, let them know why, how, what for, and that it's part of the act. When they get onstage, they are doing an act for their audience. Sometimes an interview has to be thought of in the same way.

BOB REGEHR

(Bob Regehr worked for several West Coast publicity firms before opening his own company. During that time, he handled such acts as the Mamas and the Papas and Johnny Rivers and became a well-known figure in the rock world, as well as in film, where he represented Five Easy Pieces *and* Easy Rider. *Bob is currently Warner Bros. vice-president of career development.)*

You Break an Artist by Press

I think a record company's prime responsibility to the artist is public awareness of the artist—not necessarily the record. The responsibility of breaking the record lies primarily with the promotion department and the sales department. I don't think records are harmed or enhanced by reviews or by the printed word. Records don't break by press; you *do* break an artist with press. A record is a one-time thing; an artist has longevity. I'm interested in how to guarantee that longevity. My department *always* has to look two or three years down the line.

The bulk of the publicity department's work is sticking with the Ry Cooders of the world. The music is there. There may not be a mass appeal to it, but the popularity of an artist like that will build. Randy Newman is a good example. He has never had and perhaps will never have AM radio airplay, but his popularity is built and established as a figure who is bigger than his records. It takes a new artist—if he will be a successful artist—at least a year to catch up with the fame and pace of his record. Like Gary Wright. "Dream Weaver" was a number-one hit and, at the same time, Gary was virtually unknown to the general public. It is the responsibility of Warner Bros. publicity department to build the artist's reputation once there is a foothold like that.

We have to stay on top of the situation. A record has "x" amount of life to it. For example, after two or three weeks after a record is released, if there is no reaction on it, it's quietly forgotten about. We can't allow that to happen to the artist. It's up to the publicity department to keep the excitement happening. Al Jarreau is a good example of that. He is an act we've been really involved with for a long period of time because we are convinced he is going to become a star. His record is long gone, but the publicity department works on him as if the record was released yesterday. That may require reservicing the record to our press list—getting the record back into their hands again and again. We get the name of the artist to the "opinionmakers," encourage them to keep it alive.

Breaking the New Artist

Breaking a new artist by press is extraordinarily difficult. There is a certain amount of luck involved. First of all, the music has to be there. You cannot hype anything for very long that is either not musically valid or entertaining. But we'll try, though.

We work very closely with a new act and with the management to make sure that the live act is good. That's terribly essential. Once that's established, it's our responsibility to get people out to see that act. We set up tours and generate enthusiasm within the press ranks, hoping they'll spend a few hours in a club or concert hall somewhere to see what the act can do onstage.

When conferring with a new artist, we spend a lot of time discussing the strong character points of an artist and how to bring them out. If the artist is reticent, then we work around him. If he happens to be very articulate, then we utilize him as much as possible in interviews. If the act is so suited, we will also go after television. It can enhance our goals immeasureably, but it can also

destroy them if the act doesn't come off well. But there are certain
acts who lend themselves to television. Leon Redbone broke on
"Saturday Night Live." But we've found that it's not only the
act's appearance on the show but that the audience has to be
receptive to new things—and rock on television is definitely a new
thing.

We Expanded Their Horizons

George Benson was virtually virgin coverage in the pop world.
Up until the time "Masquerade" broke, he had only been covered
in *Downbeat* and the other jazz publications. With that single in
hand, we worked all the pop publications which knew George as
an instrumentalist but not as a pop artist. We almost entirely concentrated on the pop field and let jazz lie. I'm sure we alienated
some of the more esoteric jazz writers, but that was a sacrifice we
had to make.

Fleetwood Mac almost counted as our breaking an artist but, in
fact, it was really a superresurgence of a group that had enjoyed a
previous popularity. Publicity got onto it early—as soon as we
saw it reflected in the airplay reports where they had never been
played before. We helped build the resurgence by making their
concerts an event. They were always dearly loved by the promoters as an opening act. They put on great shows and were always entertaining. It was a case of our taking them to a higher
level. Almost immediately, we started taking them around to national publications. The first one was *Newsweek,* then *People,*
then every national paper wanted to talk to them. We expanded
their horizons—took them beyond pop, gave them a prominent
awareness.

The "Yenta" Network

I always strive to have our publicity department "bunch" things.
We try to get as many things going on a particular artist in the
hope that they will all break around the same time—or, at least,
within a two-month period. Concentration of that nature, I always
find, inundates the public's awareness. If it's spread out over a
year, publicity loses its effectiveness.

This works hand in hand with bunching publicity in localities and spreading publicity from there. Michael Franks was a special project of ours with whom we worked that way. We did it because everyone at Warner Bros. felt he had a great future as a recording artist and knew we could break him. We noticed that his popularity was beginning to grow in Pittsburgh, so we rented a hotel suite in that city and began working him from there. The record went to number-one there and we began conducting more and more publicity from that suite. Now there happens to be a "yenta" network among managers, agents, and press and word went out on that network that Michael Franks was happening big in Pittsburgh. Soon thereafter, his career began spreading outward to surrounding cities and we worked that way. Of course, the media cities are basically New York and Los Angeles; however, we've found that we can also break an artist's publicity out of smaller press cities like St. Louis, Columbus, and Pittsburgh. The formulas for that are so numerous, and we just keep trying them until one works. It sounds simple, but it's not.

PAT COSTELLO

(Pat Costello is a true veteran of the progressive rock music industry. Having begun right out of high school, she assumed various record company jobs in A&R, promotion, and doing the liner notes on the backs of albums. After apprenticing with several independent publicity companies, she founded the Wartoke Concern with a group of friends and has represented such acts as Stevie Wonder, Hall and Oates, Labelle, Tom Waits, Frank Zappa and Patti Smith.)

Our First Account—Woodstock!

A few of us had been working for a publicity company and we talked, from time to time, about starting a company of our own. The opportunity arose when I was approached by somebody to work on something that was called the Woodstock Arts and Music Festival. And it became our first account. We handled the whole thing.

At that time, there were a slew of festivals being presented and a couple of them received terrible publicity. At one, the police had to use mace to control the crowd and the public became very leery of festivals. So we held a press conference at the Village Gate for network news people and members of the underground press with the promoters discussing exactly how they intended to handle Woodstock. We got national coverage on that. It sparked the demand; however, the great acts drew the bulk of the people.

Angles and Image

Basically, my job is to get my clients the best possible space in the best possible public showcases. I try to take the *real* part of my clients and build those aspects into publicity so that when they are in the public eye they don't fall short of the press which they received. I am careful not to overbuild an artist—especially a new artist—because people will become disappointed and turn off to them.

I spend an awful lot of time with an artist before I begin a campaign. Part of the reason for that is just getting to know him or her. One example is the time that I spent with the members of Labelle. I discovered so many different things about them with which I could work. I could work with them as individuals, which would have been difficult had I only seen them at a gig and then organized my campaign. I found I could work with their intense fashion sense—getting them space in fashion and women's pages. The more you get to know a person, the more angles you can see. And a lot of the new clients really don't know what they want their image to be.

When a new artist walks in, we prepare a bio and find a suitable photographer for him. There are different photographers for different kinds of people. Some photographers only shoot portrait photography, some only do live concert work, others do only album covers. We get good pictures of our client and make sure a lot of people see them. If there's a tour coming up, we begin servicing all the papers throughout the tour area as well as getting pertinent information to the national press. We follow it up with calls to all these people, discussing the artist with them, where they're going to be, what the album's like, what we feel is good about the album, what they think. And, of course, we try to get them to do reviews or stories. As the press comes in, we use the good clips to build and work on getting other stories. Some people at magazines don't follow the pop scene very closely. We throw them a name and, if they've heard of the person, we try to back up their initial interest with reviews and features, pictures and bios. We just keep hammering away until we build an image for our client.

Amazing Markets

We hit all the media possible when trying to get coverage: radio, television, all the talk shows, anything. If an artist has done a small performance or an interview which we feel is relatively good, we get a video tape of it and send it to other people who might think that the artist isn't particularly good for his or her show.

Some of the markets are really amazing. Patti Smith, one of our clients, did a Mike Douglas show and a week later, in one day, she received almost a thousand letters from kids who saw the show. Normally, you wouldn't assume that Patti's audience watches "The Mike Douglas Show," but they do.

The Price You Pay

Our fees vary. We sit down with the artist and decide what they need. If it is immediately local work, it would not be as expensive as if we'd be taking on a national tour. The going price nowadays is anywhere from $1,000 to $2,000 a month for a minimum number of months. Obviously, if an artist is not traveling and he's only doing an odd date here and there, we won't charge him as much as somebody who is doing thirty cities in ten days.

Stevie Wonder

In the beginning, being Stevie's publicist was difficult—if anyone would believe that. But nobody really wanted to know about him—right before the release of *Music of My Mind*. That's when he decided to change his image. He brought us into the studio and played us the album-to-be and we were really shocked. We really flipped out over it.

We began approaching a lot of people and some of them just said, "No! That's awful. That's not little Stevie Wonder. What's going on?" After that, he toured England and it was really not a very good tour. A lot of people were expecting to hear his early material and the reviews were mixed. We managed to pick up a few things after that—like an Associated Press feature—but not that much. Shortly thereafter, a friend of mine heard that the Stones were going out on tour and we talked about getting Steve on the bill. He asked me if I thought it was a good idea or not, and I gave him the pros and the cons as I saw them; they were about equal. Steve was not part of the rock scene at all then, and his lifestyle was extremely different from any other rock performers. Steve doesn't do any kind of drugs at all, and he had always been protected from being around it. I told him what being out with a rock band was like, and what it would be like being an opening act for the Stones. There were a great deal of chances he would be taking. I laid out what we had done so far. I thought the tour, though, was such a great opportunity for him to get to so many people in such a short period of time, and I urged him to consider it. And that was the tour that did it.

Steve doesn't have a manager—even now. He manages himself and relies on us for a lot of his decisions. Right now, it's a matter of, "Where does Stevie Wonder go from here?" It's things like that which we are sitting around talking about all the time. And publicity will come from that point on. But we always try to keep his name in the limelight even though he is a huge star. People should always know what he is doing. And that's what publicity is all about . . . getting to the people.

Forum:
The Rock Press

During the late Sixties, the rock press gained a credibility in proportion to the fluctuating income of the record industry. What began as strictly music publications geared to young people who hung on every word spoken by their current idols in exclusive interviews are now diverse periodicals; they have cultivated their own brand of volatile journalism ventilated by a new wave of writers and have expanded their reading audiences far beyond their initial musical beginnings. Interestingly enough, rock music has become only a portion of the contents of magazines like Crawdaddy, Rolling Stone, Cream, Circus, *and* Gig. *They have enlarged their provinces to cover politics, film, travel, sports, television, and other cultural forms. And, indeed, what had also begun as a tribute to the counterculture has, in those terms, rendered the word "counter" obsolete.*

Today the rock press chiefly identifies the contributors to cultural periodicals who associate themselves with music and musicians, the rock critics who offer judgments on new albums and perform-

ances. Of those periodicals, Rolling Stone *and* Crawdaddy *seem to maintain a standard of writing unparalleled in their field. They are current and are regarded by the general public, as well as by the music industry, as being trend setters within their idiom. Additionally,* Rolling Stone *has been responsible for breaking several political stories which have elicited national reverberations and scandal. Their music sections, however, remain inexorably pointed and informative, almost giving a loose definition to this era of popular music.*

And yet there is an undefined elitism which pervades their pages, an aura of divine providence which seems to encumber the rock writers and, at times, clouds their objectivity in favor of exhibiting a pedantic wittiness. This arises, in part, from the manner in which they are catered to by the record company publicity departments, in part by their past role of devil's advocate during the late 1960s' cultural revolution. Often, this indulgent disparity is overlooked by the readers who accept the built-in cockiness as an integral characteristic of rock journalism. But, in fact, it has alienated others, who have turned to publications like the New York Times, *whose straightforward classical reportage is adequate for their musical diets.*

Whatever one's preference may be, rock music has become well represented in most every phase of communications and is most prominently represented by the rock press. Whatever its stylistic slant, the rock press has successfully brought the music to the foreground. It has become the spokesman for a generation that initially rejected the printed word and, in addition to its reporting rock music, therein lies its strength.

PETER KNOBLER

(Peter Knobler, a native New Yorker, joined the rock press by answering an ad in the newspaper: Wanted, Rock and Roll Writer. *Subsequently, he began to write for an obscure Greenwich Village mimeographed paper called* Crawdaddy, *which, at that time, was published by its founder, Paul Williams. After Williams left and several other "sleazy managements and shady money*

men" took it over, Knobler convinced his father that it was wise to support it financially and become its publisher. Today, Crawdaddy boasts a circulation of over four hundred thousand readers, and Knobler is the editor.)

Cheap Thrills

In June 1972, we decided to change *Crawdaddy* to a magazine format because it was not profitable to try to compete with *Rolling Stone*. We also changed it from a biweekly to a monthly because we weren't getting sufficient advertising revenue to put it out so often and the overhead was too high. Additionally, we changed the focus of the magazine; we stopped trying to be so current and became more feature-oriented.

The first issue I did as editor featured a piece on "inside the music business," subtitled: "Cheap Thrills on a Two Year Option." It dealt with the various sections of the business: publicity, A&R, the company, the artist, and the booking agent. I was pretty naïve at the time, and I don't think the people who wrote it were tremendously more educated than I was. We learned an interesting lesson from that article: a magazine that depends largely on industry advertising has a hard time biting the hand that feeds it. There was one paragraph in that story that said, "If the record company that's interested in you as an artist doesn't have its own distribution system for getting records into the stores, run away." Now, A&M Records, which is a major record company based on independent distribution, was furious. And we didn't get any advertising from them for a year. So it proved to us that a record company will pull their advertising if we hit them where they live. Negative reviews of albums is a matter of taste, and they understand that. Negative reviews of companies are sensitive. And negative reviews of company personalities they get incensed about. So we can do exposés of other industries and of politics, but we found we cannot do a negative piece on the music industry. Our other alternative is to do puff stories on the business, which I'm simply unwilling to do. Our readers will know it's jive, and what's the sense—except to make money? And I'm not that desperate.

Why People Look to Crawdaddy

Readers today are more cynical, more aware. They are better versed in music. They have a history of rock journalism to look back on and, therefore, their standards are higher. We can't get away with, "Oh, man, this album just makes my mind trip." And an artist can't get away with saying in print, "Oh yeah, I'm really into it just to make people happy," because our readers don't believe that either.

I don't put this magazine out for myself. We try to get an idea of what people are interested in. We get that from mail, sales, and word of mouth. We look at the charts to discern what people are buying, and we have to be realistic about it. So we will say: People are buying Earth, Wind and Fire. Now, are the people who buy that group going to buy *Crawdaddy?* Maybe. People who buy Kool and The Gang are not likely to buy *Crawdaddy*. So the Top Ten is not often accurate as to the demographics of our readership. And, therefore, we have to use a lot of judgment as well. I've been doing this for six or seven years, and after that long you develop a sense of what type of story will sell the magazine.

The whole Bruce Springsteen experience (which *Crawdaddy* wrote about before the artist was well known) was our being willing to go out on a limb. Nobody had heard of Bruce, and we were so enthusiastic about him that we did a major piece and continued to support him, despite the fact that our readership couldn't possibly have wanted to see another article on Springsteen. Part of running a magazine is having your readers know that they will find something new in it. That's why I hope they read a magazine like *Crawdaddy:* 1) To find out about people and things who you *want* to know about, and 2) To find out about people who you *will* want to know about.

Another point which our magazine takes into consideration in regard to presenting a story to our readers is that a celebrity should be celebrated for only what he is good at, not just because he or she is a celebrity. Essentially, we're dealing with authority. Just because Stevie Wonder is a brilliant musician and rather a good lyricist who has interesting things to say, we would not want our readers to jump to do everything he says. We stress to our

readers to look into the face of everyone who talks to them—
directly or indirectly. We at *Crawdaddy* try to analyze what the
people in our stories are saying, who's saying it, what the effect is,
how it affects what they do, and how it affects what our readers
do. If somebody's music is affecting you strongly, then there must
be a second generation motive. You can go directly to that motive
and find something else that moves you as well. It is something
that colors the music and how the music will affect you. And by
virtue of our stories on celebrities, it gives the reader an added dimension to that person's music.

At times, *Crawdaddy* has tried to undercut its own celebrity
motives because, I think, blind celebration becomes pernicious.
The reader shouldn't believe everything *Crawdaddy* says either.
We encourage the reader to analyze, as well. That's why we do interviews—written interviews instead of question-and-answer interviews. We want to know what the writer thinks as well as what the
person being interviewed thinks. Is he giving a forthright answer?
Is he lying? Does he know what he's talking about or is he somebody deluding himself and the reader?

Crawdaddy versus Rolling Stone

As compared to *Rolling Stone, Crawdaddy* takes more chances
and has less to lose. I don't think an early Springsteen article
would have appeared in *Rolling Stone*. They take the chance of
being wrong and having all this amassed "credibility" knocked
down. In terms of politics, we are more progressive than they are,
less conventionally liberal. For instance, before *Crawdaddy* can
determine *who* to vote for, we have to determine whether or not
to vote. That's not an option for *Rolling Stone*. They just take too
much crap from all their conventional liberal supporters.

Musically, *Rolling Stone* seems very West Coast-oriented. We
try to have a broader range, although we tend to be East Coast
oriented. We're less involved in gossip. They seem to be very good
at this "Random Notes" gossip scene. I'm not interested in that.
Paul Williams said something interesting about that the first time I
met him at the old *Crawdaddy*. He said, "Gossip is just knowing
something everybody else is going to know in a day or two anyway, so what's the point." But everybody seems to love it. And

their whole magazine is based on gossip which seems to be wide-spread on every level.

We'll never do a story we hear they are going to do because they'll get it out before we will. They have a four- or five-day lead time, while we have a two-month lead time. We have overlapping readers. It's unfortunate, but it's a physical and monetary disability which we have. The kind of magazine we have takes two weeks to be printed. *Rolling Stone* takes only a couple of days. We're printed in one place, they're printed in, I think, three places around the country. So, in order for us to ship to the West Coast it goes by truck (because flying is too expensive), and it takes a week. Once it gets to the Coast, it gets broken down from central shipping points to local shipping points to newsstands. *Rolling Stone,* being more established, has a direct conduit. So four days later, there it is. So if both magazines write the same story on the same night, our readers read it six to eight weeks later, while their readers get it the next week. It's a problem for us, but we adjust the magazine that way. We know we can't compete on that level, so we try to write stories that don't date or that we have so far in advance of everybody else that we can still beat them. We did that with Southside Johnny. We made friends with them, went into the studio with them when nobody else was there, and came out with the story at the right time.

Responsibility

We feel we have a definite responsibility to our readers in terms of content. In advertising, we don't accept ads from the armed services. The Navy wanted us to run a center spread, four-color ad for a lot of money six times a year. We wouldn't give it to them, and we were turning down a lot of money. But I'd hate to have someone read *Crawdaddy* and, as a result, join the Navy. It would defeat the whole purpose of the magazine.

In terms of music, we review records seriously, not frivolously. Just because a reviewer's piece is well written doesn't mean it runs. Either it's got to state its case strongly, convincingly, or be right in our eyes. In the case of a New York *Times* theater review, some people say, "Okay, Clive Barnes likes this thing so I won't like it." The same thing should happen with our readers. "Okay,

Crawdaddy likes it. I know where *Crawdaddy* is at, so I should gauge myself accordingly." People spend money on the albums we review; therefore, our vested effort in reviewing is taken very seriously.

What We're Looking For

For a young writer today, there are a lot of smaller markets where they can develop their style and still be printed. Every major city has its own small underground press or rock magazine. But a young, undeveloped writer *must* develop chops, instinct, and must do plenty of writing to develop a professional style. I studied writing in college and worked doing stories for eight years. After a while, if you're any good at all, you develop. We look for style and content.

Concerning photographers, sure everybody today is a rock photographer, but that doesn't mean they're good rock photographers. We've seen a lot of pictures of Jimmy Page, but what we look for is a picture of Jimmy Page that says something, that exemplifies his personality and allows for visual interpretation. All these kids who show up at concerts today with cameras, they take pictures that say nothing about the individual. We're looking for levels and levels of awareness.

JOHN ROCKWELL

(*John Rockwell's roots are not found in rock and roll. He began his writing career as the classical music and dance critic at the Los Angeles* Times *while working on his PhD dissertation. Upon arriving at the New York* Times, *where his intentions were to continue writing about more classical forms of music, the paper's rock music "stringer" was on a two-week vacation and Rockwell just "fell into it." In 1974, he became the first full-time rock critic the paper has had.*)

The Critic's Role

I think any critic should write in an interesting and provocative way about subjects of interest to the audience. I don't think that the task of any critic is to mirror the taste of the audience. A fictional letter to the editor of the *Times* might well read: "How *dare* you send somebody who doesn't like rock and roll to review the Jethro Tull concert when we love Ian Anderson and everything he stands for." Well, that's a totally erroneous argument. The point is to send somebody who is interested in the field, who has a clearly delineated set of standards within that field, a lively writing style, provocative ideas, etc. A critic should not be considered within the abstract; all criticism is critical writing, so there is room for somebody who is sometimes quite off the wall.

A critic should educate the reader but not in a didactic, schoolmastery way. The way a critic predicates readers is by simply talking in an interesting way and inspiring persons who don't know everything the critic is talking about to become interested themselves.

I think the critic's primary responsibility is to the audience, not the artist. I think it would be presumptuous for me to lecture Jackson Browne on his failings as a singer. I think it is my duty to point that out in a review just to keep it straight. One of the funny things about being a critic is that it is clearly and purely subjective; nonetheless, it is carried out within the façade of objectivity—ergo, one has to "tell it like it is." Now, in that case, "like it is" is how I think it is.

Style

It seems to me that there is a whole school that argues that a rock critic should be anti-intellectual because the music calls for it. This is a sore point for me because I'm regarded as one of the more intellectual critics. I have no pretentions to want to write like a musical equivalent of the Ramones or Patti Smith. I have my style and my viewpoint, and I bring it to bear on the music.

My style is not dictated by the *Times*. The funny thing about the *Times* is that my natural style and my way of looking at the world and the audience that I wish to reach fit the paper perfectly. My style is one of formality, of no pretense of identification with the reader, a certain irony, a greater willingness to use polysyllabic words, a certain pedantic sophistication. And all of that fits into my image of myself.

What Draws Me to an Artist

I like to think, in a naïve way, that what draws me to an artist is excellence within the field the artist participates in rather than prejudices. There is no question that, given a B+ type singer, I will tend to like a woman B+ singer more than a man B+ singer. That's one of my own pure sexist prejudices. I also have the typical tendencies of white critics to be more interested in a run-of-the-mill country singer than a run-of-the-mill disco funk group. And I hate . . . I have *trouble* with real schlockarino M-O-R stuff; I just don't care about people like Barry Manilow or Peter Lemongello or Seals and Crofts. But I'll go and review them if I have to. And, thank God, the *Times* has another critic who handles the adult pop field.

I make it a point of *not* getting to know artists. I deal almost exclusively with record company PR people. They pitch stuff to me in such an incredible profusion that I wind up numb. At this point, test pressings[1] followed by calls saying that I've *got* to listen to this particular group come in with such frequency that I automatically learn to discount *just* a PR person's recommendation. I have to hear the hype from additional people as well.

I tend to allow myself to get enthusiastic. I like that quality in myself. I would rather be over- than underenthusiastic. I let myself go completely wild over Bruce Springsteen and I don't have any regrets about that at all.

Power

I don't deny that I possess a certain degree of power. What that power is seems to me to be very limited, and it is absurd to pretend that it is more than it is. First of all, no critic can make or break an artist; the radio stations have more to do with that and, more simply, public taste has more to do with that than any critic does.

A critic is part of a process by which enthusiasm is fanned for

[1] Test pressings are advance copies of an album before release that are oftentimes issued to members of the rock press.

somebody. But if I do a story about a particular club, that club's business is going to pick up. However, records are a different story. I gave Melanie a big push, but her record was a huge stiff and never even made the Top 200. So therefore, where is the power? My power exists within a possible New York context of a club date—getting people to go to a club date. The power exists as part of a process by which, when the *Times* writes about somebody, it legitimizes him or her in the eyes of *Time* and *Newsweek* and the national magazines. The fact that New York is the media center and most of the magazines like *Esquire, Atlantic, New Times,* and others who are run by "people at the top" who don't know much about rock music watch New York's media outpour— well, if Christgau[2] or I go "big" on somebody, it legitimizes that somebody in their eyes. That is becoming less of the norm now because hipper people are getting into places like *Time* and *Newsweek.* And, in that regard, my influence will lessen. But nonetheless, my criticism is part of the process which moves something from the underground to a big national phenomenon.

DAVE MARSH

(Dave Marsh grew up in Detroit, where rock and roll is most characterized by a heavy-metal approach; however, he went through his high-school days on overdoses of Elvis Presley and Chuck Berry. After a little college and some general work for local publications, he got in on the ground floor of Cream *magazine and within a few months became its editor. But Marsh was interested in the New York scene and moved to the East Coast in 1974, where he found a job as rock critic at* Newsday. *In 1975, he joined the staff of* Rolling Stone *and is currently an associate editor there.)*

We Place Things in Perspective

I operate from this presumption: *Rolling Stone* is published every two weeks; radio stations broadcast twenty-four hours a day. Therefore, *Rolling Stone* is not going to be able to give their readers an album exclusive. But what *Rolling Stone* can do is to

[2] Robert Christgau is the rock music editor of the *Village Voice.*

tout the readers on an obscure record. A record like Valerie Carter's is a good example. So is a Southside Johnny record in places other than the northeast section of the country. And I also think that *Rolling Stone* elevates the discussion of a particular record. Obviously, a new Who album will be a hit; that's not our objective—projecting hits. We raise the discussion to: what is that new Who album all about, what is its artistic worth? We place things in the perspective of what an album means in terms of the Who's career without going back and reciting history. One of the things that *Rolling Stone* has always had going for it is that it was willing to presume a lot instead of reciting historical data. Who wants to read another history of the Who? That's the great strength of *Rolling Stone,* whereas a lot of the other musical magazines are locked into the historical sense of obligation to their readers.

The Important Elements

We have a setup where we feature two or three lead record reviews with headlines and several shorter reviews. Our initial publishing process is to determine what's worth the long space and what's worth the short space. We cover the longer reviews prominently because, simply, more people want to know about those particular artists. And after that decision has been made, the most important element is getting the right writer with the right review at the right time. I determine that on the basis of having worked with the individual writers for a long period of time. After which, I decide what the artistic issue is concerning a particular grouping of reviews. For example, we recently did a review, a single review on the groups Television, Blondie, and the Ramones—which is an obvious one. That comparison adds an extra dimension and perks up a review.

Anybody who reads *Rolling Stone*'s record section buys albums and, while they may look for the magazine to tout them on the obscure stuff, they want some kind of intelligent discussion which moves them in certain directions. And the directions in which I try to lead them have more to do with artistic value than social value because social value tends to be very arbitrary. Five years ago during the Golden Age of Progressive Rock, that was a different situation. But what the magazine is interested in is:

where is rock going, where should it go, who is moving people emotionally?

To a degree, I think a *Rolling Stone* review is able to influence a reader concerning his buying or not buying an album. Additionally, some of our reviews will reassure a record company that they really *have* something worth promoting; a case in point was a Jon Landau review of Maria Muldaur's "Midnight at the Oasis." Warner Bros. Records got on the stick after they saw Jon's review. In another instance, a review by Paul Nelson showed Columbia Records that a record it was promoting in a pop market *should* have been promoted as a country album.

What I Look For

I think I look for fairly traditional values in a record. I look for good singing—because that seems to be the hardest thing for me to find—and several emotional factors. I want to hear something that, in one way or another, reflects my experience in life. I'm not terribly interested in all these English fairy-tale bands like Genesis. I look for something that I can make a connection with, that I can draw a line from Elvis Presley and Chuck Berry through the Beatles and the Rolling Stones and come out in the present. That's an instinctive process. But on the other hand, I just wrote a favorable reviews of the Genesis album *Word and Wuthering* and said that it is important to hear this English art rock which critics always dismiss. And it's totally valid to want to listen to ordinary pop songs like Elton John's "Daniel."

The artist must be articulate in a certain way. It's fine to establish a mood musically, but then the group must define it lyrically unless they choose to be purely instrumental. But I don't think that rock and roll moves in that direction anymore unless the group is doing it in three minutes like Johnny and the Hurricanes used to do.

On Jann Wenner

Jann is a phenomenon in himself. He is fantastic at capturing breaking stories and promoting them. He has an incredibly instinctive news sense, knows what makes good copy and what is rhetoric.

He's a very volatile type of guy. He operates a lot on instinct. He can't always explain why he wants to do a certain thing a certain way. But, like a lot of instinctive people, if he's 60–40 per cent correct, the 60 per cent outshines the 40. He sees things a certain way and expects it to be done. He never dictates how one should go about doing something, but he expects to see certain results.

A couple weeks ago, I was talking to him about some changes in the review section and he interrupted with, "Hey—look, it's gonna be done *this* way, *my* way. I don't want to have a random discussion about it." Of course, minutes later we were having a rational discussion about it. But his technique remains: "Let's discuss this the way I want it done and the way it eventually will be done." And he's usually right.

The Jocks' Grudge

I think that disc jockeys hate critics. The reason why is that if they don't like a particular record, they can't say so on the air. All they can do is *not* play it. A rock critic not only doesn't like a record and not only says he doesn't like it, but says why. I think disc jockeys resent that. Critics actually have the role of tastemakers, not the disc jockeys. Hence, acts that get a lot of press meet a lot of DJ resistance. I think that's what happened in the case of Bruce Springsteen. Now, the disc jockeys are forced to do an on-the-air about-face.

What It's All About

When I first began writing reviews, what gave me the right to be a critic was that I was a big fan of the music, I could write well, I could articulate what I thought, and I thought about rock and roll a little more seriously than the average listener. What gives me the right now is that I have an incredible backlog of experience.

Listeners can be their own critics, but that doesn't mean they don't need me. There's no way the average listener can bring the kind of expertise to judge something that someone who's been doing it for eight years can do. Simply, if a kid goes out and buys a new Joe Cocker album, he presupposes that because it's Joe

Cocker it will be great. Joe Cocker *was* a great singer when he first began recording and he may be now. But if that kid doesn't know anything about Ray Charles, then he doesn't know how to place Joe Cocker. I put it all into perspective for the reader. And that's what my criticism's all about.

Index

ROBERT STEPHEN SPITZ was born and raised in Reading, Pennsylvania, where, until the Beatles appeared in 1964, he estimates he was the only teen-ager listening to rock and roll. After receiving a B.A. from Albright College, he became an executive in the rock recording industry and, subsequently, has represented the careers of artists Bruce Springsteen and Elton John. Spitz has taught rock at Hunter College and the New School. He is a screenwriter, journalist, and critic whose articles appear frequently in the New York *Times Sunday Book Review, Penthouse, Viva, Crawdaddy,* and *The Saturday Review.* He lives in Manhattan with his wife, Vicki, and is currently at work on a book about Woodstock and a novel.